gluten-free girl and the chef

gluten-free girl and the chef

a love story
with 100 tempting recipes

shauna james ahern and daniel ahern

photography by lara ferroni

WILEY

JOHN WILEY & SONS, INC.

Photography © 2010 Lara Ferroni

Published by John Wiley & Sons, Inc., Hoboken, New Jersey

Published simultaneously in Canada

For general information on our other products and services or for technical support, please contact our Customer Care Department within the United States at (800) 762-2974, outside the United States at (317) 572-3993 or fax (317) 572-4002.

Wiley also publishes its books in a variety of electronic formats. Some content that appears in print may not be available in electronic books. For more information about Wiley products, visit our web site at www.wiley.com.

Design by Elizabeth Van Itallie

Library of Congress Cataloging-in-Publication Data
Ahern, Shauna James.
Gluten-free girl and the chef: a love story with 100 tempting recipes / Shauna James Ahern and Daniel Ahern; photography by Lara Ferroni.
p. cm.
Includes index.
ISBN 978-1-118-38357-5 (pbk), ISBN 978-0-470-94246-8 (ebk), ISBN 978-0-470-94248-2 (ebk), ISBN 978-0-470-94568-1 (ebk)
1. Gluten-free diet—Recipes. I. Ahern, Daniel, 1968- II. Title.
RM237.86.A338 2010
641.5'638—dc22
2009051016
Printed in The United States of America
10 9 8 7 6 5 4 3 2 1

For Lucy. Thank you for joining us at the table.

contents

at home

at the restaurant

acknowledgments

"No one who cooks, cooks alone. Even at her most solitary, a cook in the kitchen is surrounded by generations of cooks past, the advice and menus of cooks present, the wisdom of cookbook writers."

—LAURIE COLWIN

Certainly, no one ever *writes* a cookbook alone. Without the friendship and firm advice of the following people, you would not be holding this book in your hands.

Thank you to the readers of our blog, Gluten-Free Girl and the Chef, who follow our kitchen adventures and keep coming back for more food every week.

Thank you, a hundred times, to the more than 150 fans and friends who tested recipes for us. Your questions kept us on our toes and your suggestions have made these recipes more clear for readers standing at the stove. Special thanks go out to Zoë Francois for her help with the bread, Lorraine Goldberg, Julia Greene, Melanie and Eric Karlins, Nina Laden, Dr. Jean Layton, Kate McDermott, Cari Trousdale, and Lorna Yee. Tracy Chastain and Kim Malone deserve their own sentence for being the kindest, most inexhaustible recipe testers on earth. You two should do this for a living.

Thank you to Judy Amster and Matthew Amster-Burton, who read every essay in this book and weren't afraid to say when the sentences made no sense. All the funniest lines in this book actually come from Matthew. Judy, look! This sentence does not begin with an *and*. You two are incredible friends.

Thank you to our legion of friends who have stood in the kitchen with us and made us laugh throughout this entire process: Laurie Amster-Burton (and Iris), Carol Blymire, Booth Buckley and Nina Laden, Francoise Adriaan Camille and Selene Canter, Hsiao-Ching Chou and Michi Suzuki at Suzuki-Chou, Anita Crotty, Rebekah Denn and David Dickey, Cindy and Ben Etoh, Julie Jaffe, Seis and Pia Kamimura, Judy Korin, Kim Ricketts, Ashley and Gabe Rodriguez, Jon Rowley and Kate McDermott, Kaytlyn Sanders, Becky Selengut, Heidi Swanson, Quinn Thomsen and Alison Jones (plus Lila Grace), Jess Thomson, Tara Austen Weaver, Luisa Weiss, Molly Wizenberg and Brandon Pettit, Matt and Danika Wright, and Lorna Yee and Henry Lo.

A special thanks to John and Tita Woodard, Meri Escandon, Gabriel Judet-Weinshel, and Sharon Jensen, who have inspired us and put up with us for a long time.

Danny would like to thank Michel LeBourne, Pierre and Kathy Luc, Frank Kersteter, Marco Canora, Radek Cerny, and Charlie Durham for teaching him how to be the chef he has become. Also, thanks to Steve and Sheila Jagentfl, Jef Fike, and Cliff Willewerth for being the best bosses he has worked for.

He would also like to thank Carrie Nichols for being the object of his prank call, as well as Dennis and Michelle Wilson of DAM Good Pizza of Breckenridge, who made him work for two days to pay off those pizzas, and thus put him in a restaurant kitchen for the first time.

Thank you to Andy Burgess for getting Danny out to Vermont and up to Washington.

Shauna would like to thank Mr. Lester, her annoying fifth-grade teacher, who made her read the entire SRA reading series box, twice, because he didn't know what else to teach her about writing. He forced Shauna to learn it on her own, which is much better. (Thank you to Natalie Goldberg, Richard Hugo, Anne Lamott, and E.B. White, who taught her more than any classroom teacher.) Thank you as well to the administration of the Northwest School for firing Shauna, because she never would have taken the leap to become a full-time writer without that jolt.

Thank you, a thousand times over, to our families, who cheered us on through the entire process and continue to feed us. Jerry and Rosemary, Keith and Allie—thank you for being our parents. Coleen and Joe, Kevin and Patti, Kathy, Pat and Julie, Andy and Dana—brothers and sisters, all of you. Emily, Ryan, Kelly, Kyle, Patrick, Tait, Mae, Rose-

mary, Cooper, and Elliott—you have been our inspiration.

We would both like to thank Lara Ferroni, who is the most inspiring food photographer we know. We're astonished by the beauty of this book. We're also glad you became our friend through this process.

Enormous gratitude to Stacey Glick, the most determined and compassionate literary agent out there, and to Justin Schwartz, the most exacting editor we could have asked for. We have learned so much from you. The entire team at Wiley deserves our thanks as well.

Thank you to Anthony Bourdain, Julia Child, Thomas Keller, Jamie Oliver, Alfred Portale, Jean-Georges Vongerichten, and countless others, plus the legions of cooks who inspire us by stepping onto the line every night.

Finally, the biggest thanks of all goes to Lucy Marie Ahern. All is right in the world because you are here, kiddo.

introduction: dancing in the kitchen

"It seems to me that our three basic needs, for food and security and love, are so mixed and mingled and entwined that we cannot straightly think of one without the others.

So it happens that when I write of hunger, I am really writing about love and the hunger for it, and warmth and the love of it and the hunger for it; and then the warmth and richness and fine reality of hunger satisfied; and it is all one."

—M.F.K. FISHER

Time to start cooking again.

When Daniel Ahern and I first met, he was the executive chef at a small bistro in Seattle. Every month, he created a new menu, guided by the season and his palate. Fascinated by food and how to create it, Danny had spent his entire working life in front of a stove. After training at the New England Culinary Institute in Vermont, he cooked at some of the best restaurants in Colorado, in New York City, and at one of Seattle's best-loved French bistros. The highest compliment he will ever give his own food? *Eh, it's crap in a pot.* But I can say it for him. No matter what kind of food you call it—gourmet, haute cuisine, fancy schmancy—he knows how to cook it.

Soon after we met, Danny began cooking for me. After a long day at the restaurant—ten hours of prepping, whirling through dinner service, and cleaning up the kitchen for the next day—Danny arrived at my house and started swirling a sauce. When I protested that he had put in enough labor, he said calmly, "This isn't work. I'm cooking for the woman I love."

So, for months, at nearly midnight, we ate lamb chops with potato puree, beef tenderloin with port-balsamic sauce, and rich soups with white truffle honey. Thank goodness we were in the first throes of love and spent much of our time in other physical activity.

Every night, when he called from the restaurant during a break in dinner service, Danny giggled, "Guess what I'm bringing home for dinner?" The excitement in his voice told me I shouldn't bother making anything. Danny had created the roasted chicken roulade with goat cheese and arugula with me in his mind. He loves to cook because food gives people joy in the belly, and he wanted to give me joy. How could I protest?

But one night, about three months into our relationship, with Danny already moved in and the marriage proposal a funny story between us, he asked me on the phone, "So, what's for dinner tonight?"

The honeymoon was over. It was time for me to start cooking.

••

To tell the truth, I had missed cooking. The year before I met Danny, I had been in the kitchen nearly every evening, music playing and my hands dancing. After I was diagnosed with celiac disease, I said yes to food, with great enthusiasm. Told I should never eat gluten again if I wanted to save my life, I vowed to taste everything I could eat, rather than focusing on what I could not. I started a food blog—*that will keep you cooking, knowing you have to post a photograph and recipe nearly every day*—and reveled in my food discoveries. My friends loved the fact that I had to give up gluten because I cooked chicken thighs in pomegranate molasses or seafood stew from scratch or chocolate banana bread on a whim. Someone had to come over for dinner every night to keep my refrigerator from bursting with leftovers.

When I had been sick and tired, I could not cook. TV dinners crowded the freezer and the vegetables came in a bag, already chopped. I hated chopping onions because they left my fingers smelly; I never made stock from scratch. Until I had to give up gluten, I had never cooked a meal without following a recipe, and I never felt full.

But in the year before I met Danny, I stopped worrying about how long it took to put dinner on the table. Instead,

I enjoyed the smell of fresh ginger on the wooden cutting board, the sight of spinach wilting in hot oil, the feel of artichoke leaves brushed into melted butter, and the sound of roast chicken skin crisping in a hot oven.

Over the course of that year, I fell passionately in love with food. I had always loved it from afar, the way a pubescent girl loves that cute boy in the photo she tore out from *Tiger Beat* and tacked to her wall. But the year after I stopped eating gluten, I started to cook food, for the first time. The crush had become real love, imperfect and glorious.

••

On the day when Danny wanted to know what I was making for dinner, however, I seized up in fear. What do you make for a chef? My confidence crumbled. After watching him make world-class meals in a matter of minutes on our stove at midnight, I didn't know what to do.

I did the only thing I knew how to do; I looked to the words of other people.

The living room was cluttered with cookbooks, spines cracked open and flung away in panic. All the food magazines I had been meaning to read were now dog-eared with recipes I could make. I wanted something sure to impress, with ingredients in season. None of the recipes seemed right. What was I going to do?

As the afternoon wound down, and I still hadn't been shopping, I settled on something. A fancy egg dish, baked in a ramekin, with pungent cheese and fine-diced chives as a garnish. I hesitated for a moment, because it did seem like a lot of powerful cheese for such a tiny dish. However, the recipe was from a well-known food writer and had been published in one of the nation's leading newspapers, so I figured I was safe. Danny was sure to like this.

By the time he came home, I was all atwitter. After kissing him, I pointed toward the ramekins on the stove, "I made us dinner!" He looked at me gratefully, grabbed a spoon, and gulped down a bite.

He paused for a moment, a pained expression on his face. And then he made his way to the other side of the kitchen, stopped in front of the trash can, and spit out the food.

I knew when I opened the package of Stinking Bishop that the ¼ cup per ramekin the recipe called for was too much. The cheese smelled of wet socks and oozed out of the package like the Blob taking over that small-town movie theater. Why did I think Danny would like this?

I wanted to make the recipe I thought would impress him. A food blogger with a following, I wanted to rush to the moment where he would cover me with kisses and say how great I was.

Instead, he spit it out.

••

When I taught writing to high school students, I told them nearly every day, "Write to connect, not to impress." However, when it came to cooking for the chef, I didn't know how to follow my own advice.

If I had been cooking to connect with Danny, I would have made him a big pan of meatloaf. At the end of a long day of cooking, during which he usually forgets to eat, Danny needs more than a tiny ramekin of a refined dish, with a small salad on the side. If I had wanted to make him truly happy, I should have made him a big plate of nachos. He would have dug in and smiled at me with sour cream on his lips.

I could have chosen a recipe from one of my cookbooks stained with food and enjoyed my time in the kitchen. Instead, I spent time cooking to impress him, so he would think I knew what I was doing.

••

When Danny saw my tears, he gathered me into his arms and held me close. He comforted me, because he knew how. I babbled about bungling the meal, and how little I knew, and how intimidated I was by his skills.

"But sweetie, I can't write like you can. I can't even spell. I've been doing this for twenty years. Why do you expect to be as good at cooking as I am?"

That stopped me. I didn't know.

Why was I trying to compete? Why couldn't I just cook something and let it be imperfect? I had written an entire book about slowing down and being comfortable in the kitchen. But starting a new life with Danny, I had to learn it all over again. I had to learn it in my hands, this time, not my head.

Danny kissed my teary cheeks and hugged me close again. Then he pulled back and said, "Look, I intend to be with you the rest of my life. If you really want to know food, and know how to cook it, during the time we are together, I will teach you everything I know."

• •

Danny had an eager student on his hands.

The longer I loved him, the more I realized he knew, and the more I wanted to learn. After a lifetime of low energy and subsisting on food instead of living in it, I gobbled up new ingredients and longed to understand classic techniques. I wanted to eat anything that I could: wa-termelon gazpacho; poussin with red quinoa and rhubarb; shiso-cranberry sorbet. I wanted every bite to be memorable. Through endless explorations on my website and in enormous black notebooks I filled with recipes clipped from magazines and tasting notes from restaurants, I had become voracious.

Luckily for both of us, Danny didn't set up tutorials or give me homework. The learning was more liquid. I listened to Danny talk about his seafood purveyors with respect, and then I watched the way he cleaned the fish. I listened to Danny as he chose produce at the farmers' market, mumbling under his breath about the quality of the leeks and what he would do with them in the fish special. I listened to Danny when he talked about the dishes that sold well at the restaurant and the ones only a few customers wanted.

the importance of *mise en place*

This is probably the most important technique you can learn if you want to be a good cook. You'd think the secret to cooking like a chef would be something flashier, like how to sear a great piece of meat or make an astonishing presentation on the plate. But really, if you learn to prepare all your ingredients in advance and have them arranged in a clean fashion before you, cooking will be efficient. This will give you more time to pay attention to the sensory details in the act.

When I first met Shauna, she'd put a hot pan on the burner and then start chopping her onions with the oil getting hot in the pan. She'd run from the stove to the refrigerator while a dish was simmering, always a bit frantic. Even during parties she was running around, covered in flour, sweaty, and missing ingredients. Once I'd taught her to set up a mise en place first, she worked twice as fast, cleaned up more easily, and enjoyed the process more. Her onions didn't burn, either.

Have you ever wondered why recipes are written with a list of ingredients first? It's not just for your shopping trip. In this book, each of the ingredients has directions like "finely diced" for the carrots, or "peeled and roughly chopped" for the onions. Those are guidelines for how to set up a mise en place in advance. You can sometimes even prepare your ingredients the morning or night before you are going to make a dish, so you can start cooking right away when you come home from work. Chefs could not survive dinner service without an organized mise en place at their station. Treat your kitchen like this. The food will taste better if you're free to pay more attention to the cooking.

Sometimes I took notes as he cooked and asked more questions than a two-year-old. He walked me through a process and I scribbled words in my reporter's notebook, like his personal Girl Friday.

He loved this. No one had ever paid as much attention to his talents and passion. No one had ever asked him about the dishwashers in the restaurants where he worked, or his favorite grains, or what his process was for choosing the soup of the day. Over the months and years we knew each other, I watched the stumbling shy chef become a confident man, sure in his love.

Our lessons came through loving each other. When you fall in love, you want to know everything about that person. You want to devour him, sometimes, to make him part of you. Loving Danny meant being as endlessly curious about food as he was, and understanding the arduous life of someone who works in a restaurant. Mostly, I paid attention to his time at the restaurant. It fascinated me, his days of physical sensation and hard manual labor, so different than mine.

• •

Chefs work hard. They have scars and burns on their hands. They are frequently exhausted. They are working-class heroes, with jobs that mean they sear foie gras and mop the floors, all in one shift. They aren't paid well, certainly not well enough to eat the meals their companions cook in other high-end restaurants. Chefs are a band of brothers—men and women both—who have a work ethic most people never have. Most of us eat in restaurants as a means of escape. But for chefs, as well as servers and dishwashers, the restaurant is not theater. The restaurant is home, a grungy labor-of-love home, where the work is never completed, and the inhabitants are always capable of more.

Chefs just love to cook.

• •

It took knowing Danny to make me understand: chefs (and good home cooks) enjoy the entire process. Danny is happy in the kitchen by himself, peeling and chopping a pile of onions. Cooking sometimes means screwing up, and burning the sauce, and realizing it's because he wasn't paying attention, and starting over. Good cooking comes from a stockpot sitting on the back of the stove, slowly simmering for hours.

People who don't cook well try to rush through it, to get dinner on the table. That's why there are so many pre-cooked and half-baked and already chopped foods in packages in our culture. People want to skip the mundane stuff, rush through the process, and be done with it. But what delight there is in listening to the sizzle of oil in a skillet, in feeling the heat on our faces from the burners on the stove, in plopping an egg yolk in the hand and feeling the sticky white fall between the fingers. Sometimes the best part of cooking is standing in the kitchen, humming, and opening the oven to check on the roast.

I thought that Danny would teach me fancy techniques, using ingredients I had never heard of before. There was some of that, and you'll see those in this book. But mostly, the learning came from practice, from repetition, from taking a task and making it muscle memory. After cooking with him, watching him, and writing up these recipes with him, I started to see that the best food in the world came from the simplest tasks done right: searing, roasting, braising, stewing, sautéing until soft and translucent, straining, reducing.

Danny taught me that flavor comes from freshness, that it's far better to have a simple preparation with great ingredients than a fancy-pants flourish of a dish with something out of season and old oil. He taught me how to take shortcuts, how to stretch stock, how to compromise and let the food be less than perfect, if it's necessary. Danny is the one who taught me how to eat in season, how to develop relationships with the people who grow and make and sell our food, and how to enjoy being in the kitchen.

• •

Really, that's the main lesson he taught me, my favorite lesson in the world: enjoy this.

Together.

baked eggs with taleggio

VARIATIONS
There are so many semisoft cheeses you could use in place of the Taleggio, making a different dish every time: pecorino fresco, smoked Gouda, drunken goat cheese, or Manchego.

SUGGESTIONS
To make this a dinner, serve with roasted potatoes, latkes, or a salad.

Baked eggs with cheese is comfort and pleasure, easy to make and something to savor. Yours will always be good if you choose the right cheese. Cheese that is especially pungent, so much so that the smell makes your mouth pucker, might make your loved one skip his or her dinner.

Taleggio, however, is a slice of heaven on earth. This Italian semisoft cheese with a washed rind has a strong aroma, but the flavor is mild. The buttery cheese oozes when heated, so the creaminess weaves in with the eggs and makes a basic dish spectacular.

No one will spit this out. • *Feeds 4*

4 teaspoons unsalted butter
8 tablespoons heavy cream
4 ounces Taleggio cheese, sliced into
   4 equal pieces

8 large eggs
4 teaspoons finely chopped fresh thyme
Kosher salt and cracked black pepper

Preparing to bake. Preheat the oven to 375°F. Grease four 1-cup ramekins with ½ teaspoon butter each. Bring a small pot of water to boil, and reduce the heat to a simmer.

Filling the ramekins. Pour 1 tablespoon of the cream into each ramekin. Cut each slice of the Taleggio in half and put 2 pieces on top of the cream in each ramekin. Plop 2 eggs into each ramekin. Top with the chopped thyme. Top each dish with the remaining cream and ½ teaspoon of butter.

Baking. Place the ramekins into a baking dish. Pour the simmering hot water into the dish, enough to fill the dish halfway up the sides of the ramekins. Bake the eggs in the oven until the eggs are cooked and jiggle just a bit, 7 to 10 minutes. There should be no hint of uncoagulated egg. (Ask your guests how they like their eggs.) Season with salt and pepper and serve.

why is this book gluten-free?

After Danny and I fell in love, he turned his restaurant gluten-free. He decided to do this on his own. I didn't ask him. Since we share a passion for food, he didn't like creating a dish that he could only describe to me at the end of the night. So he took the all-purpose flour out of the kitchen and replaced it with a blend of sorghum flour, tapioca flour, potato starch, and sweet rice flour, plus some xanthan gum. He started cooking with grains he had never known before. He made sure that nothing with wheat in it touched the cutting board at his station, so no one would have to worry about cross-contamination.

In taking gluten away from his restaurant, he learned—as I continue to learn—that a little deprivation breeds creativity. Not only did he start cooking with ingredients he had never heard of before—quinoa, teff, and amaranth, for a start—but his food grew more refined. He loves to cook because his food can give people joy in the belly. Imagine the joy that people who fear they cannot dine in a restaurant feel when they eat his food. Often, he called me from the restaurant, moved, to tell me about the gluten-free couple who came in for their thirtieth wedding anniversary, or the young woman that came in for her first meal after diagnosis. With choices like pork campagne, pan-roasted rib eye with an artichoke-potato gratin, or prosciutto-wrapped king salmon with a wild mushroom risotto, these people did not feel deprived. They felt well fed and loved.

This book is born from that experience.

· ·

You may be wondering—*what the heck is gluten?* Gluten is the elastic protein in wheat, rye, barley, triticale, spelt, kamut, and farro. Most of us don't even know what kamut is, so it's pretty easy to avoid. However, wheat is in nearly everything in our culture, it seems. Try to make it through a day of coffee shops, lunch at the office, and airport layovers without eating anything on a bun or breaded. It's nearly impossible in some places. Then, when you add worrying about whether or not the young kid at the sandwich place made your tuna salad with breadcrumbs still in his fingers from the last baguette he sliced, your options have shrunk to almost nothing.

There are thousands upon thousands of us dealing every day with the dominance of wheat in our country's diet, whether we have wheat allergies, gluten sensitivities, or gluten intolerance. *Hundreds of thousands.*

I have celiac sprue, an auto-immune disorder that makes it impossible for my body to digest gluten. In fact, my body reacts to gluten as if a poison has entered my system, and sends out antibodies to destroy it. Sadly, however, my body ends up damaging itself instead. It only takes half a teaspoon of gluten to make me sick for three days. A lifetime of someone with celiac eating gluten can lead to over 250 different symptoms and medical conditions, including gastrointestinal problems, infertility, chronic fatigue, anemia, peripheral neuropathy, seizures, migraines, depression, and colon cancer.

Clearly, that sandwich isn't worth it.

According to the Celiac Disease Center of Columbia University, 1 out of 133 Americans suffers from celiac. Some scientists are starting to suggest that the number may be more like 1 out of 100. However, most of us are suffering from celiac without knowing it. Because medical schools taught prospective doctors for decades that the incidence of celiac is 1 in 5,000 people, with a narrowly defined set of symptoms, most doctors still don't think of celiac when someone comes in complaining. At this time, only 5 percent of people with celiac have been officially diagnosed.

The numbers are on the rise, however. Have you noticed the phrase *gluten-free* popping up everywhere these days? In nearly every national story I read about this increase in gluten-free products, the writer adopts a world-weary cynicism and wonders if this isn't all just a fad. Nope. The reason you see so many more gluten-free foods and products on the market is that people are finally finding out what ails them. They're mad as hell and they don't want to take it anymore. We want good food that is safe for us and still delicious.

I'm one of the lucky ones. I know what I have. However, for years before my diagnosis, I languished with low energy and constant medical ailments. In the six months before I finally learned what ailed me, I suffered so much that I spent more time in doctors' offices than the classroom where I taught. The people who loved me thought I was dying. When I found out I had to give up gluten, I had already been through multiple CT scans and emergency-room visits, experienced fears of cancer and kidney failure, and endured more pain than I can describe.

I had two choices. I could make my life an endless mourning of the loss of convenience foods and familiar meals, or I could dive into food and come up grinning.

You probably know which route I took.

There are many good gluten-free baking books already out there, with recipes for snickerdoodles and sandwich bread that work pretty well. We applaud the work of those folks. However, when I first started eating without gluten, I found that I wanted more than just substitute baked goods, especially because many of them were pale imitations, rather than actual food.

I wanted to eat. I didn't want to nibble on beige food for the rest of my life. Instead of longing for the meals of my youth, or the breadsticks at chain restaurants, I decided to try everything I *can* eat. If it doesn't have gluten in it, I eat it.

I say *yes*.

• •

After I fell in love with Danny, a talented chef more interested in food than anyone I know, my food horizons only widened. Instead of decrying the fact that most breakfast cereals on the market had gluten in them, I asked Danny to teach me how to make pork sausage from scratch, as well as eggs over easy with roasted potatoes. What did I care if canned soups had gluten in them? I preferred to eat homemade pumpkin soup when the air was crisp and the leaves were falling from the trees. Instead of buying TV dinners, I learned from Danny how to braise a pork shoulder into a tender stew with potatoes, cabbage, and caraway. The leftovers from that meal fed me for days, much better than the foil-covered plastic trays ever could. Upset that not one food available at big-chain coffee shops was gluten-free (even the fruit cup had granola in it), we baked apple-rosemary muffins and brought them with us for munching when we met friends.

Celiac is the only disease I know of where eating well is the healing. If I could heal myself through food, I might as well learn to cook duck confit with Umbrian lentils, cassoulet from scratch, and blue cheese cheesecake with a fig crust. When I was first diagnosed, I believed from the literature that I read that I would never eat in a restaurant again. *Too dangerous.* A funny irony that I ended up marrying a chef.

However, after those first few months together, when Danny brought home dinner every night, I stopped eating at his restaurant all the time. I preferred our time together to be side by side, the two of us chopping onions or fresh herbs, talking about our days with music playing in the back-ground. I wanted to eat the best food I could, *in our home.*

That's what we want to share with you in this book.

• •

Along with all this, sometimes you still want a piece of crusty warm bread with butter.

In the more than two years it took us to create this book, we learned enormously about how to make bread, the varieties of gluten-free flours, and the different tricks it takes to make a great gluten-free pizza dough. We'll be sharing those with you throughout the book, in recipe descriptions and sidebars on technique.

Knowing about the different flours in the book will help you through these pages as well. There are dozens of gluten-free flours available to U.S. consumers now, with more ease every day. Instead of suggesting a multitude of flours throughout this book, however, we have chosen to focus on a few that we think make the best baked goods. If you are just beginning, therefore, you won't have to buy an entire pantry full of flours in little bags.

• •

Almond flour. Take raw, blanched almonds, grind them to a fine flour (but not so much that they become almond butter), and you have almond flour. This and other nut flours—such as chestnut and hazelnut, macadamia and pistachio—add protein and vibrant taste to gluten-free baking.

Brown rice flour. Ground from whole-grain brown rice, this flour contains protein and good nutrients to ensure your baked goods are made of more than white starches. We use a brown rice flour ground superfine to avoid the grittiness that rice flour can have.

Corn flour. This was the secret ingredient in the astonishing baked goods we enjoyed in Italy. Ground from dried corn, this whole-grain flour adds a depth of taste and texture to the gluten-free crackers (and pizza dough) we created for this book. Note: this is not the same as masa harina, the lime-soaked flour used to make corn tortillas. Do not substitute.

Cornstarch. Most of us already have this in our homes, for thickening gravies or making puddings. When used as a gluten-free flour, cornstarch can create a consistent texture in baked goods.

Guar gum. The seeds of the guar plant make a granular powder when dried and ground. Take a look at many processed foods—such as commercial ice creams and puddings—and you will see guar gum on the list of ingredients as a binder. In small amounts, guar gum can somewhat mimic the elastic effects of gluten. If gums give you digestive upset, substitute an equal amount of psyllium husks for the guar gum.

Millet flour. Mild and ever-so-slightly sweet, millet is an adaptable grain. It's inexpensive and takes on the flavors of the foods around it. Millet flour gives gluten-free breads a good crumb.

Potato starch. The white starch that exudes from potatoes, when extruded by machines and put into little bags, helps gluten-free bakers to create light goods. This is not to be confused with potato flour, which is dried potatoes ground into a flour. If you want the taste of potatoes, choose potato flour.

Psyllium husks. This one might surprise you. The husk around the seeds of the psyllium plant (also known as plantago ovata) are great for gluten-free cooking. This insoluble fiber expands in water, becoming a thick gel. When you use it in small quantities as a dry ingredient in baking, it binds the ingredients together, mimicking some of the properties of gluten. You may not be familiar with the name but you know this stuff. Think Metamucil.) If xanthan and guar gum give you digestive upset, as they do me, you can substitute psyllium whole husks (or the powdered form) in the place of xanthan and guar gum in the recipes in this book. You will probably find it in the health section of your grocery store.

Sweet rice flour. This flour, which is mainly found in the Asian sections of the grocery store, is ground from mochi rice, which is a short-grain rice. The starchiness of that sticky rice makes the flour essential for gluten-free baking. Smooth and finely ground, sweet rice flour thickens sauces and gravies so well that no one eating them can tell they are gluten-free.

Sorghum flour. To us, sorghum flour is the closest in texture to whole wheat pastry flour of any of the gluten-free flours. We use it in many baked goods we create. Some people, however, detect a bitter taste in sorghum flour, so you should try some for yourself.

Tapioca flour. What we in the West call tapioca comes from a plant originally from Asia, known as cassava. (In South America, it is known as manioc.) When the root has been dried, it is ground into a white flour. This tapioca flour, also known as tapioca starch, has a similar starchy quality to potato starch.

Teff flour. As a flour, teff is nearly miraculous. The fine flour—ground from the tiny seeds—almost dissolve in baking, giving it a slightly gelatinous quality. This binds the baked goods in a somewhat similar fashion to gluten. Teff flour is essential in quick breads.

Xanthan gum. Geeky chefs in love with molecular gastronomy adore xanthan gum. So do commercial food producers, who put xanthan gum in salad dressings, frozen foods, and even toothpaste as a stabilizer, since it binds everything together in a uniform consistency. Now, you can buy some for your gluten-free baked goods. If gums give you digestive upset, substitute an equal amount of psyllium husks for the xanthan gum.

• •

If you want your gluten-free baking to be the best it can be, bake by weight instead of measuring cups. We have included the weights of each gluten-free flour in ounces and grams in the recipes for baked goods. If you try to substitute ½ cup of brown rice flour for ½ cup of sorghum flour, the baked good will be too heavy by nearly 2 ounces. This makes a difference in the ratio of flours to fats to eggs and probably means you won't have good waffles. Trust us. We have learned this the hard way. Please substitute your own flours for ours with the same number of ounces or grams written in a recipe.

Finally, know this. Every single recipe in this book, but particularly the ones for focaccia or pancakes, tart dough or fresh pasta, has been made, changed, tweaked, and tested at least 25 times before it made it onto these pages.

Please make each recipe exactly as written, at least once, before you play with it. We have chosen every ingredient with great care. After you feel confident with the recipe, feel free to play. We have. You'll see that some of the photographs might vary slightly from the ingredient list given. In the moment of creating them, we came up with something new.

We want you to play. That's what this is all about—enjoying yourself in the kitchen.

Now, start cooking.

at home

that first bite

We tell everyone that we fell in love at first sight. That's not entirely true. Oh sure, in hindsight, it was clear. I knew from the first moment I met Danny that something felt different. *Right*. However, it wasn't the Bobby Brady "I kissed a girl and saw fireworks" love at first sight. I felt comfortable with the man, comfortable enough to hit him on the arm and tease him about how much sugar he was pouring into his coffee before I even said hello. We had been writing e-mails back and forth for ten days, but they had not been long, revealing e-mails. I'd like to claim that you could sense the passion simmering beneath the surface

of every literary sentence. But for the most part, they were prosaic. Danny wrote about cooking the entire menu in a kitchen the size of a boat galley, and I shared the food I was making for my friend Sharon's visit (roast chicken salad with walnut oil, cauliflower with smoked paprika and cocoa powder, blood-orange sorbet). He asked if I had an ice-cream maker. I told him that I had learned to put an egg white in sorbet to make it more frothy. The fact that he mentioned his nieces and nephews intrigued me (a man who loves his family?), as did the fact that he noticed how I wrote about my nephew on my website (he likes kids?). But for the most part, his e-mails could have been text messages instead of letters—they were brief and to the point. We were both interested, but I had nothing invested. I didn't expect much.

You see, I had been meeting people through that online dating service for six weeks. Every one of them had been a dud. At thirty-nine, I was starting to accept the fact that I was never going to meet the love of my life, but I was hoping for more than a man who claimed to be one thing (single, in his forties, sober) and was another (married, in his early sixties, roaring drunk throughout the entire date). Just before Danny wrote to me, I'd given up. No more.

He was the last one to write and the only one with kind eyes.

Still, by the time I walked into the coffee shop to meet him, I carried a thick knuckle of wariness with me. This isn't going to work, I kept repeating in my head. Maybe that's why I felt so comfortable with him, because I was sure that I would never see him again. What did I have to lose?

Danny walked in with simmering optimism. He had felt the primal tug when he first saw my photo, he told me later. Shy from years behind a stove, he walked to our date with hope and nervousness both.

"I had bad hair, and I smoked. Of course I was nervous."

We talked about food and why we love it, why I was a teacher, and why he was a chef. I looked down at the table and noticed he had only a little hair on his forearms. I saw the burns and scars on his fingers and wrists. And I caught myself thinking, If we're going to date, he's going to have to change that hair immediately. (Danny was the only man since the 1980s to use handfuls of mousse, other than aging members of metal bands.) But I caught myself; I was thinking about dating him.

When we parted ways, in the middle of the day on a busy intersection in Seattle, I expected him to say good-bye and not ask for my number. Good, I thought, then I'll be done dating. Instead, he gave me his card and chased after it when the wind blew it out of my hands. And when we said good-bye, he leaned toward me and hugged me. He held me, close, with all the strength of a chef with good hands, and the kindness of a good man. There was no artifice in that hug. He just held me.

I walked away dazed. So did he.

He called me the next day. "I wanted to call you that afternoon, but Cliff told me to wait. I shouldn't look too eager." I made him wait until the day after that for me to call him back. I wanted to be sure. We haven't stopped talking since.

On our second date, he kissed me, late in the warm afternoon at the end of a wine tasting, both of us a little tipsy. "I had that line from the Kenny Chesney song stuck in my head all day: 'Cause it's the first long kiss on a second date'." Danny tells me I ate pork belly for the first time with him at Union, the restaurant across the street from the wine tasting, but I don't remember anything but the feel of his hand on my leg.

A few days later, we met outside my school and walked downtown toward Pike Place Market, holding hands. I had spent all the moments in between thinking about him, talking to him, cooking with him in my mind. Later,

he told me that he had made the latest recipe from my website—a tomato, Gruyère, and fava bean salad—as the special at the restaurant the night after we met. We chatted all day, in between his prepping sessions and my classes, mostly laughing. That sunlit spring day, I felt as though I knew him.

At the market, we gathered Concord grapes from Sosio's, Mt. Tam cheese from Beecher's, and gluten-free crackers for a spontaneous picnic. We sat in the little park by the water, drunks and crack addicts sprawled on the hill behind us. We fed cheese to each other off our fingers. We giggled and kissed in broad daylight, people walking by.

As we stood up to leave—he had to get to the restaurant to start working, even though it was only 12:30—he handed me a little white container. He had made me food—white beans braised in extra-virgin olive oil.

I took the beans home, nervous the entire bus ride. With all our talking and sharing stories, I still had not eaten any of his food. What if he wasn't any good? Watching him pick out the cheese and grapes, I knew he paid attention to every detail, the way that someone who doesn't talk that much notices everything instead. But I really liked this guy. Hell, like wasn't the word. I was deeply smitten, already falling, stirring him into my life. But if he couldn't cook beans?

He had told me to heat them up slightly. "Toss them in a little saucepan, gentle, until they are just warmed." As I heated the beans, rosemary wafted to my nose, a warm scent that could only come from hours of cooking. I hesitated before I tried them, the fork halfway to my mouth. Here it was, the moment of truth. I closed my eyes and took a bite.

The first layer of those beans felt crisp against my teeth, but when I bit down, the softness oozed out. I swallowed, my eyes still closed, but in pleasure this time.

braised white beans

VARIATIONS
You could try this with black beans instead of the cannellini and play with the flavors—try chiles and cumin, with a little lime zest. You don't have to use the Parmesan rind if you don't have one, but the next time you get to the bottom of your Parmesan, throw the rind in the freezer to save for making these beans.

Before I met Shauna, I had never read a food blog before. I was blown away by the idea that someone would write up recipes and take photographs of food, then update the site almost every day. I knew I wanted to bring her food. I thought about making her some elaborate recipe, with luxury ingredients sure to impress. But that's not me. And I wanted to show her who I am.

One slow night at the restaurant, I was fooling around with the extra white beans I had lying around. We were doing food and wine from Tuscany that month, so I had the rind of a good Parmesan cheese. I figured that if I simmered the beans in good extra-virgin olive oil with the Parm, this might taste like Italy. I let the beans braise overnight on the pilot light of the gas stove. That slow simmer yielded beans with a meaty, creamy tenderness and a little crunch on top.

I have to tell you, in all honesty, that I have never been able to replicate those beans. We've made the braised white beans a dozen different ways while writing this book, and none of our methods have produced beans exactly like the ones I made that night. It must have been something about the moment, the hope of her loving those beans, and me. This recipe comes close, though. • *Feeds 4*

1 cup dried cannellini beans, soaked overnight in cold water
1 small nub Parmesan cheese rind (about the size of half a thumb)
3 cups olive oil (you want a mild to peppery oil, not fruity)

3 cloves garlic, peeled
2 sprigs fresh rosemary
4 to 5 sprigs fresh thyme
Salt and freshly ground black pepper

Cooking the beans. Drain the beans. Pour the beans into a large saucepan along with the Parmesan cheese rind. Cover the beans with the oil and set over medium-high heat. When the oil starts to bubble, turn the stove to its lowest possible setting. Allow the beans to simmer, with only the occasional bubble rising to the surface, until they are soft and tender, 1 ½ to 2 hours.

Seasoning the beans. Throw the garlic, rosemary, and thyme into the saucepan. Season with salt and pepper and stir everything in. Grab a spoon full of beans, drain the oil from the spoon, taste the beans, and season with more salt and pepper, if necessary. Take the saucepan off the heat and allow the herbs to mingle with the beans as the oil cools down. Allow the beans and oil to fully cool before you eat them, about 1 hour. When you serve the beans, drain them from the oil. Reserve the oil and store any uneaten beans in the oil in the refrigerator.

the foods we used to woo each other

One afternoon, when school had finished for the day, I walked home in a sunlit trance, stopping every five minutes to take photographs of buds on trees and flowers in bloom, sending them to Danny on his cell phone.

When Danny saw those photos on his phone, he sent me back a picture of the ducks that crossed the street in front of his restaurant, in pairs. With it, he sent a message: "Hey, those breasts look plump and tasty. And those legs are perfect for confit."

May should be the time we drop the ball at midnight and celebrate in the streets. January is a lousy time to start

the new year. Dreary skies and dwindling light in the late afternoon make that celebration feel fake and cold. In May, finally, there are leafy green vegetables in the market again.

Danny and I didn't romance each other with tulips and cherry blossoms. He made me bouquets of pea vines and handed me fava beans. We walked around the market, holding hands, and picked out the first asparagus to eat with halibut cheeks. Danny fed me my first dandelion greens (in big salads with slivers of pâté and Marcona almonds), green garlic (folded into risotto), and ramps (grilled with coho salmon). He loved tasting the strawberries on my lips.

I know. It's enough to make you want to turn away, all that love. But that time truly was a birth for both of us. I was a few months away from forty, and Danny's family thought he would never find someone if he continued to work twelve hours a day, six days a week at a restaurant. Falling in love always feels like a bedazzling whirl of a jumble, but it means more when you thought it would never happen. A few weeks earlier, separately, we had both started to feel like the wilted vegetables in the back of the refrigerator. Now, together, we were like young salad greens sprouting up.

Normally, when you first start dating someone, you might go to the movies and dinners at restaurants. But Danny and I didn't see our first movie in a theater for nearly eight months, and we only went to a handful of restaurants in those first few months. For one thing, we couldn't afford to eat out much. Chefs are woefully underpaid for their work, as are teachers. On top of that, Danny wanted a break from that life, to spend his days off with me in a less confined space. Still, one Sunday morning we wandered around the market, sampling cheeses at the festival of local producers. Hungry after the appetizers, we wandered into a popular French restaurant and put in our names for a table. We hadn't thought this through. It was Mother's Day, and the restaurant was serving brunch. We were so much in love that we didn't care about the two-hour wait for lukewarm eggs. After that, though, we didn't go out much.

Instead, we snuggled in together, late at night, after Danny was done. I taught high school then, and I had to be awake at 6 a.m. on weekdays. However, I wasn't going to miss the chance to dance with my man because of an exam the next morning. Instead, I napped in the afternoon, graded as many papers as I could, and hopped on a bus to meet him in front of his apartment. Every time he stepped off his bus, with a to-go container in his hand, my heart flopped like a fish on a dock. I stood on my tiptoes to kiss him, and he held me close as we walked to his apartment.

If you have any illusions about the home kitchens of chefs, with gleaming appliances and pantries stocked with luxury items, think again. Danny's refrigerator was nearly bare. Some almost-empty pizza boxes sat on the top shelf, with a six-pack of cheap beer below them. On the bottom shelf was a withered salad in a plastic box, with a small tub of ranch dressing. In the sink, coffee mugs with an inch of old orange juice sat next to wine glasses with purple rings, the tannins gathered at the bottom of each glass. He didn't even have a real salt shaker, just the cardboard one that says SALT on the side, with little pictures of vegetables, from the convenience store up the street.

Danny apologized and kept the kitchen door closed against the mess he threw in there so I wouldn't see it. I didn't care. I just wanted to be with him. We rarely cooked in that kitchen, anyway. He brought home food from the restaurant. One night, he stepped off the bus with a soup container. He grinned when he handed it to me, and said, "Take a whiff."

I thought back to that date we had spent at Pike Place Market, where we stopped in the tiny stand selling all things truffle. As we dipped our noses into jars and tasted lavish oils, he hummed a song under his breath. "What's that you're singing?" I asked.

He leaned in and sang, in a low voice: "Out the blue you came to me and blew away life's misery out the blue life's energy. Out the blue you came to me."

I gasped. Not just because he was singing so out of tune (I'm not trying to be mean—you can ask him—he can't sing), but because he was singing one of John Lennon's most obscure songs, a love song I had always loved, but no one else ever knew.

I leaned in for a kiss, but he put his finger, dipped in white truffle honey, into my mouth instead. We had to buy the jar, of course.

So that evening, when he opened the container, I smelled the potato-leek soup he had made for the restaurant's nightly special. On top, just dolloped, was a bit of the white truffle honey. He spooned it into my mouth as if he were feeding a baby. Creamy potatoes, a tickle of sweetness, and the earthy quality of the truffle—it was so good.

The next morning, we ran for the bus, because we had slept too late again. I remember nuzzling into him, my hair wet, our eyes sleepy, and I was clutching leftover soup in my hand, for lunch.

potato-leek soup with white truffle honey

VARIATIONS
You could make
this with blue
potatoes, which
would color the
soup a purple-gray
color. If you cannot
eat dairy, you can
omit the cream and
use stock or more
water instead—
this won't give
you a creamy, rich
consistency, but
the soup will still
be good.

SUGGESTIONS
You could make
fried leeks to
garnish the soup.
Or homemade
potato chips would
be a great tasting
presentation.

The truffle honey makes this unbelievable, but if you can't find it, simply savor this as a great potato-leek soup. Potatoes, leeks, onions, a bit of herbage—this is simple but rewarding. As a cook, you need some soups in your repertoire, and this is a hearty, comforting one to have.

• *Feeds 6 to 8*

4 leeks, white part only, cut in half
   lengthwise
¼ cup extra-virgin olive oil
1 medium yellow onion, peeled and
   medium diced
5 cloves garlic, smashed and peeled
1 tablespoon chopped fresh rosemary
1 tablespoon chopped fresh sage

1 tablespoon chopped fresh thyme
3 pounds Yukon gold potatoes, peeled
   and quartered
2 cups heavy cream
2 tablespoons cold unsalted butter
Kosher salt and cracked black pepper
2 to 3 tablespoons truffle honey (optional)
1 tablespoon finely chopped fresh chives

Preparing the leeks. Chop the leeks. Place in a bowl full of cold water and allow them to sit for 20 minutes. Drain the leeks, pat dry, and chop roughly.

Sautéing the vegetables. Set a large stockpot over medium heat. Pour in 2 tablespoons of the olive oil. Add the onion and garlic to the hot oil and cook, stirring to ensure they do not burn, for 1 minute. Add the leeks and cook, stirring. When the onion and leeks are softened, toss in the rosemary, sage, and thyme. Cook until the herbs release their fragrance into the room, about 2 minutes. Tumble in the potatoes. Add enough water to cover by 1 inch.

Cooking the soup. Raise the heat to high and bring the soup to a boil. Cook until your paring knife slides right through one of the potatoes, about 15 minutes; do not overcook the potatoes or you will have watery soup. When the potatoes are done, stop whatever you are doing and puree the soup.

Pureeing the soup. Puree the soup in a blender in batches, pouring the remaining 2 tablespoons of olive oil into the blender as the blender is running. Press each batch through a fine-mesh sieve back into a large bowl. Repeat until all the soup is pureed and pour it back in the pot.

Finishing the soup. Add the cream to the soup and stir to blend. Bring the soup to a boil, then turn down the heat to medium. Simmer, stirring occasionally, for 10 to 15 minutes. Whisk in the cold butter. Taste the soup and season with salt and pepper. Remove the soup from the heat.

To serve, ladle the soup into bowls. Garnish each bowl of soup with 1 teaspoon of the truffle honey (if using) and the chives.

how to cook potatoes

You can never go wrong with potatoes, unless you over-cook them. That is such a waste. Here's what to do to ensure you can eat great potatoes.

Start with good potatoes. Try different kinds—there are thousands in the world. It's not all about russets. Try Russian bananas, purple Peruvians, red Lasordas, German Butterballs, and Mountain Rose. We love Yukon golds, most days, but we also like to go to the farmers' market and try new varieties.

• Start with cold water when you boil potatoes. Adding them to boiling hot water releases the starches imme-diately, which leads to gummy potatoes. Potato starch is good for gluten-free baking but not for mashed potatoes.

• Pour in lots of salt to cook the potatoes. The water should taste like the ocean. Salt brings the flavor out of potatoes. If you don't season them properly during cook-ing, you'll add more and more salt later, and then you'll have overly salted potatoes.

• I like to parboil the potatoes before roasting, until the potato slides off the knife. That makes the insides softer, and the outsides crisp. A contrast in texture makes food more interesting.

• If you mash the potatoes with a fork or potato mash-er, there's still a chance of lumps. If you use a handheld mixer, you're beating the starch out of them. For the best results, try pushing the potatoes through a ricer or food mill. They emerge as squiggles of potato, ready to mash on their own. You don't even need cream because they will be so smooth. You can also push them through a fine-mesh sieve with the back of a ramekin or a large wooden spoon.

Respect the potato and it will treat you right.

grocery shopping as foreplay

In the middle of picking out produce one day, Danny grabbed a cucumber and wiggled his eyebrows lasciviously. Of course, I giggled.

We stood in front of the cheese section for fifteen minutes, nibbling on Drunken Goat and Cocoa Cardona, comparing notes and wondering about Manchego for the macaroni and cheese.

We walked down the condiment aisle, arms slung around backs, hands tucked into each other's pockets.

Danny sent me off on a mission: we'd forgotten the green onions. I ran back to the arranged piles of fruits and vegetables, rooted around for the greenest bunch, and made my way back to him. Turning the corner, I thought, Oh, there he is. And he bloomed again before my eyes.

At the checkout counter, we played our favorite game—looking into other people's carts. We wondered, What are they having for dinner tonight? We whispered

behind our hands and laughed into each other's shoulders. Sometimes ideas popped into our heads when we saw someone else's meal in composite pieces. Danny would run back to the aisles this time.

Everything at the grocery store seemed brighter, and more exciting, when we were looking at it through each other's eyes. When two people are first dating, they open their worlds to each other. Some people show each other their record collections. Others have litmus tests with movies. ("I swear, if you don't like *Waiting for Guffman*, I don't know how this is going to work.") We sauntered through grocery stores and showed each other our favorite mustards.

Of course, we like music and movies too. Danny loved country music, which I always thought was for bumpkins and loud patriots. When he played me love songs, I changed my mind. Many a time we've been in the car and listened to an achingly open ballad, and I've turned to him with tears in my eyes and said, "Your damned country music." My father taught film when I was a kid, so I grew up watching old movies projected on the living room wall, through a 16-mm clackety-clack projector. I've introduced Danny to Buster Keaton and *Harold and Maude*, two essentials of my world. He's given me back the comics section of the newspaper (I hadn't read them since I was a kid; he reads them every morning), *South Park*, and M*A*S*H. I've shared Buddhist principles, Eddie Izzard, and how to upload photographs on Flickr with him. We share much more together than just our love of food.

But food—talking about it, shopping for it, cooking it, savoring it, and discussing it afterwards—is a big part of who we both are, separately, but especially together. For us, going to the grocery store is foreplay. Danny taught me not to walk into the market with a recipe or set idea of what we would be eating. I watched him invent dishes every time we went to the store, and I started to prefer his way. Go with a list and you are completing a task. Go with an open mind and you start discovering.

Shopping with him became my favorite game. Sometimes I'd watch him stalk the aisles, hunting down his prey. Local baby arugula appeared for the first time all year. He stuffed a bag full. What protein went well with it?

I might have chosen a more expensive cut of meat, but as he scanned the lit refrigerator case, his eyes opened wide and he reached in for chicken breasts. He couldn't speak. I learned over time that the longer he went without words—too absorbed in his thoughts to answer, no matter how many times I asked "What? What did you think of?"—the better the idea.

"Do you have a meat pounder at your house?" he asked me. I laughed. Luckily, I did. I had bought it once for a recipe I intended to make but never did.

"Good. We'll need goat cheese," he said, as he put chicken breasts into the basket and started moving, immediately. I followed. We found a tangy local goat cheese, some firm zucchini, and a can of San Marzano tomatoes. He picked up another jug of Italian extra-virgin olive oil and made his way to the checkout counter. I followed him with a bag of Yukon gold potatoes and a bottle of wine.

Every ingredient was simple. But he wanted those ingredients, and only those. At home, he pounded out the chicken breast with my meat pounder and made us chicken roulade with goat cheese and arugula, roasted potatoes, and a simple pan-dripping sauce with the leftover veal stock he had brought home from the restaurant. He made something far more interesting than I would have by following my recipe.

Even when he wasn't with me at the grocery store, I began to look at food differently as I shopped for dinner parties with friends. I started playing, looking to the mundane ingredients as much as the fancy and new. What could I do with these? I was learning so much from him.

We assume a lot about the people we love, don't we? It didn't occur to me, until much later, that he could be as excited about shopping for food as I was. He was the chef. Of course he was commanding in a grocery store.

"Sweetie, did you forget how I was eating when you met me?" He never cooked in his own home, so he never went to the store. Instead, when he was away from the restaurant, he ate corn dogs and rotisserie chicken from the convenience store down the street, Taco Bell burritos, Subway sandwiches, and cheap burgers from Dick's. To shop at a well-lit store stocked with fresh produce and great vinegars was a revelation for him.

"Besides, I was with you. It was such a wonderful experience. We were doing something together, as a couple. Your eyes would light up when I'd say, 'Have you tried this before?' And then we'd take the food to your house, cook together, dance, and laugh. And then we'd eat. I'd never had so much fun in my life."

Neither one of us had ever been shopping with someone who loved food as much as we did. Most people just didn't understand. Food keeps us alive, all of us, in a literal way. But for Danny and me, sharing food together brought us alive.

roasted chicken roulade with goat cheese and arugula

VARIATIONS
If the taste of chèvre is too tangy for you, you could use fresh ricotta here. Spinach could be the bit of green in place of the arugula.

SUGGESTIONS
Serve with mashed potatoes or jasmine rice.

The word *roulade* scares people because it sounds too fancy to make at home. But roulade just means rolling up a thinly sliced piece of meat. That's why you have to pound the chicken thin, so you can roll it really tight.

When you are pounding, focus on the thickest part of the breast. Pound it away from you. Keep the meat pounder down, but hold it so that it is angling away from you. If you pound the breast directly, in the center, you will not flatten the whole thing evenly. If you want the chicken breast even thinner after pounding, take out a rolling pin and flatten it that way.

You can use this rolling technique to make any variety of dishes. You can stuff fish, chicken, or pork with mushrooms, breadcrumbs, or even other forms of meat. Brown the meat before baking or braising it in wine or stock—that's your template. Experiment from there. • *Feeds 4*

4 tablespoons extra-virgin olive oil
1 small shallot, peeled and sliced
2 cloves garlic, peeled and sliced
2 tablespoons chiffonade fresh basil
¼ pound arugula
Kosher salt and cracked black pepper

½ cup soft goat cheese (chèvre)
4 chicken breasts, skin on
½ cup fortified wine (Madeira or Marsala)
2 cups chicken stock
2 tablespoons butter

Sautéing the vegetables. Set a large sauté pan over medium-high heat. Pour in 2 tablespoons of the oil. Add the shallot and garlic to the hot oil and cook, stirring, until the shallot is softened and translucent, about 2 minutes. Toss in the basil and cook, stirring, until it releases its fragrance, about 1 minute. Throw in the arugula and cook until wilted, about 1 minute more. Season with salt and pepper and take a taste. Season more, if necessary. Remove the pan from the heat.

Finishing the filling. Allow the vegetables to come to room temperature. Fold in the goat cheese to coat the vegetables. (If you fold the goat cheese into hot, just-sautéed vegetables, you will have melted goat cheese.)

Preheating the oven. Turn the oven to 450°F.

Pounding, stuffing, and rolling the chicken breasts. Put the chicken breasts skin side down on a piece of plastic wrap, then cover them with another piece of plastic wrap. Pound the breasts with a meat pounder, pounding away from you, until they are spread out to a ½-inch thickness. Season both sides of the meat with salt and pepper.

Put about 2 tablespoons of the cooked vegetable mixture in the middle of each chicken breast, lengthwise. Don't spread out the stuffing all the way to the edges because it will burn when you cook the breast. Center the stuffing both lengthwise and horizontally.

Roll the chicken breast from the bottom up, tightening toward you between each roll. If you have tightened the chicken breasts well enough, you won't need a toothpick, but it's okay to use one.

Searing the chicken breasts. Set a large oven-safe sauté pan over high heat. Pour in the remaining 2 tablespoons of oil. Put the rolled chicken breasts in the hot oil. Sear until the chicken is browned on the bottom, 3 to 4 minutes. Flip the chicken breasts. Slide the sauté pan into the oven. Cook the chicken breasts until the internal temperature reaches 155°F, the meat is white, and the juices are running clear, 7 to 8 minutes. Remove from the oven and set the chicken breasts aside on a plate.

Making the pan-dripping sauce. Drain the grease from the sauté pan, leaving the crispy bits and browned parts in the pan. Pour in the wine, scraping up the goodness from the bottom. Set over medium heat and cook until the wine has almost entirely evaporated. Pour in the chicken stock and cook until bubbling. Whisk in the remaining cooked vegetables. Swirl in the butter until it is fully incorporated. Taste the sauce and season with salt and pepper, if necessary.

To serve, swirl ¼ cup of sauce on each plate and top with a chicken breast.

watching him cook

"The first time I stepped foot in your kitchen, I imagined what it would be like to cook with you. I didn't need to see the rest of the house before I said yes. Spacious and filled with light, with a little nook with skylights—that kitchen felt like home."

The second story of a large house, with the windows facing west to meet the Olympic Mountains, that apartment was my sanctuary for three years before I met Danny. It sat on the top of a hill, in one of Seattle's most charming neighborhoods. All around my little place were lovely homes with large yards and people who smiled as they walked by with strollers. Down the street was Macrina Bakery, one of the best in Seattle. I ate their buttermilk biscuits and kalamata olive loaf nearly every day, until I found out I had celiac and could not eat gluten anymore. Across the street from my apartment was Ken's, a small grocery I visited frequently where every checkout person became a friend.

For three years, I lived there alone, including the dark months of pain after a terrible car accident when I could barely walk. I ate a

lot of frozen dinners in those months, replenished when I could hobble across the street to the store. Briefly, one summer, Danny worked at a restaurant three blocks from my front door. He swears that every Monday, when a coworker gave him a ride to do inventory, he stared up at that house and wondered who lived there.

Just before I met Danny, friends helped me paint the wall above the stove a bright spring green. A crew from the Food Network was coming to film me for a show they were doing on people whose lives were transformed by food. I wanted a vivid backdrop for the shots of me cooking. I didn't know then how much time Danny and I would spend looking at that green wall, or that photographs of both of our toddler nephews would hang above the stove.

Late at night, after eleven, I stood at the living room windows, craning my neck to look for the bus. At the time we met, Danny didn't drive; he hadn't since he was a young man. And my car had gone kaput. So our romance was conducted by bus, at first. All evening, when he had the time, he called me, to tell me stories and dirty jokes. I knew where he was, and that his hunger had kicked in on Third Avenue. I couldn't wait to hear the whoosh of the bus sliding to a stop beneath my house. Sometimes, we couldn't stand it, and he grabbed a cab from the restaurant instead.

And when he came through the door of the house, he kissed me. (We'll skip the next part.) When we made it to the kitchen, he pulled white boxes from his battered backpack and started unpacking them. Roast chicken breast (an "airline" breast, which he taught me means the entire breast plus the wing to the first joint) with crisp skin, potato puree, and first-of-the-season asparagus. That late at night, he mostly reheated our meal, but he was dancing in front of the stove.

I loved watching him flip food without a spatula or any hesitation. He moved backward on the balls of his feet, watching the sauté pan, and shimmied forward without moving his feet. In the moment in between, he tossed everything in the pan into the air and watched it settle down perfectly. Every time, I stared.

On his days off, however, he started everything from scratch in that kitchen. Watching him chop onions made me sit up and take notice. He chopped his onions with a surgical precision and wonderful relaxation in his body. He had the intent focus of an athlete who makes it look like he could have run that 100-meter dash ten seconds faster if he had broken a sweat. When I chopped onions, I focused so intently that I almost looked angry, but I hacked at the poor vegetables so badly that it looked like a scene from a Sam Peckinpah movie.

As he started to stir and swirl the sauce, we talked. But after a few moments, I quieted down. He needed to focus, to really feel the food. Goofy and sweet, shy and sometimes passive, Danny grew powerful in front of the stove. He never barked out orders or became controlling. He loved it when I wanted to work next to him, and he forgave my slovenly chopping. His silence, his concentration, and his every balletic movement made it clear to me: he was home. I wanted to be around that calm as much as I could.

As much as I worried at first that he was working in front of the stove after a long day at the restaurant, I learned to stop protesting. He loved it. He rarely had the chance to see someone so love his food. "I felt like I was cooking for somebody who really appreciated what I did, not just someone who had paid for it. Food became more personal for me with every meal."

One lazy Monday afternoon, about six weeks after we met, Danny made me a frisée salad with a warm bacon vinaigrette.

After one bite, I turned to him and said, "Oh, would you just move in with me?"

"Yes," he said. "Yes."

why dicing vegetables correctly matters

Shauna used to wreak havoc on onions with a blunt knife. I let her do so, until she asked me for help. "What's the difference between a fine dice and a rough chop? Why does it matter?"

If you are sautéing vegetables and all the onion pieces are different sizes from haphazard chopping, then the smaller pieces will burn and the larger pieces will tend toward raw. That affects the taste. It also affects the presentation of the food. When you see vegetables diced precisely in a dish, you know that someone took the time to make this meal special for you. You want to make your food look appealing for your family and friends.

Often roughly chopped vegetables are not going to be served that way. Those vegetables might be pureed later or pulled from the sauce, so it's okay for them to be imperfect. But still, for even cooking, it's best to chop them thoughtfully, fairly close in size.

Mainly, you have to practice and allow yourself imperfection. I probably chopped fifty pounds of onions before I could chop comfortably, in a fast rhythm. But do practice. This really does matter to your cooking.

veal goulash

VARIATIONS
Pecorino fresco is only available in the spring, but you can also use fresh mozzarella in this recipe to equally good effect.

SUGGESTIONS
Instead of the veal, try ground beef, pork, buffalo, or venison for a different goulash.

The first time I was at Shauna's house, we cooked together. Her roast chicken made me yell with delight. My roasted yellow pepper potato puree seemed to do the trick for her too.

The next time I was at her house, however, we made veal goulash. We both ate goulash as kids, but it didn't taste like this. I had never made this before; I created it with her. Shauna had never eaten veal before this dish. She said it was evocative of every other meat she had tasted before it. The melted pecorino knocked me back in my seat with its softness. And of course, the pasta was gluten-free, so Shauna could dig into the dish.

We both slammed our forks into the goulash and moaned. Reminiscent of comfort, with a twist of culinary adventure—soft, rich, and memorable—this is the perfect meal for new lovers.
• *Feeds 4*

6 tablespoons extra-virgin olive oil
1 pound ground veal
½ large yellow onion, peeled and small diced
9 cloves garlic, peeled and thinly sliced
1 tablespoon finely chopped fresh thyme
1 tablespoon finely chopped fresh rosemary
1 tablespoon finely chopped fresh sage
6 medium ripe tomatoes
1 medium yellow onion, peeled and finely chopped

1 stalk celery, finely chopped
½ medium carrot, peeled and finely chopped
2 teaspoons smoked paprika (Pimentón de la Vera)
1 tablespoon chiffonade basil
Kosher salt and cracked black pepper
2 cups uncooked gluten-free fusilli pasta
½ pound pecorino fresco cheese (see Variations)

Browning the ground veal. Set a large sauté pan over medium heat. Pour in 2 tablespoons of the oil. Add the ground veal to the hot oil. Cook, stirring to break up the meat, until it is browned, about 10 minutes. Strain the cooked meat and set it aside. Drain the grease from the pan.

Sautéing the vegetables. Pour 2 more tablespoons of the oil into the pan. Add the diced onion and two-thirds of the garlic to the hot oil. Cook, stirring, until the onion is softened and translucent, about 5 minutes. Toss in the thyme, rosemary, and sage and cook, stirring occasionally, until the herbs release their fragrance, 2 to 3 minutes. Spoon the veal back into the pan, stir, and set the pan aside.

Blanching and chopping the tomatoes. Bring a large saucepan of salted water to a boil, using enough salt to make the water taste like the ocean. Mark a small X on the bottom of the tomatoes with a paring knife. Add the tomatoes to the salted water and cook until the skin starts to slip off, just 5 to 10 seconds. (Don't let the tomatoes stay in the water for much longer, or you will start to cook them.) Transfer the tomatoes to a bowl of ice water to cool quickly.

Remove the tomato skins, which should slip off fairly easily. Cut the tomatoes in half and remove the seeds. To chop the tomatoes, slice each tomato one way, and then slice them the other way.

Preheating the oven. Turn the oven to 500°F.

Making the tomato sauce. Set a large saucepan over medium-high heat. Pour in the remaining 2 tablespoons of oil. Add the finely chopped onion, celery, carrot, and the remaining garlic to the hot oil. Cook, stirring, until the vegetables are softened, about 5 minutes. Sprinkle in the smoked paprika and cook until the spice begins to perfume the air. Throw in the basil and cook until it becomes fragrant, about 1 minute. Scoop in all but 1 cup of the chopped tomatoes. Cook over medium heat until the tomatoes are softened, about 10 minutes.

Transfer the tomato and vegetable mixture to a blender and puree, in batches if necessary. Pour the sauce back into the saucepan and taste it. Season with salt and pepper, if necessary.

Assembling the goulash. Add the cooked veal to the tomato sauce. Bring the mixture to a gentle boil. Taste and season with salt and pepper, if necessary. Add the remaining chopped tomato to the sauce for a slightly chunky texture. Stir in the pasta.

Cooking the goulash. Pour the tomato sauce, ground veal, and pasta into a 9 x 12-inch baking dish. Top the goulash with thick slices of the pecorino fresco cheese. Bake the goulash in the oven until the cheese has melted and become bubbly, about 10 minutes.

losing him to an open kitchen

One Friday evening, Danny called me from the restaurant after the rush of dinner service had passed. Jazzed after a good night, he talked fast. "Hey, I just read that Tilth has opened. You want to go for dinner?"

Go out to dinner on a Friday night? That never happened. Danny and I never dated like other people—all our best times outside the house were on Monday afternoons. By that time, my house was our home, so we had every late evening together. But a date? That was as rare as the ahi tuna we had eaten the night before.

"Hell, yeah!" I answered. "When can I come pick you up?"

Finally, the long bus rides had ended. I had found a car. Whistling to the Beatles as I rounded the curve around the lake, I thought about the stories I had saved up all day. No matter what happened, it reminded me of Danny. And seeing him lock the front door

of the restaurant and turn toward me filled me with a joy I couldn't describe.

We chattered all the way across town. Tilth was the much-anticipated restaurant of Maria Hines, one of *Food and Wine*'s best new chefs. Only the second restaurant in the nation to be certified organic, Tilth composed its menu almost entirely of ingredients from local farms and ranches. I anticipated long conversations about the grass-fed hanger steak, the duck burgers, the sweet carrot risotto, and the corn crème brûlée with candied bacon.

We walked into the cozy green house and saw every table taken. This was only Tilth's second day in business

and the place was packed. The only seats were at the bar, in front of the open kitchen. At least there were two together.

I wiggled onto the bar stool and leaned toward Danny, ready to start a conversation. But he was somewhere far away. Mouth slightly open, eyes focused, Danny was staring at the kitchen.

My eyes turned toward where he was looking. I saw a gleaming-clean space, fairly small, with quiet people working hard. Heads bent down, they placed ingredients methodically, moved plates without clinking them, and seemed to communicate without words. They all looked as focused and relaxed in their bodies as Danny was in our kitchen.

I saw why he was mesmerized, and I accepted it. We weren't going to be talking all night.

When I was a kid and we went to a restaurant, my mother threw a fit if we were seated at a table by the kitchen. She was convinced it was the worst spot in the place. She didn't want to see what actually transpired behind closed doors. I think she worried that the chefs were spitting in our food when she made a fuss about something not being hot enough. (Danny swears he has never seen this in a professional kitchen.) Danny's dad always asked to be moved, as well, because he couldn't hear the conversation above the sounds of the kitchen. Most people regard eating in restaurants as escape, or even theater. They don't want to see how it happens.

Danny has to look at the kitchen in every restaurant we visit. Sometimes the owners and other chefs grow suspicious, as if he's a spy. But he just wants to see how they all live. His kitchen was the smallest one in Seattle. There wasn't room for much staff. I think he was lonesome for chef companions.

"Besides, I learn so much. You get to see how other people do stuff. Going out to eat just makes me want to cook more."

Danny always sees details I could never catch. "I can tell if there is tension in the air, if the staff gets along well, if they are behind on something, if they forgot something. I love to hear the squawking between everybody."

He tells me about a time he was walking downtown and passed a fabulous restaurant where there's a window into the kitchen the size of the wall. "I watched it one time, and this guy was just fucking buried. In the weeds. You could tell because he was sweating and whoever was expediting was talking only to him. Oh, the facial expressions. I just stood there watching, thinking, 'Oh, you poor bastard.' I would never wish that upon anybody."

Danny has taught me to avoid restaurants based on the way the staff looks. "If there's a chef with his jacket hanging outside his apron, covered in grease, working at a station with sour cream hanging off his 9-pan, your food is going to taste like that too." How chefs command the kitchen is an indication of how the whole place is run.

"Something as simple as how a restaurant makes potato puree tells you everything you need to know. A lot of restaurants use bain maries to keep mashed potatoes warm. But if you hear this distinct sound like clunk clunk crink, you know it's the lid coming off the bain marie and a spoon hitting the metal sides. That means the steam from the potato puree is going to form as water on the lid of the container, drip down into the potatoes, and make them sodden and disgusting. Keep the lid off, and the potatoes won't be watery. Or better yet, rice all the potatoes ahead of time and make them up to order."

He notices everything.

Mostly, Danny is entranced by the fluid motion of a good kitchen. He can tell when the staff is busy, and if the cooks are good or not. He watches the way they whirl together without words, how they float instead of stutter-stepping around, and how they move as one organism. Danny loves to watch another team at work, unguarded, dancing, collaborating.

However, the way he watches kitchens is more than professional curiosity. Seeing his fellow chefs at work gives him an indication of the food we're going to eat. If he can tell that the people behind the stoves are not putting their heart into their work, we're going to eat mediocre food. "When I watch a good kitchen at work, I feel that I'm going to have a great meal, because the people in there care about what they are doing. That food is going to be memorable."

I don't mind anymore, the way we sit in silence, side by side, when we go out to eat in restaurants with open kitchens. We have plenty of time to talk at other times. When we watch a kitchen together, I learn about food, and about how Danny thinks.

potato puree

VARIATIONS
If you cannot eat dairy, try goat's milk or rice milk instead of the milk. Soy creamer might work instead of the heavy cream.

SUGGESTIONS
Mashed potatoes go well with nearly everything. For Danny, potatoes are pretty close to the essence of life.

Serving overcooked, watery potatoes is a sin. I've been to so many restaurants where they overcook potatoes, and it's inexcusable. If they overcook the potatoes, what else are they doing wrong? Potato puree is simple. But if you can't do it right, it ruins your entire meal.

Use Yukon golds for potato puree. Russets are starchier, so it's easier to overcook them. Russets are also dirty, so you have to wash them before you can peel them. Yukons have a lovely buttery flavor that makes potato puree even better.

Drain the potatoes properly. If you don't drain them well and you rice them, they are going to take on the water they were cooked in. Let them steam dry for a few minutes instead of rushing to rice them right away.

(Danny doesn't want me to tell you this, but when he cooked at Gramercy Tavern, Marco Canora said that Danny made the best potato puree in the place. I have to say, I agree. I've never had mashed potatoes like the ones he makes at home.) • *Feeds 4*

5 large Yukon gold potatoes, peeled
½ cup whole milk
½ cup heavy cream
4 tablespoons (½ stick) unsalted butter, softened

2 to 3 tablespoons extra-virgin olive oil
Kosher salt and cracked black pepper
3 tablespoons fine-chopped fresh chives (optional)

Preparing the potatoes. Cut the potatoes in half lengthwise. Make slices at every 1-inch interval. The slices should be about the same size, so toss the stubby ends.

Cooking the potatoes. Pour 12 cups of cold water into a large pot; the potatoes need room to bounce around. Add enough salt to make the water taste like the ocean. Add the potatoes to the water. Bring the water to a boil over high heat, then reduce the heat to medium-high. Simmer until you can slide a knife right through one of the potato pieces without any force, 10 to 15 minutes.

Draining the potatoes. Pour the potatoes into a large colander and shake to make sure all the water is out. Let the colander sit in the sink for 3 to 4 minutes to steam the potatoes dry.

Ricing the potatoes. If you own a potato ricer or food mill, push the potatoes through. If the potato is cooked properly, you should have to use a bit of muscle. If you do not own a ricer or food mill, push the potatoes through a fine-mesh sieve with the back of a ramekin or a large wooden spoon.

Heating the cream. Heat up the milk and cream in a small saucepan on medium heat until the mixture begins to boil. Remove from the heat.

Finishing the potatoes. Place the potatoes back in the large pot. Stir the softened butter into the potatoes. Pour in the hot milk mixture, folding it in with a rubber spatula. Add the oil and continue to fold. When the potatoes and liquids are fully combined, taste the potatoes. Season with salt and pepper, perhaps about 2 teaspoons each. Taste again until the potatoes are how you like them. (Oh darn, you have to keep trying spoonfuls of potatoes.) Top with the chopped chives, if you wish.

eating through the seasons together

During the school year, when the alarm clock threw me out of bed at 6 a.m., I resented the darkness outside my window. It always took me twenty minutes to remember how good it is to be alive.

However, in June, I wake up when the sun hits my eyes and feel Danny stirring beside me. Nothing makes me happier than turning toward him and seeing his face. I kiss his forehead, whisper "I love you," and climb over him in the bed. He always sleeps later, after a long night at the restaurant. Besides, I still like some time in the kitchen alone.

One morning, I went downstairs to grab the newspaper, shaking the hair out of my eyes. In the kitchen, the daily movement of emptying the filter and running the water awakes me even more. As the liquid started dripping, and the kitchen filled with the smell of fresh coffee, I pulled out a muffin tin. Fat raspberries sat on the counter, left over from the farmers' market the day before. I pulled flours from the shelf, scooted the softened butter toward me, grabbed the sugar, and oiled the tin. By the time the coffeepot was full, the muffins were in the oven, already rising. And after I had drunk my first cup, I piled raspberry muffins with brown sugar on a plate, and carried them, along with the newspaper and two cups of hot coffee, into the bedroom.

Danny kissed me with a happy sigh, and we settled in, under the covers, our legs touching, to read the newspaper and lie in bed all morning.

It's so easy to eat in season during the summer. Most days, all we need is a handful of cherries and a hunk of good cheese to make a lunch. We can never keep up with all the fresh vegetables. Pints of fresh berries sit on farmers' stands in abandoned bounty. It's a breeze to follow the dietary recommendations every health magazine suggests: eat lots of fruits and vegetables, nothing fried, with a little meat and fish.

Tomatoes in summer are rich and meaty, a sensory experience like no other. All I need is a thick slice of a warm heirloom tomato, a pinch of sea salt, and a napkin to wipe off my chin after I eat it. A complicated dish for the height of summer? Slices of tomato, shreds of fresh mozzarella, whole basil leaves, and a drizzle of fruity extra-virgin olive oil. That's satisfaction on a plate.

But tomatoes in December taste like water with a thin skin of balloon. Not only that, but those flavorless tomatoes cost $4.99 a pound, and they've been transported from Mexico or Chile. The savoy cabbage and celery root are just $1.99 a pound, grown twenty miles away. In Seattle, in winter, that's what is coming out of the ground. Danny taught me this.

Good chefs insist on the best ingredients, and flavor comes from freshness. Watching Danny make up menus every month, I saw how he crafted the dishes he served around what was available. No one who came to his restaurant once a month ate the same dishes again. By October, he was tired of tomatoes, since we had sated ourselves on them until they were gone. And he is too fascinated by food to cook with the same ingredients all year long.

Good chefs insist on the best ingredients.

Besides, eating in season saves money. Tom Douglas, one of the most successful chef/owners in Seattle, says that he makes only a 4 percent profit on his five restaurants in town. If he constantly bought food out of season, he'd only make a 2 percent profit.

Before I met Danny, I always swore I wouldn't marry a man until I had been through an entire season cycle with him. It's easy to fall in love in spring, feel warm and fuzzy under the covers on a long summer morning. The long winter reveals more than June ever could.

I still believed this. But living with Danny, I looked forward to the new tastes he would introduce me to in February and March.

eating in season

Flavor comes from freshness. Eating in season is one of the easiest, and least expensive, ways to improve the quality of your food immediately.

If you bite into a pear in the middle of its peak season, it's not going to be overly soft or mushy, or have bruises you could put your finger into. Instead, it will have a bit of crunch at first, followed by softness. Touch your teeth into it and the flesh comes away. Buy a pear six months later, and you're going to have to bite down with all your force. You're going to break your damn teeth. And then there's no flavor. All that work, and there's no reward.

When people talk about eating in season, they usually talk about summer produce, because they think about the bounty. It's easy to eat in season in August, with tomatoes, peaches, and watermelon. During other times of the year, eating in season may seem tougher, but it gives you the chance to explore foods you don't know as well, such as sunchokes, savoy cabbage, and celery root. Broccoli, cauliflower, and citrus fruits are all winter produce too.

If you don't know what food is in season, and you don't have a farmers' market near you, look at the delivery trucks in front of your favorite restaurant. Go look up their website (Charlie's Produce in Seattle, for example). They might have a page called something like Hot Picks, highlighting what is best that week. Go to the store with those foods in mind and you'll be eating in season.

You will spend less money for more flavor if you buy fruits and vegetables in season. In most cases, this means you will be supporting your local farmers, as well.

millet tabouleh

VARIATIONS
You could make this dish with red quinoa, instead of millet, which would add great color. If you can't find smoked paprika, you could use sweet paprika.

SUGGESTIONS
This would go well with baked fish, poached prawns, or lobster tail. You could even serve it with grilled skinless chicken breasts.

Most people think of millet as birdseed. It's one of those grains I never thought I would try. But then I met Shauna, and she needed to be gluten-free, and I wanted to use everything I could. Millet is grainier than couscous, but it's also neutral in taste, so it picks up the flavors of the foods with which it is combined. It puffs up when cooked and fluffs up well.

Since most people don't crave it, millet is relatively cheap, certainly in comparison to more popular grains. You feel good about your health for eating it. Besides, it's a heck of a lot better than wheat germ. • *Feeds 4*

2 cups millet
2¾ teaspoons kosher salt
4 medium tomatoes, or enough to make 1 cup chopped
6 green onions, small diced (about 1 cup)
1 long English cucumber, peeled, seeded, and small diced

2 tablespoons chopped fresh Italian parsley
½ tablespoon chopped fresh mint
1 lemon, zest grated and juiced
¼ teaspoon smoked paprika (Pimentón de la Vera)
3 tablespoons extra-virgin olive oil
¼ teaspoon cracked black pepper

Cooking the millet. Place the millet in a large saucepan with 4½ cups water and 2 teaspoons of the kosher salt. After the mixture has come to a boil, stir the millet and reduce the heat to low. Simmer until the millet has absorbed all the water and turned fluffy, about 25 minutes. Set aside to cool, then transfer to the refrigerator to chill until it is cold.

Blanching and chopping the tomatoes. Fill a large saucepan with water and add enough salt to make it taste like the ocean. Bring the water to a boil. Mark a small X on the bottom of each tomato with a paring knife. Add the tomatoes to the boiling water and cook until the skin starts to slip off, 5 to 10 seconds; don't let the tomatoes stay in the water for much longer, or you will start to cook them. Transfer the tomatoes to a bowl of ice water to cool quickly.

Remove the skins from the tomatoes, which should slip off fairly easily. Cut the tomatoes in half and remove the seeds. Chop the tomatoes.

Preparing the salad. Add the chopped tomatoes, green onions, cucumber, parsley, mint, and lemon zest to the millet. Pinch the smoked paprika over the salad. Make a quick dressing by combining the lemon juice, oil, the remaining salt, and the pepper. Pour over the salad and toss.

living in the northwest

Some days it slides out of the sky, skipping across the tops of puddles and soaking our hair. Some mornings start out with sprinkles, escalate to showers, and step back into mist by the end of the evening. And then there are the seven-day stretches of salt gray sky, the air thick with moisture-laden clouds that won't let go. Those stretches of February can drive you mad sometimes, especially because you've been eating kale for what feels like forty days and forty nights.

When people say, "Oh, you live in Seattle—doesn't it rain all the time?" I say yes. Yes, it does. It takes too long to clarify: "You're talking about the winter, and winter everywhere is hard. At least ours is rain instead of ten below zero." But I just nod and smile because, frankly, I don't want everyone moving here.

If you saw Seattle in July and August, you'd be here in a minute. All those days of rain and showers and more rain and showers yield an explosion of life during the summer. The dark green trees that provide the only color during the winter are outshined during the summer by lilac bushes fat with blossoms, bright kayaks dotting the surface of Lake Union, and a sky so lucid blue until ten at night that there is no word for it.

And then there is the food. Morel mushrooms and long stalks of asparagus in late May. Small strawberries in June, deep red inside, a burst of sunlight condensed into a bite. Tiny huckleberries in August, to tuck into goat's milk yogurt with vanilla sugar. Baby rainbow carrots, Japanese eggplant, cucumbers and tomatillos for salsa. Everyone's garden zucchini grows to the size of baseball bats, and no one will take the extras. Miner's lettuce, pepper cress, and lobster mushrooms. And the salmon. Oh, the salmon.

The damn rain is worth it.

Both Danny and I chose this area deliberately. If somehow Louisiana had been our home, we would be waxing poetic about crayfish and gumbo. The deserts of Arizona? Squashes, beans, and corn. If Minnesota had called our names, we would craft recipes for wild rice and gluten-free lefse. When we're lucky, we find our homes. Seattle just happens to be ours.

Danny remembers coming to Seattle from Colorado by a slow train, passing lush state parks, rivers with names like Skookumchuck and Stilliguamish, and cows chewing on green fields. When the train cruised by the Columbia, he thought of Woody Guthrie, but he also thought of the salmon swimming toward the sea.

"Seattle seemed like heaven, even though I was sharing a room with a high school friend at first. There was just such richness here. And it was good to get out of the snow."

For years, I had been living in Manhattan, living out loud and late into the night. I shopped for knishes at Yonah Schimmel's, ate bagels with smoked salmon with my best friend in our kitchen, and devoured Chinese food from cartons, pizza from Sal and Carmine's, and pastrami sandwiches from Katz's on the Lower East Side. Everything tasted exciting. Thank goodness I rollerbladed in Central Park every day. Still, I never felt well (now I know it was all that gluten), and I never entirely felt at home. I felt like a starstruck fan instead.

One afternoon, I was tutoring a student in a coffee shop on the Upper East Side. He needed help preparing for the vocabulary section of the SAT, and I was trying to teach him how to decode the words. We came to *terrestrial*. He had never heard of it. When I asked him what *extraterrestrial* meant, he said, "Aliens?" Close enough.

"If those are not from Earth, then *terrestrial* means Earth." As I said this, I swept my hand toward the window, to illustrate the Earth. And I noticed, in a flash, that I couldn't actually see the ground anywhere. Every square inch was concrete and glass. That's the moment I decided I needed to move back home.

Danny could have easily risen up the ranks of the fine-dining restaurant in Denver where he was the sous chef, moved to another as head chef, and maybe owned his own

restaurant in a wealthy ski town someday. I could have stayed in New York for years to come, maybe married a man who owned a brownstone in Brooklyn. But both of us felt drawn to the Pacific Northwest by the food.

During our first summer together, we visited our friends Nina and Booth, who live part of the time on an island about three hours north of Seattle. Danny, who normally worked six days a week, had three days away from the restaurant, which was closed for the Labor Day weekend. Our dear friends shared their rural island, where we could walk down the middle of the road toward the beach, knowing there were no cars coming. In the mornings, we sat on their balcony drinking our coffee, watching orca whales spouting. We went out in their small boat and pulled up one Dungeness crab scrabbling,

its claws opening and closing, in the green metal pot.

In the evening, we gathered together before sunset and ate roasted corn brushed with butter infused with chili powder and chives from the garden, Caesar salads topped with smoked salmon skin, and the crab we caught that afternoon, thrown in a pot of boiling water and plunked down in front of us, with a bowl of drawn lemon butter. For dessert, we ate warm gluten-free crumble with the blackberries we had picked off the vine in the driveway earlier that afternoon.

Afterwards, under the stars that dotted the black night sky like the freckles that splash across Danny's back, we lounged in a hot tub with our two friends, floating and laughing, feeling grateful.

blackberry-peach crumble

VARIATIONS
You can make a fruit crumble with any number of fruits: blueberries, raspberries, and strawberries for an early summer crumble; or pears and apples for the autumn. If you cannot eat butter, you can make this with a nondairy "butter." You can replace the sour cream and crème fraîche with a goat's milk yogurt.

SUGGESTIONS
This goes well with anything, but it's particularly good with a meal of fresh-caught Dungeness crab.

We felt the warmth of the sun on our fingers, the prickles of the berries, the juice already spilling. And the taste—dark sweetness and a hint of tartness. Blackberry.

When we went to Sosio's in Pike Place Market and saw the sign over the peaches (Oh my God, they're so good), I caught the eye of my favorite produce guy and he knew. He cut off a slice, then extended it toward me with juice-dripping fingers. I bit into the fuzzy flesh and let the peach juice drip.

It might seem like a sin to cook this fruit, since it's so perfect eaten from the hand. But a crumble is wonderful. The fruits release their juices when they are bubbling and baked. In Seattle the evenings grow cool, even in summer. There's nothing like the taste of warm berries and peaches, with a crumble crust and crème fraîche. • *Feeds 4*

CRUMBLE TOPPING
¼ cup sorghum flour (32g/1oz)
¼ cup tapioca flour (30g/1oz)
¼ cup potato starch (48g/1.7oz)
¼ cup sweet rice flour (51g/1.1oz)
¼ cup almond flour (28g/1oz)
¼ cup sugar
1 teaspoon fine sea salt
¼ teaspoon ground cinnamon
3 tablespoons frozen unsalted butter, cut into pieces
¼ cup sour cream

FILLING
2 pints fresh blackberries
2 to 3 large juicy peaches, pits removed and sliced
2 tablespoons sugar
½ lemon, zest grated and juiced
2 teaspoons cornstarch

CRÈME FRAÎCHE TOPPING
½ cup crème fraîche
1 tablespoon honey, or more to taste
Smidge ground cloves

Forming the crumble. Sift the sorghum flour, tapioca flour, potato starch, sweet rice flour, and almond flour into a large bowl. Combine with the sugar, salt, and cinnamon. Grate the frozen butter into the flour and stir until the mixture has the texture of coarse cornmeal. Spoon in the sour cream and stir with a rubber spatula until the mixture has the consistency of damp breadcrumbs.

Preheating the oven. Turn the oven to 350°F.

Preparing the filling. Marry the berries and peaches in a large bowl. In another bowl, mix together the sugar, lemon zest and juice, and cornstarch. Add this mixture to the fruit and stir to coat.

Baking the crumble. Place the fruit filling in a 9-inch pie pan. Sprinkle the crumble topping over the fruit. Slide the pan into the oven and bake until the fruit is bubbling, the juices are thickening, and the crumble topping is browning, 25 to 30 minutes. Let the crumble cool while you prepare the crème fraîche topping.

Preparing the crème fraîche topping and serving. Stir the crème fraîche, honey, and cloves together. Taste and add more honey if you like it sweeter. Top each warm serving of crumble with a dollop of the honeyed crème fraîche.

you're marrying a chef

When he asked me, he did it by accident.
At the end of the evening, after a long Monday together, Danny made us a spectacular dinner. Pan-roasted beef tenderloin on top of mashed potatoes, with a port-veal-stock reduction sauce, and balsamic onions and soft chèvre on top. Oh, this man. Just before we ate, he started to slice up some bread to go with his meal.

You have to understand—this was a big deal.

Celiac sprue (also known as celiac disease) is an autoimmune disorder, which means that my body attacks itself if I have any gluten. If I were to eat gluten regularly, I could suffer from a litany of physical ailments, other autoimmune disorders, lymphoma, or even colon cancer. Perfectly healthful for most people, the smallest amount of gluten—the elastic protein in wheat, rye, barley, triticale, spelt, kamut, and farro—can make me terribly ill. I don't mean slices of bread, I mean twelve breadcrumbs. All it takes is half a teaspoon of gluten for me to be sick for three days. That makes eating in a restaurant a daring decision and shopping an endless scrutiny of labels on any food packaging. Fresh whole food is much more important to me than a theoretical discussion of how Americans should eat. If I don't have fresh meats, vegetables, cheeses, and grains, I can't eat.

But cross-contamination is the worst. If someone on the line in a restaurant makes a salad with croutons for one customer, and makes another without them for me, without changing his gloves or cleaning out the bowl, I get sick. If I eat French fries made in the same oil as anything made with gluten, such as onion rings, then I am in bed in pain that night. If the packaged candy I eat was rolled out in the factory on conveyor belts dusted with flour, I'm down for the weekend. (Celiac affects about 1 out of 100 Americans, so you probably know someone who has to deal with this on a daily basis as well.)

So when I went gluten-free, for the first year not a bit of gluten ever darkened my door. My house was a gluten-free zone. Until Danny moved in.

He had been eating bread in my house for a while. By this time, it was our house, anyway. I never complained if he ate gluten. I wanted him to say yes to any food he could eat. But if he eats bread or drinks beer, we have to wait until he has brushed his teeth before we can kiss. Just the breadcrumbs in his mouth would make me sick.

And so that night, feeling particularly close to him after a long day together, I complained for the first time. "Oh, do you have to eat bread tonight?"

Without really turning around, he said, "Honey, you're marrying a chef. You're going to have to get used to the fact that he's going to eat bread."

"What?!" I said. I turned him around and looked in his eyes, already smiling. "What did you just say?"

He turned red and said, "I said that I'm going to eat bread."

We danced around the kitchen, giggling, not saying it. After all, we had both known, and had been hinting at it, since our first night together. A few weeks earlier, in a moment of exuberance, Danny had said, "I can't wait until our families meet."

I laughed. "When exactly is that going to happen?"

He blushed. "Oh, at some big party."

To tell the truth, I had known early on that this was the man I would marry. I could not imagine my life without our laughter, his kindness, and our shared love of humanity. Not to mention the kick-ass meals. It was only a matter of time.

But he had just spoken it out loud. Sort of. I didn't press him to say more. He would find his time.

Together, we sat down in the living room to eat our dinner. He put on an episode of *South Park*, the one called "Cartman's Mom Is a Dirty Slut," to be precise. I started laughing immediately, and then I took a bite of the food.

Glorious. Layers of taste, like years of memories tumbling together. Every flavor alive.

He watched me eat, as he always does. When he saw again how much I loved his food, and thus loved him, he put down his plate. "Oh, what the hell," he said. And then he kneeled on the floor before me.

And in the act of putting one knee on the floor—forgive me if you find this offensive, but the truth is important to tell—he inadvertently let out a fart. A loud, juicy fart.

We both laughed, and then I started crying.

"Shauna Marie James, will you marry me?"

"Yes, of course I will. But do you think we could turn *South Park* off?"

••

"I thought I would have to wait until I could take you to the Eiffel Tower. I certainly thought that I needed a diamond before I could ask for your hand."

We danced around the living room, giddy with excitement, at a loss for words. Suddenly he stopped.

"Wait, this can't be real yet. I don't have a ring."

I kissed him and said, "Wait a second."

I ran back to the bedroom and dug around in the dresser drawer. There it was. The summer before, I had been shopping at a thrift store with my friend Tita. We moseyed through the racks of clothes and chipped pots and pans, talking. As we approached the smudgy glass cases of used jewelry, I stopped—a silver ring with a sky blue glass stone shined up at me. It fit me perfectly; it cost ten dollars. I bought it.

But when I took it home, I knew I couldn't wear it. It was an engagement ring. Other than secretly slipping it on my finger sometimes and walking around the apartment by myself with my hand held out, I never wore it.

I ran into the living room and held it up for Danny to see. "Will this do for you?"

"Are you kidding me?" he exclaimed. "Is it okay for you?"

Neither one of us knew it would happen so soon. No one could have predicted that it would happen by accident. But that his marriage proposal was born from food? That never surprised us.

Our life together started in compromise.

"Do you have to eat bread?" (You know that will make me sick, and I'd like to stay well.)

"Sweetie, you're marrying a chef. He's going to eat bread." (I acknowledge you, and I'll make sure you don't get sick. But you still have to let me be who I am.)

He thought he would wait until he could take me to Paris, with a big ring in his pocket, and we were at the top of the Eiffel Tower. But that was like the movies—a preplanned itinerary to fit into what every little girl (and the boy who watched chick flicks) thought she should have.

Instead, we got *South Park*, a ring from the thrift store, his knee resting on the carpet that needed vacuuming, and a fart.

It was better than I could ever have hoped.

pan-seared beef tenderloin with port sauce and balsamic onions

VARIATIONS
This dish would work well with rib-eye, porterhouse, or top sirloin steaks in place of the tenderloin. If you don't want to use veal stock, you can substitute chicken stock, but the sauce might take longer to reduce. You might also have to thicken it with a cornstarch slurry (cornstarch mixed with cold water, then mixed into the stock for 1 to 2 minutes).

SUGGESTIONS
Whenever we eat this, we serve it with Potato Puree (see page 43). In fact, these pota-toes really should be part of the dish. The balsamic onions can also top lamb, hamburgers, or chicken as well. And the port sauce enhances ostrich or venison.

I made this dish for Shauna the night I proposed (even though I didn't know I was going to) because I knew she would love it. The first time I ate this flavor combination was at Gramercy Tavern. As I worked, I set aside some scraps to eat later. There's a rich meatiness to the balsamic onions, as well as the tender beef, and the veal stock in the port sauce rounds it all out. All the textures and flavors blend together.

This dish is one of my favorites to cook for people I love. The night I first made it for Shauna, she swooned. And I didn't need the bread after all. • *Feeds 4*

BALSAMIC ONIONS
3 tablespoons olive oil
2 large red onions, peeled and sliced
3 tablespoons brown sugar
½ cup balsamic vinegar
Kosher salt and cracked black pepper

BEEF TENDERLOIN
8 pieces beef tenderloin, 3 to 3½ ounces each
   (these are called medallions)

Kosher salt and cracked black pepper
4 tablespoons canola oil

PORT REDUCTION SAUCE
1 cup port
2 cups veal stock (see page 148)
Kosher salt and cracked black pepper
2 tablespoons butter

Caramelizing the onions. Set a large sauté pan over high heat. Pour in the olive oil. When the oil starts to smoke, add the onions. Cook, stirring occasionally, until the onions have wilted and shrunk, have turned dark blue or purple in color, and smell sweet, 7 to 8 minutes. Add the brown sugar to the pan and cook, stirring, until the sugar begins to melt into the onions.

Finishing the onions. Pour the vinegar into the pan and cook, stirring occasionally and tasting continually, until the liquid is reduced and thickened, but not burnt, about 7 minutes; if you reduce it too much, it becomes tarry with a burnt taste, and instead you want a strong balsamic flavor, followed by the sweetness of the onions. Season with salt and pepper, if necessary. Set aside.

Searing the beef tenderloin. Season the tenderloin medallions with salt and pepper. Set 2 large sauté pans over high heat. Pour the canola oil into the hot pans. Put the tenderloin pieces in the hot oil; don't crowd the pans, or the beef will boil in the oil, and that wastes a good piece of beef. Cook until the bottom of each piece has a lovely brown crust, 2 to 3 minutes. Flip over the tenderloin pieces. For medium-rare doneness, the medallions should have a little firm push at the center when pressed, but with softness all around, and the internal temperature should be 150°F. Remove the pans from the heat, transfer the beef to a plate, and allow the beef to rest while you prepare the sauce.

Certified organics
Walla
walla onions
$3.00
bunch

Reducing the port. Pour ½ cup of the port into each pan, scraping the goodness from the bottom. When you have deglazed both pans, pour the contents of one pan into the other. Set the pan with the port over medium heat and simmer until the port is reduced by half its volume.

Finishing the sauce. Scoop the balsamic onions into the reduced port. Pour in the veal stock. Simmer until the liquid is reduced by half its volume. Taste the sauce and season with salt and pepper, if necessary. Drop in the butter and whisk the sauce until the butter is fully incorporated.

To serve, spoon the sauce with the onions onto each plate. Place 2 tenderloin pieces on top of each serving.

the importance of ingredients

In the dead of February, I ran out of ideas. Exuberant as I am about food, discovering as I go, I had no idea what to write for my weekly blog posts. Each week on our food website, Gluten-Free Girl and the Chef, I write a story and recipe, based on the foods in season we are eating. Winter root vegetables excite me in December, with their knobbly shapes and hard-to-love skins and the sweet way they slip into soups and surprise us. By the end of February, however, I cannot look at one more parsnip.

Even Danny was done with winter. He didn't wake up and start wondering what to cook that day. Instead, he just wanted to curl up in bed for another hour. I started to worry that he didn't love his job anymore. Maybe it was time for a new restaurant?

"Don't worry. This happens every year. February and March are the dead times for chefs."

So we played games, stayed away from the rain, and ate whatever appealed to us most. One Saturday at the farmers' market, I spotted a dark green savoy cabbage. Ruffled like an Elizabethan collar, curved inward like the neck of a demure young girl, this was the most stunning cabbage I had ever seen. I had to buy it, just to take a photograph.

At home, however, I found I had no idea what to do with it. We could have made coleslaw with Danny's winter recipe, but I wanted something different.

So I asked my readers.

On that Monday, I put up a small piece about savoy cabbage, with the photograph of the one we had found. And I asked, "What do you cook with it? What do you suggest?"

When I opened my e-mail the next day, I found I had been inundated with ideas. Cabbage rolls with bacon-studded rice. Cabbage chiffonade, quick sautéed with Worcestershire sauce. Cabbage wraps with tiny-diced chicken, green onions, bok choy, and sweet and sour chile sauce inside. And I also received this suggestion, which moved me with the memories it evoked, even though they weren't mine:

I've never tried savoy cabbage, but I bet it would work great in the dish my Russian grandmother made—stuffed cabbage. She made a mixture of ground beef, onions, cooked rice, and salt and pepper. She removed the thick stem from the cabbage leaf and then rolled a handful of beef mixture in the leaf. She placed all the stuffed cabbage packages into a stock pan and covered them with a homemade tomato sauce. Sometimes she'd add raisins to the tomato sauce. The stuffed cabbage cooks on the stovetop until all is tender. —NINA

Danny's mother made stuffed cabbage when he was a kid, as did mine. I made some that evening.

All through that winter and beyond, I published an ingredient post on our website. With a photograph of food that moves me that day—eggplants, beets, avocados—I tell a story and open the floor to everyone else. What do you like to cook with this ingredient?

Every week, those pieces inspire more comments than any others combined. A few people post links to specific recipes. But most offer lyrical memories, evoked from a single ingredient, like this post:

My birthday is in July, perfect strawberry season in England. Every year of my childhood, my grandmother, a wonderful baker, and I would go strawberry picking the day before my birthday, and she would make me a strawberry cream sponge cake to have on my special day. I miss my grandmother, and I miss those cakes, but the first strawberries of the season always take me back to those happy, happy times. —NICOLA

The week I posted up popcorn, I thought I had lost it. Who the hell was going to have something passionate to say about popcorn? Well, at least seventy-five people did, including the person who sent this recipe:

Thinly slice 8 to 10 cloves of garlic, and cook them in butter and extra-virgin olive oil on the stovetop until they turn a little golden and crisp. Take them out with a slotted spoon and add either fresh sprigs of rosemary or (my favorite) whole fresh sage leaves (about 40 or so, ¼ cup). Cook the sage in the butter for about a minute or two, until crispy. Pour the whole thing over the popcorn. Toss in the garlic flakes, too. I've been meaning to add a little fresh grated Locatelli Romano to this. —ADDLER

Every single week, I learn a new way to eat food, even the foods I eat on an almost daily basis.

We will never run out of ingredients. Berries, pumpkins, squashes, cinnamon, cherries, venison, wild mushrooms, buffalo, walnut oil, frisée—every one of these could start a multitude of dishes.

Reading about suggestions with chickpeas, olives, and wild rice gave me enough ideas to make it through March, still excited about the dinners we ate when Danny came home from the restaurant.

how to choose the best ingredients

Chefs have dedicated staff members who know important techniques, but the biggest difference between chefs and most home cooks is the ingredients they use. Food doesn't have to be expensive or luxurious to be good. You don't need to eat foie gras, oysters, and caviar to eat well.

When I met Shauna, she was making her vinaigrettes with expensive bottles of extra-virgin olive oil that emptied quickly. At the restaurant, I use mostly canola oil, which is cheaper, and some extra-virgin olive oil. It's a waste to use high-quality extra-virgin olive oil for all your sautéing. Try a pomace oil, or grapeseed oil, which has a higher smoke point anyway. Choose your ingredients wisely.

Don't buy expensive ingredients just for the sake of it. Truffle oil, for example, seems luxurious, but almost all truffle oils are chemically induced. There are a few exceptions, but the tiny truffle oil bottles you see in high-end grocery stores are filled with extra-virgin olive oil enhanced with the chemical smell of truffles.

Keep your kitchen stocked and make a few changes. Champagne vinegar is much better than the white vinegar that comes in the gallon jug. Fresh spices really make a difference in the taste of the food, so toss out anything in your pantry that's been there for too long. A good sea salt finishes a dish well, and you can also buy a big box of kosher salt instead of the iodized stuff that has no taste.

And again, foods in season are the most important ingredients.

Once in a while, buy an ingredient for your pantry that will allow you to experiment; try Banyuls vinegar, pomegranate molasses, Piment d'Espelette, gomashio, fresh wasabi. You want something that will spike your attention and wake up your senses.

pasta with anchovies, lemon, and olives

VARIATIONS

If you cannot eat dairy, you can substitute a nondairy spread for the butter. Any combination of olives will do well here—find your favorites.

SUGGESTIONS

This sauce is also good with grilled or roasted chicken, smoked salmon, or seared prawns.

People are afraid of anchovies. They remember super-fishy bites from Caesar salads or bad chain pizza. But eating a good anchovy is a different experience than you imagine. Anchovies are distinctively fishy, but the texture is more like a meat than a fish. They are as salty as the sea, but more like the ocean water around ports. This is the food of a working man in a cloth cap taking a lunch break.

Anchovies are perfect for making a pasta dish, because the oil they are packed in helps to flavor the sauce. You won't be eating chunks of fish, because the anchovies will melt away in the hot pasta. You'll just have that indelible taste of the Mediterranean, indolent summer warmed by the sun. • *Feeds 4*

1 pound uncooked fresh gluten-free fettuccine (see page 60) or 1 pound dried gluten-free fettuccine
4 tablespoons extra-virgin olive oil
4 shallots, peeled and thinly sliced
3 cloves garlic, peeled and thinly sliced
1 cup pitted mixed Greek olives, roughly chopped
2 ounces anchovies, chopped, oil reserved

¼ cup capers
1 teaspoon cracked black pepper
¼ cup dry white wine
2 lemons, zest grated and juiced
2 tablespoons butter
½ cup pine nuts, toasted
1 tablespoon chiffonade fresh sorrel or basil

Cooking the pasta. Bring a large pot of salted water to a boil. Toss in the pasta. Cook until the pasta is slightly al dente, about 5 minutes. Drain the pasta well, then toss with 2 tablespoons of the oil. Set aside.

Sautéing the vegetables. Set a large sauté pan over medium heat. Pour in the remaining 2 tablespoons of oil. Add the shallots and garlic and cook, stirring frequently, until the shallots are softened and translucent, 2 to 3 minutes.

Making the sauce. Toss in the olives, anchovies, and reserved anchovy oil and stir. After a moment, add the capers and pepper to the pan and cook, stirring, until everything releases its smells, 1 to 2 minutes.

Pour in the wine to deglaze the pan, scraping the goodness from the bottom. Squeeze in the lemon juice and simmer until the liquid is reduced by about a third of its volume, about 1 minute. Swirl in the butter, which will emulsify the sauce.

Tossing with the pasta. Add the pasta to the sauce. Toss with tongs until the pasta is hot and coated with the sauce. Remove from the heat. Add the pine nuts, lemon zest, and sorrel and stir just a bit before serving.

fresh gluten-free pasta

VARIATIONS
You have some wiggle room with different flours here. Tapioca flour works as a replacement for the potato starch, as does cornstarch. You might try sorghum or brown rice if you cannot eat corn. However, be sure to substitute by weight instead of volume.

SUGGESTIONS
You can easily double or even triple this recipe for more pasta. Work with the pasta in batches if you do.

When you find out you cannot eat gluten, one of the first foods you worry about living without is pasta. There's a certain mourning involved, imagining a trip to Italy without a mound of fresh fettuccine.

Guess what? The Italians make great gluten-free pasta, since many of their citizens have celiac sprue. You can buy a package of gluten-free pasta at the *farmacia* and take it to the best restaurant in town, where they will make the pasta of the day for you.

When we first started making pasta, we tried our favorite gluten pasta recipes with gluten-free flours, without much success. It took us about fifteen different recipes and wranglings with flour combinations before we figured out the right ratio of flours to liquids. Now, at least once a week, when we want a quick meal, we pull out flours and make homemade pasta. • *Feeds 4*

⅔ cup (70g/2.5oz) corn flour
½ cup (70g/2.5oz) quinoa flour
½ cup (60g/2.125oz) potato starch
2 teaspoons xanthan gum

1 teaspoon guar gum
1 teaspoon fine sea salt
2 large eggs
4 egg yolks from large eggs

Combining the flours. Sift the corn flour, quinoa flour, and potato starch into a large bowl. Add the xanthan gum, guar gum, and salt and stir. Sift the entire mixture into the bowl of a stand mixer.

Forming the pasta dough. Put the eggs and egg yolks into the bowl of dry ingredients. Run the stand mixer on medium speed with a paddle attachment until the dough feels fully formed, about 3 minutes. The final dough should feel firm yet still pliable, a little like playdough.

Making the pasta. If you are using a pasta machine, cut the ball of dough into quarters and roll out each piece of dough to about a ½-inch thickness. We like to roll out each piece between 2 pieces of parchment paper. Lightly flour both sides of the dough with a bit more potato starch. Run the dough through the machine, increasing the setting each time, until the dough is paper-thin and long. If the pasta sheet starts to break, it is thin enough.

If you are making the dough by hand, we suggest you cut the ball of dough into 8 pieces, and then cut each of those pieces in half, so they are about the size of golf balls. Roll out each piece of dough as thin as you possibly can.

For fettuccine, use the fettuccine setting on the pasta machine. If you are cutting the dough by hand, you want ribbons of pasta, about ¼-inch wide. For spaghetti, use the spaghetti setting on the pasta machine. If you are cutting the dough by hand, you want thin strings of pasta.

For ravioli, cut the rolled-out pasta into 2-inch-square pieces. Dollop the filling in the middle of a square of pasta. Brush the edges of the pasta with an egg wash. Place another pasta square on top and press down, crimping the edges. (Having a ravioli cutter on hand helps with this process.)

For lasagna, leave the pasta in long sheets.

To cook the pasta, bring a large pot of salted water to a boil. Put the pasta shape of your

choice into the boiling water. When the pasta rises to the surface, take a little piece and taste it. You should be able to bite into it without it falling apart. (With gluten-free pasta, it's a fine line. One moment it's al dente, and the next it's one big ball of mush, so watch the pot.) Cooking times will vary for the different shapes. Fettuccine generally takes 4 to 5 minutes, spaghetti 3 to 4 minutes. Ravioli takes a little longer, about 5 to 6 minutes. The cooking times will differ in each kitchen, depending on how thin you were able to roll out the dough. Let your taste be the judge.

sunday afternoon

The sun is shining through the skylights. Danny and I are in the kitchen, music playing—*Songs in the Key of Life*—and we are dancing. Our knives are chopping staccato rhythms on the cutting boards. Our hips are swaying and our lips are smiling. Friends are coming over. We have the day off—he from the restaurant, and me from the computer. We are home.

He is chopping stalks of asparagus, just come into season. The woody bottoms he scoops into a metal bowl. The tender tips he sets aside. He starts an asparagus stock. Before I met him, making stock from scratch felt impossible, an endeavor for an afternoon of cookbook consulting and perhaps some pulling of hair. But in his hands, it is effortless. He slivers and cuts, nudging leeks and onions into the stockpot with his broad palms, and then setting them all to simmer.

For the first few months we were in each other's lives, I watched him, awed by his economy of movement and the tender attention he pays to every vegetable before him. He has, within his body, twenty years of muscle memory, the daily making of veal stock and pureed potatoes and beef tenderloin done medium-rare. He has been cooking every day since he was twenty. But in the end, nothing makes him happier than being in our kitchen, with me, making food together.

Now I am cooking beside him. After months of awed watching and taking notes—then cooking on my own when he was at work—I am comfortable enough to be more than his prep cook. No one wants to be put on a pedestal forever. He's far too imperfect for me to make him a

cooking god. Standing beside him, instead of gazing up at him, makes me love him more.

I bend down to the white cutting board before me, and I begin to slither the fleshy mango in my hands. What is the color of a mango? Orange is too boring, and it doesn't come close. There's something of summer sunset, and egg yolk, and a Crayola color I cannot remember the name of—but that's not all. I bend down closer, my nose almost against the mango. I hear a little giggle to my left, and I know he's laughing with me. We must look ridiculous. But cooking is a way of paying attention, of really being in this world. When you look closely at a mango and inhale its scent, everything else stops. Life feels rich and easy.

I walk to the living room to turn up the music—*Abbey Road* this time—and when I return, Danny has already finished the asparagus stock. "How did you do that?" I ask him, incredulous. He just grins. Today is not the day for lessons or recipes. It is Sunday, and we are cooking.

Winter had yielded a month ago, and then relented. Spring has rushed right in. Finally. After the long months of flat gray skies, the sun extends onto the floor like an ample cat, rolling slowly, stretching all its limbs.

When I first met him, Danny worked six days a week, including Sundays. But that was a schedule for a single man, ready to devote his entire life to the restaurant. His one day off was spent sleeping, rising at noon, maybe watching a movie with me, and cooking for us both. Just when his body began to unclench, he had to gather his strength again for work the next day. With a bit of nudging and a lot of cajoling from me, he convinced the owner to hire an assistant to help him three evenings a week and take over on Sundays. Since I am no longer teaching high school, writing full-time instead, this means we can actually experience a weekend in our own way.

And so this afternoon in our kitchen is the beginning of two days together, just after our first anniversary of having met. While most people are spending Sunday afternoons starting to mourn the end of the weekend, we are just beginning.

We had talked all morning about what to make that evening. The veal goulash from the first time he cooked in this kitchen? Soft pecorino fresco was back in the markets. But goulash felt too heavy in this May sunshine. We never grew tired of eating crisp pork belly, especially in bed at midnight. But one of our guests was a vegetarian, so that was out. Garlic flan felt more like a winter dish. In the end, we decided on a chilled millet salad with mango and jícama, asparagus soup, and a lemongrass ice cream.

Our friends are due soon. The dishwasher needs emptying and there are still dirty dishes in the sink. We haven't mopped the floor in days. However, the best friends are the ones who are happy to be there, even when the house is a little cluttered. The best kitchens are the ones that are used well.

The CDs have shifted position, and suddenly we are listening to the Marc Cohn song "True Companion." Danny never lets it play without opening his arms and asking me to dance. We look in each other's eyes, intently. We dance as solemnly and slowly as we did as seventh graders, our feet shuffling slightly. To some songs, we jump around the living room, all angles and elbows, nothing else mattering but the joy in our bodies.

Danny knows how to dance. Just after he proposed to me, we attended the wedding of friends. Fresh to the idea of marrying each other, we both grew teary-eyed at the rituals and words spoken aloud. Later in the evening, the dance floor filled with gawky dancers, the women more at ease

than the men in suits, jerking their fists in rigid syncopation. I turned toward him and asked him to dance, which we had never done in public. He demurred. I assumed he couldn't do any better than the "white guy at the wedding reception" we were witnessing before us. After another drink, he agreed. He glided onto the small floor, turned toward me, and began to move in fluid motion, his face unguarded and his body a fascinating gyration. I shouted above the music: "Why didn't you tell me you know how to dance?!" He just grinned his shy grin, and then turned his eyes toward me, luring me in. As he gripped my hands and moved me around the dance floor, his hips enticing me toward more, I thought to myself: Why am I surprised? He lives in his body, all day long, paying attention to his senses, unafraid to act on what he knows.

We danced, unabashed and laughing, all night long.

But in this moment, in our kitchen, we hold each other close and dance quietly. We still both grow a little teary at this song. And then he makes a joke I could never explain outside that moment, and I laugh so hard I double over.

We go back to the cooking. Within a few moments, the house will be filled with people. A toddler will absorb our attention for hours. We will be surrounded by people we love.

But the guests aren't here, quite yet. We are alone, and laughing. And when I look over, he has finished the vivid green asparagus soup. It gleams and looks like the color of grass, condensed. He swirls it with the ladle, to stir it one more time, before he lets me take a taste. It's sunlight through green leaves, the peals of giggles from a three-year-old, a certain earthiness, the taste of spontaneity. Locally grown asparagus is only available two months out of the year in Seattle, and we are enjoying it, fully. He's laced it with pepper, for a little kick. It's not thin and reedy, the way some asparagus soups sit in the mouth. This one has presence.

I kiss him. He can taste the soup on my lips, and he approves. We hold each other for a moment, and say out loud how lucky we feel. Then we go back to making food.

chilled asparagus soup

VARIATIONS
If you don't have any chicken stock on hand, you can use water in its place. You can also substitute a packaged vegetable stock for the asparagus stock in this recipe, if you must; however, homemade stock always tastes better than boxed stock.

SUGGESTIONS
A dollop of crème fraîche would be great as a garnish for this soup, as would a swirl of great extra-virgin olive oil or some chopped hard-boiled egg. This soup would be a good starter for a lamb dish, to make the spring theme complete.

Please make this soup only when asparagus is in the peak of its season, which is May and June in Seattle. People who eat this soup in January are nuts. If you are buying asparagus in January, you are buying it from somewhere in South America. The shippers spray it with gases to keep it "fresh" until it makes it to the store shelves. Just because some of your local restaurants are serving asparagus out of season doesn't mean you should eat it. Be patient. Eating in season allows you to eat the food in its prime. • *Feeds 6*

3 tablespoons canola oil
3 pounds asparagus, stalks trimmed (save the tough stems)
2 carrots, peeled and roughly chopped
3 stalks celery, roughly chopped
2 medium yellow onions, peeled and roughly chopped
6 cups chicken stock

2 tablespoons thinly sliced garlic
1 medium potato, peeled and roughly chopped
1½ tablespoons chopped fresh tarragon
2 cups loosely packed spinach
4 tablespoons extra-virgin olive oil
Salt and freshly ground black pepper

Making the asparagus stock. Set a large pot over medium heat. Add 1½ tablespoons of the canola oil. When the oil is hot enough to swirl around the pan as easily as water, add the tough asparagus stems, half of the carrots, a third of the celery, and a quarter of the onions and cook, stirring, until they are softened, about 10 minutes. Pour in the chicken stock, reduce the heat, and simmer for 30 minutes. Strain the vegetables and set aside the stock. Discard the vegetables.

Sautéing the vegetables. In the same empty pot over medium heat, add the remaining 1½ tablespoons of canola oil. When the oil is hot, add the remaining carrot, celery, and onions, as well as the garlic, and cook until they are softened, about 5 minutes. Add the potato and tarragon and cover with the reserved asparagus stock. Bring to a boil and cook the soup until you can pierce the potato and it slides off your knife, about 15 minutes.

Cooking the asparagus and spinach. Add the asparagus stalks to the soup. Cook until the stalks are fork-tender, 3 to 4 minutes. Drop in the spinach and cook until it wilts.

Pureeing and chilling the soup. Puree the soup in batches, either with a blender or food processor, adding some of the olive oil to each batch. Season with salt and pepper, using your taste buds to reveal when the soup is properly seasoned.

Place the soup in a large bowl and slide it into the refrigerator. Allow the soup to chill thoroughly before serving.

slowing down

If you rush making food, nine times out of ten, it will turn out lousy.

You can't rush a stock by boiling it and cutting corners, or it will turn out cloudy and there won't be any flavor.

If you rush the yeast rising, it's only going to be a so-so bread. (And with gluten-free bread, you need all the advantages you can get.)

If you try to rush something that you are roasting, like vegetables, then there's a good chance it's going to burn.

If you rush risotto, you will end up with a mushy outer taste and the inside of the rice will be crunchy.

The point of cooking food is to enjoy it: the process, the anticipation, and the taste. If you can pay attention and be there instead of focusing on being done, you can cook better food. If you're really in a rush, make a bologna sandwich.

You might see a bustling restaurant kitchen at work and think the chefs and cooks are rushing, but they're not. It's a controlled, quick work, a purposeful movement. If they cook herky-jerky, confused and searching, tossing things and swearing, you will taste it in the food.

If you rush the food to the table, just to get dinner started at six, what will your family remember about your food? Just that it was there.

As the Reverend Horton Heat sang, "Ain't no reason not to take it slow."

come on over and bring some bacon

Danny stood at the stove frying bacon. I was at the left of the sink, cutting bacon into precise quarter-inch pieces. Earlier in the day, I had tried to coat slices of smoky bacon in melted chocolate, but that hadn't worked. The chocolate wasn't tempered correctly, and it ran off the strips in unattractive drips. It tasted great though: bacon + chocolate = good.

We looked up at the clock. Only one more hour until the bacon party.

We love having parties. I adore the sight of friends standing in the kitchen, backs against the counter, a plate of food in one hand, the other making gestures as they talk to the people next to them. Something good happens when you bring a disparate group of people together and give them food. As our circle of friends grew, we didn't have time to see people one couple at a time. Danny's work in the evenings really cut into our social calendar, so we invited groups of people to our house to eat.

At first, we tried throwing dinner parties. Certainly, it's a lovely gesture to cook food all afternoon and place it before guests who can sit without lifting a finger. However, since Danny is a chef who worked six days a week, having a dinner party meant that Danny didn't have a day off. Danny loves tasting other people's food. And he likes his rest. Besides, we just couldn't afford to throw frequent dinner parties.

And so we began having potlucks. Our plates are mismatched, picked up in thrift stores. Our kitchen is, at best, in a state of slightly controlled chaos. We don't own enough silverware to give everyone a fork, so we have to resort to plastic cutlery we wash and reuse. "Bring whatever you want," we tell our friends.

People feel relaxed at a potluck and we love seeing what people do with food. If you ask twenty-five people to bring their favorite flavor in the world, you have twenty-five different dishes. Even if there happen to be two lasagnas, they will not taste the same. Our friends Matthew and Laurie's audacious five-year-old daughter, Iris, has been eating spicy Thai food, sushi from a conveyor belt, and duck confit for as long as she could eat. For God's sake, she once plucked the eyeball out of a whole cooked fish and ate it with aplomb. When she grows up and takes a dish to a potluck, it's going to be unfamiliar to most people there. But they'll want to take a taste, as long as she goes light on the eyeballs.

So we started inviting our friends over on long Sunday afternoons, saying, "Bring food." We wanted the feeling of the Amish barn raising, without the barn. Our new home was perfect for parties. We stumbled on it through a barista at a coffee shop who had become a friend. (I know, how Seattle.) One of her closest friends had spent the previous year renovating a cottage from the 1930s, two blocks from a river, across the street from a park, in a far-from-hip neighborhood fifteen minutes outside of the city. We hadn't intended to venture that far. The house was cozy, but a bit small, and the kitchen was a little dark. But when we saw the backyard, we had to move in. Sprawling and lush, the green yard contained two apple trees, a Bosc pear tree, an Asian pear tree, a gnarled old blueberry bush, red currant bushes, rhubarb plants, an Italian plum tree, grapevines, and a big plot for a garden.

"Yes," we said together.

It was the perfect place for potlucks. At our first one, our friends arrived with plates in their hands. Iris said, "Hi, it's nice to see you," and pushed us aside to run out to the tree house. Danny's eighty-five-year-old uncle showed up next. The backyard filled up quickly, and we were thankful the air was late-spring warm.

I used to have this idea that only chefs know how to cook well. Danny certainly knows how to push a pan on the stove, but so do most of our friends. The people who gather at our parties are high school teachers, painters, photographers, librarians, real estate agents, veterinarians, software engineers, and journalists. And yes, some of them are also chefs and fellow food bloggers, some of whom might post photos of the food they made on their own blogs. They all create tastes that leave us wanting more.

After a few potlucks, we started giving homework. (You can't take the teacher out of me entirely.) We asked our friends to focus their food on a single ingredient. Inspired by the comments readers left on the Monday posts of my website, we had ingredient-themed potlucks.

The first one was the potato party. Honestly, I can only think of a few days that Danny and I have been together that we have not eaten potatoes. Danny doesn't know how to live without them. So he was thrilled to see the house filled with potato latkes, purple potato-gnocchi, potato-leek soup, and homemade potato chips. Our friend Jess made potato lollipops by roasting tiny potatoes with mustard and spearing them on sticks.

For the citrus party, we had Buddha's hands and kumquats on the mantelpiece as decorations and drank lemonade and ate tangy sorbets and fruit salads. But our tongues were too masked by the tartness at the end of the party to even talk.

The winter root party was probably the healthiest of the bunch, but it was also the least well attended.

The best attended? No question. The bacon party. We had candied bacon, potato gratin with bacon, twice-baked potatoes with bacon, dates stuffed with goat cheese and wrapped in bacon, deconstructed BLTs, and cups crafted out of bacon with little salads inside. The topper, however, was the bacon-wrapped bacon: braised pork belly roasted with bacon slices. Everyone chattered happily for hours, and then we sat sluggish, a layer of bacon fat in our bellies. It was worth it, though.

Everyone who attends the parties agrees: being forced to focus on one ingredient makes the cooking more creative. And we have so many other ingredient parties to throw: an asparagus party in May, a winter greens party, a wiener party, a ginger party. How about a tea party, where everyone has to cook something with tea?

As much as Danny knows about food, he always wants to learn more. And me? I'm just a beginner, and I hope I always will be. It's inspiring to see what other people cook.

Besides, we love the leftovers.

what cut of meat do i use?

Tough cuts of meat require wet cooking. Braise a pork shoulder, make a stew with chuck roast, or poach lamb tongue in stock. The toughest cuts of meat come from the parts of the animals that move. Braising or stewing tough cuts of meat over many hours breaks down the connective tissues in the muscles, turning them tender. Shoulder, shanks, butt, chuck, and legs: these are by no means bad cuts of meat. In fact, braised short ribs have been a darling dish of chefs for the last decade. It's simply that these cuts of meat require slow, wet cooking to become tender. If you know how to braise, you can save money on meat.

Tender cuts of meat require dry cooking. Grill a T-bone, sear a veal chop, or roast a pork tenderloin. These cuts of meat require quick cooking to keep their tenderness. Any other technique would ruin that meat. You wouldn't braise a prime rib. By the same token, don't put medallions of beef into the oven without searing them first. They would boil in the oil. Tenderloin, sirloin, short loin, loin—these more expensive meats require close attention.

bacon-wrapped pork belly

VARIATIONS
You cannot substitute anything for the pork belly or the bacon in this dish. That would be like substituting duck for filet mignon, or a soy burger for a ground beef burger.

SUGGESTIONS
Cut this into bite-size pieces for a party. This might be the most-talked-about finger food you will ever serve. Serve it with a big salad—you're going to need some roughage after eating this.

Whenever Shauna asked me to describe this dish, all I wanted to say was, "Oh yeah, baby." But she insisted I had to say more, so here goes. It's pork belly. And bacon. It's searing and braising and roasting, three meat techniques in one. What's not to love?

No one should be eating this every day. It's a once-every-few-months splurge. (Shauna says once a year.)

The idea for this dish came to us from our friend Matthew Amster-Burton, who had learned of it from Seattle chef Lorna Yee. (She's now a friend too, in part because of this dish.). The original dish was Asian inspired, with star anise, ginger, and tamari. We chose to go a different route, more French, more rustic. This dish reminds us of Matthew's daughter, Iris, our clever five-year-old friend. It's a smart-alecky dish. Who else is going to wrap bacon in bacon but a smart aleck?

• *Feeds 4*

1 quart chicken stock
1 tablespoon extra-virgin olive oil
1 carrot, peeled and large diced
½ medium yellow onion, peeled and large diced
1 stalk celery, large diced
5 cloves garlic, smashed and peeled
1 teaspoon tomato paste
1 medium sprig fresh rosemary

3 sprigs fresh sage
4 pieces fresh pork belly, about 6 ounces each
2 teaspoons unsalted butter
2 teaspoons apple cider vinegar
1 teaspoon chiffonade fresh sage
Salt and freshly ground black pepper
12 slices smoked bacon
1 tablespoon canola oil

Preparing to braise. Preheat the oven to 425°F. Bring the chicken stock to a boil in a large saucepan on high heat, then turn off the heat.

Sautéing the vegetables. Set a large sauté pan over medium heat. Pour in the olive oil. Put the carrot, onion, celery, and garlic in the pan. Cook, stirring, until they are golden brown, 10 to 15 minutes, and add the tomato paste, rosemary and sage sprigs. Cook, stirring until the vegetables are coated and the herbs are fragrant, 2 to 3 minutes.

Braising the belly. Transfer the vegetable mixture to a casserole dish. Place the pork belly pieces on top of the vegetables. Pour in the chicken stock. Cover the dish with aluminum foil and slide it into the oven. Braise the pork belly until you can squeeze tongs easily into the meat, with little resistance, 1½ to 2 hours. Remove from the oven.

Making the sauce. Strain the stock and let it sit for a few moments, allowing the fat to rise to the surface. Skim the fat off the stock and pour the stock into a large saucepan. Bring to a simmer and cook until the sauce is reduced enough to thickly coat the back of a spoon, about 15 minutes. Add the butter, vinegar, and chiffonade sage. Taste the sauce and season it with salt and pepper accordingly. Let the sauce sit on the back of the stove while you finish the pork belly.

(continued on next page)

Wrapping the pork belly pieces in bacon. Place 3 slices of bacon per pork belly on a plate, overlapping them like ribbons. Season each piece of pork belly with salt and pepper on both sides. Place each pork belly piece, skin side down, in the middle of the bacon. Fold the bottom part of the bacon ribbon up over the belly, and then bring the top down.

Roasting the bacon-wrapped pork belly. Pour the canola oil into a clean, oven-safe sauté pan or baking dish. Put the bacon-wrapped pork belly, seam side down, into the pan. Slide the pan into the oven. Cook, turning halfway through, until the bacon is crisp, 10 to 15 minutes. Take care not to burn yourself, because the bacon fat will continue rendering, spitting hot fat.

To serve, spoon a bit of sauce over each piece of belly.

the chef and the gluten-free girl get hitched and run off to italy

We always knew our wedding would be slightly unusual. Danny had worked for a catering company briefly, and he shuddered at the thought of the two of us married in a big hall, with nice little tablecloths, matching flower arrangements, and a hired band. The food at those affairs is nearly always dreadful, or at best mediocre. I refused to have a wedding where everyone sat politely through a generic service, just waiting to reach the open bar.

Even if we had chosen a local caterer who shared our food sensibilities, Danny would have found it difficult not to check on the food throughout the wedding. I would have worried about gluten cross-contamination in the caterer's kitchen. A marriage should start with three days in the bedroom—not the bathroom.

Inspired by the parties we held at our house every month, we imagined standing together, arms intertwined, surrounded by our favorite people and the food they made for us.

Plus, we'd save like a million dollars.

The night before the wedding, my dear friend Sharon and I lined up cubes of softened butter, mason jars filled with brown sugar, a bottle of vanilla extract, cartons of eggs, and bags of sorghum and teff flour. I turned on the KitchenAid and started flinging in ingredients. The gluten-free flour was flying that night, as we made an enormous chocolate-banana wedding cake.

The next morning, the sky dawned blue. Danny frosted the cake with chocolate ganache. When he greeted me at the altar, and I expected him to whisper sweetness in my ear, he leaned in and said, "I'm sweating like a pig." We married each other, telling stories and laughing with a backyard full of people we love. Instead of throwing rice, our friends and family set off whoopee cushions.

The food worked out fine. People arrived bearing bowls of baba ghanoush, plates of just-cooked collard greens, and platters of roasted green beans with caramelized onions. We ate ripe watermelon, sweet corn with basil, and a Moroccan lentil salad. Our friends Don and Michelle, who own the restaurant Volterra, roasted an entire lamb for us with fennel pollen and chiles, along with a side of fava bean aioli, as well as portobello mushroom caps with fresh mozzarella. The tables were laden with plates of food, beckoning and enticing. And there was gluten-free beer.

As one of our friends later said of the food at our wedding, "Wowie wow wow."

Danny and I agreed.

Besides, we had saved up enough money by not hiring caterers that we could go to Italy for our honeymoon.

When we told folks we were going to Italy, most of them had the same response. The gluten-free girl in Italy? The land of pizza and pasta? As my friend Matthew said, "Why not honeymoon in the Pillsbury factory and get it over with?"

But I had done my research. Besides pizza and pasta, food

in Italy also means grilled sardines, chickpea crepes, vanilla panna cotta with fresh berries, and forest chicken roasted in myrtle and wild thyme. Since a significant percentage of Italian people suffer from celiac, the Italians make the best gluten-free food in the world. In the culture that loves and lives in food, eating gluten-free is graciously easy.

The first day we stayed at an *agroturismo* in the hills above Assisi, we enjoyed the most local meal we had ever eaten: scrambled eggs laid by the chickens outside the door, tomatoes and zucchini from the garden, and olive oil produced on the farm. So what if the wine tasted faintly of the smell of the pig outside? We knew where it came from.

For breakfast most mornings, Danny and I dined on locally made prosciutto, fresh cheese, and chocolate croissants. That's right—gluten-free chocolate croissants.

We walked in the Central Market in Florence from one stand to another, sampling bloomy cheeses, slices of Parma ham, truffle salts, and fruity olive oils that slithered over the sides of our tongues like a sweet stream in spring.

Tender risotto, strewn with wild mushrooms, was delivered sizzling to the table. The sweet dreaminess of fresh buffalo mozzarella, in creamy ropes on small saucers, was available everywhere we turned. At dusk we shared lentils with smoked mussels, a cheese plate, and a saucer full of salumi. Heirloom tomatoes came in saturated colors: lime greens with dark green stripes, mid-July-sunshine yellows, warm oranges like terra-cotta tiles on Umbrian roofs.

Walking down the main street of Norcia, I grabbed Danny's hand. "My god, my love, that smell." He nodded and kissed me. Truffles. The entire street smelled like truffles.

The first time Danny ever kissed me, he came up for air and said, "You taste like truffles." At that point, I had never eaten them. In Norcia we ate truffles together.

We have never eaten so well in our lives.

How did this happen? It wasn't because we were eating in the best restaurants in Italy. We did splurge at a couple of expensive ones during the trip. *The honeymoon*, we'd say to ourselves, and not look at the bill. However, most of our meals did not cost that much. We ate well because we were in Italy, not because we were hanging out with "foodies." As far as we could tell, no one in Umbria or Rome was a foodie. Frankly, the mamas were the best cooks of all. It's just that everyone in Italy seemed to love food.

Our honeymoon was a sacred time of fullness, sweet and filled with light. In eleven delicious days of eating through Italy with Danny, I never once grew sick. We ate in restaurants for lunch and dinner, every day, and I never suffered from cross-contamination. All I had to say was "*Io sono celiaco*," and people took care of me. Not only that, but no one made me feel freakish or set apart. Eating gluten-free—safely and well—was simply a fact in Italy.

We returned home with a new vision of the world.

It should be as gracefully easy to live gluten-free, here in the States, as it was for me in Italy. No bride should have to worry about growing sick from the catered food at her own wedding.

We have work to do.

La dolce vita, senza glutine. It's possible, people. Let's live it.

how to season food

If you ask me to name the one ingredient I must always have in my kitchen, it's going to be salt. Salt is a humble ingredient, but food just wouldn't taste good without it. When food is bland, we instinctively add salt. Everyone has a different set of taste buds. When I smoked, my food was much saltier than it is now. Someone who is a supertaster can only stand the tiniest pinch. So if a recipe says "season with salt," that means something different to each person eating. You have to learn to trust your own taste.

Salt and pepper bring out the essential flavors of a food. If you are making a potato leek soup, you want to taste the potatoes, the leek, a little of the onions, and the celery—you want a taste of everything. You don't want food to taste salty; you want it to taste fully like itself.

Don't put salt in an overnight marinade. That will ruin the food by sucking out the moisture.

Potatoes, vegetables, rice, and other grains need seasoning while cooking. You should cook potatoes in water that tastes like the ocean. Rice is a smaller grain and absorbs salt faster, so don't use as much salt. In general, I use 1 tablespoon of salt per quart of water for rice and other grains.

Don't salt stocks or any other liquid that you will be reducing. In the reducing, the saltiness will become more intensified, and then you cannot play with the seasoning at the end if it's been oversalted.

Meats, fish, and grilling vegetables require seasoning just before you cook them. If you put a piece of steak on the grill without seasoning it, you're going to have flavorless steak.

When you season food, hold your hand up high, at least as high as your belly button or even as high as your chest, in order to spread the salt and pepper evenly all over. If you were to use the same amount of salt an inch above the plate, one area of the meat would be too salty and the rest of it underseasoned.

Some foods are seasoned at the end of the cooking process: soups, sauces, risotto, and vegetables that have not been blanched. With these, you want to simply crunch in a bit of salt and pepper, and taste. Add some more, and taste.

We recommend kosher salt for most seasoning and sea salt for finishing. Freshly cracked black pepper is best.

The key to seasoning is how the food tastes to *you*.

braised veal cheeks with stuffed squash blossoms

VARIATIONS
You can use chicken stock in place of the veal stock if you want a lighter taste. If you cannot eat dairy, you can use a nondairy butter substitute in the risotto and finish the sauce with extra-virgin olive oil instead of butter. Beef cheeks would also work well in this dish.

SUGGESTIONS
The Wild Mushroom Risotto (see page 207) would be fantastic in the squash blossoms.

For months, we anticipated our first meal in Italy. After being in the airplane for half a day, eating lousy food and drinking cheap airline wine, we would have been happy with merely decent food. But when the waitress at the Trimani wine bar in Rome set down the plate of braised veal cheeks with risotto-stuffed squash blossoms, I knew we were in Italy at last.

The veal cheeks had all but melted in the braising sauce. The risotto oozed out of the blossoms. Instinctively, I curved my arm around my plate and prevented Shauna from sharing. I had never done this before, but this dish was more than I could resist. The first bite tasted like my first hug with Shauna. I opened my arm and let her have a bite. That's when we fell in love with Italy.

• *Feeds 4*

2½ cups dry white wine
1½ quarts veal stock (see page 148)
1 tomato, quartered
½ head garlic
½ bunch fresh thyme
1 bay leaf
1½ pounds veal cheeks
8 tablespoons (1 stick) unsalted butter
3 tablespoons extra-virgin olive oil
½ medium yellow onion, peeled and finely diced

1 leek, white part only, finely diced
2 cloves garlic, peeled and chopped
1 tablespoon chopped fresh tarragon
1 cup Arborio rice
2 teaspoons sun-dried tomato paste
1½ quarts chicken stock
Kosher salt and cracked black pepper
½ cup julienned sun-dried tomatoes
½ cup freshly grated Parmesan cheese
8 large squash blossoms
1 tablespoon chopped fresh tarragon

Preheating the oven. Turn the oven to 375°F.

Braising the veal cheeks. In a Dutch oven over high heat, combine 2 cups of the wine, the veal stock, tomato, garlic, thyme, and bay leaf. Bring the liquid to a boil. Add the veal cheeks and bring the liquid to a boil again. Cover the Dutch oven and slide it into the oven. Cook until the veal cheeks are meltingly tender, about 1½ hours.

Making the risotto. While the veal cheeks are braising, set a large saucepan over high heat. Add 2 tablespoons of the butter and 1 tablespoon of the oil. Add the onion, leek, and garlic and cook over medium-low heat, stirring occasionally, until the onion and leek are translucent, about 8 minutes. Stir in the tarragon and cook until it is fragrant, about 1 minute.

Add the Arborio rice and cook, stirring occasionally, until the rice is entirely coated, about 2 minutes. Add the sun-dried tomato paste and stir to coat the rice with it. Pour in the remaining ½ cup of wine and cook until it is reduced by half its volume, about 5 minutes.

Pour the chicken stock into the rice, 1 cup at a time, stirring gently until the stock is absorbed into the rice; wait for each cup of stock to be absorbed before adding the next cup. Continue this process until all the stock is absorbed. The risotto should be chewy and soft, but not mushy. Season

the risotto with salt and pepper, about 1 teaspoon, and taste it. Sprinkle on more, if necessary.

Add the sun-dried tomatoes, 4 tablespoons of the butter, and the Parmesan cheese. Stir gently until everything is completely incorporated. Cover for 2 minutes to allow the risotto to become creamy. Take off the lid and allow the risotto to stay warm while you finish the braising liquid.

Reducing the braising liquid. When the veal cheeks are done, remove them from the Dutch oven. Keep the oven on at 375°F. Set the pot over high heat. Bring the liquid to a boil, then reduce the heat and simmer to reduce the liquid while you cook and stuff the squash blossoms.

Cooking the squash blossoms. Cut the squash blossoms in half lengthwise. Lightly coat them with the remaining 2 tablespoons of oil and salt and pepper. Place the squash blossoms in an oven-safe skillet with ¼ cup of hot water. Slide the skillet into the oven and bake until the blossoms are softened, about 5 minutes.

Stuffing the squash blossoms. Place the blossoms on a cutting board. Stuff each blossom with ½ cup of the risotto. Roll up the squash blossoms.

Making the sauce. Toss the remaining 2 tablespoons of butter and the tarragon into the sauce and stir until the butter has emulsified. Taste and then season with salt and pepper, if necessary.

To serve, spoon some sauce onto each plate. Place a squash blossom on the sauce and arrange the veal cheeks around the blossom.

planning the menu

We call it his time of the month.

For a few days at the end of every month, Danny grows a little grumpy. He broods. He needs more time to himself. He sits with his chin in his hand, leaning in, reading intently. At least a dozen cookbooks sit on the couch, looked through and abandoned. He stores everything—meals we have eaten at potlucks and friends' restaurants, spontaneous dinners at home, recipes I read to him from the *New York Times*—in his brain and thinks about it again.

But he doesn't start writing until it's almost too late. He writes fast, in ballpoint pen, on paper with shreds on the edges from being ripped out of a notebook, and uses his own unique spelling.

It's time for the new menu.

Every month Danny creates the menu anew for the restaurant—five appetizers, five entrées, and three desserts. Once the menu is in action, he will also create a new soup every day, a pâté every day, and a fish special and pasta special every day. But during his time of the month, it's the backbone of the menu that consumes his thoughts.

He starts by calling his seafood purveyors. "What's going to be coming in next month? You don't want to serve halibut in January. That would defeat the entire point." And then he calls the produce guys. "What's going to be good? How much local fruits and vegetables will they have?" Danny also watches the weather, all across the nation. "You might hear something—oh look, the people in Florida are having 30°F weather. That's going to affect the citrus crop."

Danny has to think about how the restaurant has been doing financially, and how much he can spend. Rising gasoline prices mean that every purveyor now adds a surcharge on deliveries. Should he raise the price of every item on the menu by a dollar? What are the rest of the chefs in town doing about this?

And then he has to think about the region of the world the menu will feature, to pair with that month's wines. If it's South Africa, what spices would make that food come alive? He never wants his food to be an imitation, a false front of taste. It has to be authentic, which means research about a culture and its food. No wonder his brow is furrowed for days.

After a couple of months of knowing him, I started wondering why he put himself through this. Couldn't he just let a menu work for two or three months, instead of growing anxious and pulling out flavor combinations from places I can't name?

It takes a while to know someone. He had to explain. "If I worked in a place that always had the same menu, I'd go crazy. Denny's hasn't changed its menu, ever, and they still have customers. Some people need familiarity. I just think it's boring."

People who are bored when they are cooking are not going to give you the greatest food. He told me stories about working the line at some places when he was younger. "Take the paper off a hamburger patty and put it on the grill caked with burnt meat that hasn't been cleaned in a week. Throw the potato skins in the fryer and let them sit there for three to five minutes. Put the bacon under the broiler. Slap a pickle on the burger. If you do a menu like that, repeating it over and over, and there's never any change, you could be stoned and do it fine. A bunch of the line cooks I've worked with were stoned the entire time on the line."

Of course, there are great restaurants that have the same menu for years because the chef is obsessed with perfecting those dishes, but Danny is too excited about food to not play with it every month. That's his way of being alive and paying attention. Knowing he had to do this, I gave him space on those days and any help I could. And I started watching to learn how he crafted a menu.

"Start with the most prominent ingredient. Most of the time, it's the protein. If you want to make a film, everything falls in place when you find your main actor." Salmon season starts next month. On Saturday, he saw lovely purple potatoes. The asparagus this year is fat and happy. He just started working with Italian black rice at home, and he likes the way it turns a dark purple on the plate. He thinks about how the ingredients will work together, and says, "Purples and greens, the pink of the fish. Hmm. Chickpeas would add an extra hit, plus some baby bok choy for another shade of green."

Danny also gets inspired as he shops for fresh ingredients. "I'm walking through the market, and I'm hit by this beautiful basil, a profusion of smell. I think, Sweet Jesus! I have to do something with that. I'm tired of making pesto. So I take the basil, some beautiful Italian parsley, garlic, eggs from Skagit River, some fresh-squeezed lemon juice, and some spinach for really great color and make a basil sauce, like a runny mayonnaise. I drizzle that over the dish."

That's one entrée done. Now, he needs to do it again, and make sure all the entrées work together.

Danny rarely repeats flavors across menus. "You can make a great movie with entirely unknown actors. I love introducing people to sunchokes, pomelos, kumquats, sturgeon, veal cheeks, squash blossoms. I want people to be surprised by each bite. But it shouldn't be so new that they are confused." He wants to create a dance on the plate, thinking about texture, smell, and color as much as taste. "I want people to experience the sweet chew of scallops, the way the chanterelle mushrooms have a bite then fall apart in the mouth, the creaminess of the risotto, the buttery texture of lobster, and the crunch of apple. I don't want people to eat my food and the next day think, Wait, what did I have to eat?" There are the avant garde chefs, the ones who experiment with foams and glucose syrup, irony on a plate. That's not Danny, and that's not the neighborhood in Seattle where his restaurant is. He's the solid independent chef who cooks straightforward food, done right. With the best ingredients in season, his food is trustworthy, with unexpected twists of flavor.

"A lot of times what ends up on the menu at Chez Panisse may not sound that impressive in words. Food isn't about words. It's in the mouth. It's about doing."

The first day of the new menu, Danny dances like a frenetic Fred Astaire. He starts working late in the morning, preparing everything. "I'm finally releasing my story into the world." And then he plays, for days, fine-tuning, working all the kinks out. "The corn risotto has too much corn, let's add more rice." Until, by the end of the first week, the menu has reached perfect precision for him, just what he wanted.

By the end of the second week, he's thinking about next month's menu instead.

Everything in our life goes back to the restaurant.

crisp pork belly with wild rice, cabbage, sour cherries, and honey-sage gastrique

VARIATIONS
Instead of dried sour cherries, you could easily use plain dried cherries—apricots or apples would work well too. Napa cabbage could substitute for the savoy cabbage.

SUGGESTIONS
The honey-sage gastrique would go well with foie gras, good fish, and grilled chicken.

About three years ago, nearly every chef in the country fell in love with pork belly. It's a wonderful way to use the pig. It's cheap, it's full of flavor, and you don't need a big piece—eating eight ounces of pork belly would be disgusting. So a beautifully seared piece of pork belly impresses diners and keeps food costs down at the same time.

By the time this book is published, I'm sure that many restaurants will have moved on from pork belly and gone on to the next trend, but I will still be serving it because pork belly is one of the most satisfying cuts of meat I work with. And this dish will always satisfy.

The wild rice here cuts the fattiness of the belly. The gastrique adds a spoonful of sweetness, with an intensified tang of vinegar, to accompany the sour cherries. You're going to enjoy this.
• *Feeds 4*

HONEY-SAGE GASTRIQUE
½ cup sugar
1 cup sherry vinegar
2 tablespoons honey
2 tablespoons chiffonade fresh sage
Kosher salt and cracked black pepper

WILD RICE
2 cups wild rice
2 shallots, peeled and thinly sliced
1 teaspoon finely chopped fresh thyme
3½ cups chicken stock
Kosher salt and cracked black pepper

PORK BELLY
4 pieces fresh pork belly, about 6 ounces each
Kosher salt and cracked black pepper
4 tablespoons extra-virgin olive oil
1 carrot, peeled and large diced
½ medium yellow onion, peeled and large diced
1 stalk celery, large diced
5 cloves garlic, smashed and peeled
1 medium sprig fresh rosemary
3 sprigs fresh sage
1 teaspoon tomato paste
3 cups thinly sliced savoy cabbage
¼ cup dried sour cherries

Making the gastrique. Put the sugar and ½ cup of water in a large saucepan over medium-high heat and cook, stirring occasionally, until the mixture becomes caramel in color, 5 to 10 minutes. Pull the pan off the heat and slowly pour in the vinegar, stirring gently. Watch the mixture closely, because it will want to boil over; don't let it. Once the vinegar is incorporated into the caramel, spoon in the honey and 1 tablespoon of the sage. Set the pan over medium heat and cook until the liquid begins to thicken. When it's close to the consistency of molasses, remove the pan from the heat.

Taste the gastrique. Season it with salt and pepper, if necessary. Strain the gastrique, which should be lovely and thick. Set it aside for later use.

Making the wild rice. Rinse the rice under cold water for 15 minutes, which will reduce the starchiness.

Sautéing the shallots. Set a large saucepan over medium heat. Add the shallots and cook, stirring occasionally, until they are softened and translucent, 4 to 5 minutes. Toss in the thyme and cook until it is fragrant, about 1 minute more.

Cooking the rice. Scoop the rice into the saucepan and stir to coat. Pour in enough chicken stock to cover by 1 inch. Bring the liquid to a boil, reduce the heat to low, and simmer until the rice is tender, about 45 minutes. Strain the rice from the liquid. Taste and season with salt and pepper, if necessary. Set the rice aside.

Preparing to cook the pork belly. If you bought frozen pork belly, make sure it is thoroughly thawed and season with salt and pepper. Bring the chicken stock to a boil in a large saucepan on high heat. Preheat the oven to 425°F.

Sautéing the vegetables. Set a large sauté pan over medium-high heat. Pour in 2 tablespoons of the oil, then put in the carrot, onion, celery, and garlic. Cook, stirring, until the vegetables are golden brown and softened, about 5 minutes. Toss in the rosemary and sage and cook until they are fragrant, about 1 minute. Add the tomato paste and stir to coat the vegetables.

Braising the bellies. Transfer the vegetables and pork belly pieces to a baking dish and pour the chicken stock on top. Cover with aluminum foil. Transfer to the oven and braise the pork belly pieces until you can take tongs to the side of one of the pork belly pieces and squeeze easily with little resistance, 1½ to 2 hours.

Searing the bellies. Remove the bellies from the baking dish, reserving the stock, and allow them to cool a bit. Pat dry the skin side of the bellies. Set a large oven-safe sauté pan over medium-high heat. Pour in the remaining 2 tablespoons of olive oil. Put the bellies, skin side down, into the hot oil. Sear them until the bottom has crisped to a golden brown, then turn the bellies over. Drain off the fat. Add 1 cup of the reserved chicken stock, just enough for a thin layer of liquid at the bottom of the pan. Place the belly pieces in the oven until they are soft and juicy, 5 to 10 minutes.

Heating the rice. Set a large sauté pan over high heat. Add the wild rice and ½ cup of water. As the rice is reheating, toss in the savoy cabbage and drop in the dried sour cherries. Taste the rice and season with salt and pepper, if necessary.

To serve, mound rice in the center of each of 4 plates and drizzle on the gastrique. Divide the remaining chiffonade sage among the 4 plates. Place the belly piece on top.

at the restaurant

waking up hungry

Sunlight is coming through the window, nudging my eyes, and urging me to rise. I turn toward Danny, who is still sleeping. His eyes open, and he smiles. He reaches for me with a sleepy wave of his hand. Snuggling in, I think once again how beautiful he is, how lucky I am.

He's thinking about the fish special for the day.

"Five orders of sturgeon left. What can I do with it? Jeremy dropped off those black trumpets yesterday. Risotto with those. Maybe some mâche. Bacon vinaigrette? Or maybe something lighter. That risotto will be heavy. We're going to the farmers' market today, right?"

Lying there, eyes still closed, he has already begun his day at the restaurant. The connection Danny has with the restaurant never ends. He is a chef and chefs never rest. Sometimes he wakes up in the middle of the night with an idea and stumbles into the living room to write it down on a scrap of paper, or to send a text message to himself. Pasta specials, or the pot of stock he left on the pilot light the night before, dance through his head. "It won't burn down, right?" he asks. Before he is fully awake, he figures out what to do with the leftover Brussels sprouts, thinks about calling his seafood purveyors, and remembers the dishes he ran out of the night before and so has to begin again.

Luckily, I understand. When I was teaching, I dreamed about Dostoyevsky essay exams. Sentences sing in my head. Our minds rarely turn off.

How long does it take for him to wake up and start thinking about the restaurant? Maybe three minutes. Just enough time to fling his arm over me and say "I love you. Good morning."

We haven't been awake that long before one thought hits us both: breakfast. I pad into the kitchen, past the dishes piled high from dinner the night before, and pull the filter from the coffeemaker.

Danny grabs the paper from the lawn, leaves some bird feed out for the rooster and hen that wander up our front steps by nine. He reads me headlines from the newspaper as I finish the coffee, especially when it's Wednesday's food section.

"Hon, what do you want for breakfast?" I call to him.

"Um . . . what do we have in the refrigerator?"

I pull open the door and bend forward to explore. "Smoked salmon left over. The slaw from last night. Frozen berries. Yogurt . . ." He isn't making a sound. I wait for it.

"Do we have eggs?" he calls out, as he flips to the comics.

"Yep. We have six of them. Do you want pancakes?"

Some morning, he answers yes. When I offer waffles, he is intrigued by those, sometimes. If I ever ask him if he wants some oatmeal, he waits a moment before quietly saying, "No, thank you."

Well, at least he was raised to be polite.

Most mornings, he says, as though he has never said it before, "Do you know what would be really good? Eggs. Eggs would be wonderful."

I laugh. We do this every morning. "Do you want bacon or sausages?"

"Sausages. We need sausages."

I pull some homemade sausages from the refrigerator and start the water. Then I ask the inevitable question. "Do you want potatoes?"

"What do you think?" he says with a laugh from the living room.

Yawning, I poke my head around the door and ask him how he wants them.

These mornings taste more satisfying than the mornings we spent alone. Danny rarely ate breakfast. Well, not unless you count coffee and cigarettes as breakfast. (He quit smoking after we met.) If he ate before he reached the restaurant, he grabbed a breakfast sandwich from a chain store. Mostly, he went hungry. Breakfast for me, on weekdays, generally meant a slice of gluten-free toast (the bread from the refrigerated section of the grocery store, more of a texture than a taste) with a quick skim of peanut butter,

wrapped in a paper towel, and coffee in a travel mug. On the weekends, I took my time, but the weekday mornings never left me satisfied.

Now, every morning brims with good food and hot coffee. I certainly don't mind the parade of eggs every morning. Our doctor told us that eggs are far better for us than people believe. So we dig our forks into sunny scrambled eggs, or poached eggs on toast, or eggs over easy draped on roasted potatoes. Sometimes, I place a plate of pancakes or waffles before him, dripping with syrup, or a bowl full of warm apple-rosemary muffins. Each morning dawns open, a surprise. I never know what is going to happen. I'd never trade these breakfasts for the old days, even if Danny is thinking about fish specials while we eat.

roasted potatoes with eggs over easy

VARIATIONS
You can use canola or grapeseed oil instead of the olive oil. Try different herbs every time you make these.

SUGGESTIONS
Don't overcook the potatoes. Don't worry if they're not perfect. If the eggs stick, use a bit more oil and a rubber spatula to free them from the pan. I've made my share of eggs over easy, and some of them still come out imperfect. Practice.

We must have potatoes in this house. It would be an Irish sin to not have potatoes. Shauna once lived with an Irish actor who insisted that every meal be accompanied by potatoes. Even if he went to a restaurant where the chef made risotto, he needed potatoes on the side. She didn't mind it either. Potatoes with butter is one of life's simplest pleasures.

When I first began working in restaurants as a cook, in my late teens, I was the breakfast cook two days a week at a great greasy spoon called the Horseshoe. That's when my mother taught me the phrase, "If you dance, you have to pay the fiddler." Even if I was hung over and exhausted, I had to make the eggs well. I knew how breakfast service would be by how my first over-easy eggs came out. Focus, dance on the balls of the feet, and flip. It's still how I judge my day, by how the eggs come out.

If someone wants to come to my restaurant to work for me, the first thing I'd say is, "Cook me an egg." If you can't do a nice egg over easy, and you burn the potatoes, you're not going to be paying attention to the rest of your day. • *Feeds 4*

ROASTED POTATOES
¼ cup kosher salt
2½ pounds Yukon gold potatoes, cut into large bite-size cubes
5 cloves garlic, peeled
1 sprig fresh rosemary

½ medium yellow onion, peeled, sliced, and core removed (French cut)
2 tablespoons extra-virgin olive oil

EGGS
8 tablespoons extra-virgin olive oil
8 large eggs

Preheating the oven. Turn the oven to 450°F.

Blanching the potatoes. Fill a large saucepan three-quarters full with cold water. Pour in the salt. (You might need more. The water should taste like the ocean.) Put the potatoes in the cold water with 2 cloves of the garlic and the rosemary and set the pan over high heat.

Bring to a boil and cook the potatoes until fork-tender, about 20 minutes. Drain the potatoes immediately.

Roasting the potatoes. Set a large oven-safe sauté pan over high heat. When the pan starts to smoke, toss the potatoes into the pan. Throw in the onion and the remaining 3 cloves of garlic and toss them both around. Add the oil and toss to coat.

Slide the pan into the oven. Toss the potatoes around in the pan, making sure that none of them stick. Roast the potatoes until they are browned and crisp on all sides, without burning the garlic or onions, 7 to 8 minutes. Remove the potatoes from the pan and discard the garlic and onion.

Cooking the eggs. Set a small sauté pan over medium-high heat. Pour in 2 tablespoons of the oil and swirl it around the pan; don't put too much oil in the pan or you might get burned when you flip the eggs. Crack 2 of the eggs into a small bowl. Slowly pour the eggs into the hot pan.

Allow the whites to coagulate; they should turn white as a sheet and firm up. Swirl the eggs around the pan, slowly and gently. Bring the yolks toward the top half of the pan.

Take the sauté pan away from the heat, swirl it, and tilt the pan away from you a bit and downward. To flip the eggs, gently but quickly step forward onto the balls of your feet, and flip the eggs up and toward you, moving back on your feet as you do it. Move the yolks to the top of the pan and flip them again.

If the eggs flip the first time, you're going to have a good day.

If they flip perfectly and are glossy and shiny, it's going to be a beautiful day.

To serve, place the potatoes on a plate and slide the eggs out onto them. Repeat with the remaining oil and eggs.

multigrain waffles

VARIATIONS
Play with other whole-grain flours for this mix— that's what we do every time we make waffles—but keep the potato starch and sweet rice flour so the mix will be light. If you cannot eat dairy, use a vegan sour cream; for the buttermilk, add 1 tablespoon of lemon juice or apple cider vinegar to soy or rice milk and let it stand for 15 minutes before using; and use extra oil in place of the butter.

SUGGESTIONS
We like to serve butter, good Vermont maple syrup, and a homemade fruit compote with these waffles. You might prefer brown sugar, or you could add 2 tablespoons of good cocoa powder in the batter to make these into dessert waffles.

One of the ironies of going gluten-free is that you will be forced to start eating more whole grains than ever before in your life. Without enriched white flour, you have to turn to more interesting grains. Teff, originally from Ethiopia, is the smallest grain in the world. It's also packed with a nutritious wallop: one-quarter cup of whole grain teff has one-third of the iron you need for the day. Eating these waffles will improve your health.

The teff flour is dark and has a taste almost like molasses. Here you have waffles that taste like more than cardboard.

We both grew up eating Eggos sometimes. If you miss that convenience, you can make up a big batch of these waffles ahead of time and freeze them in airtight containers. Bingo—healthy toaster waffles! • *Makes 8 waffles*

¾ cup (90g/3oz) tapioca flour
½ cup (57g/2oz) sorghum flour
½ cup (57g/2oz) oat flour
    (make sure it's certified gluten-free)
⅓ cup (30g/1oz) teff flour
2 teaspoons xanthan gum
½ teaspoon guar gum
1 tablespoon baking powder
1 teaspoon salt

3 tablespoons sugar
1 cup (8 ounces) milk
2 large eggs
1 teaspoon vanilla extract
4 tablespoons (½ stick or 2 ounces)
    unsalted butter, melted and cooled
Walnut or canola oil, or butter for
    greasing the pan

Combining the dry ingredients. Put the tapioca flour, sorghum flour, oat flour, and teff flour into a small bowl. Stir, then sift through a fine-mesh sieve into a larger bowl. Add the xanthan gum, guar gum, baking powder, salt, and sugar into the flours. Combine them all together. Set aside.

Combining the liquids. Put the milk, eggs, and vanilla into a small bowl. Whisk together. Add the melted butter and stir again.

Finishing the batter. Make a well in the center of the dry ingredients. Pour in the liquids. Stir until combined.

Patience. Let the pancake batter stand for at least 1 hour before cooking the pancakes. (For best results, make the batter the night before you intend to eat them.)

Making the waffles. Turn on the waffle iron. When it has come to heat, brush both surfaces of the waffle iron with oil or butter. (We like walnut oil here.) Pour about ⅓ cup of the waffle batter into the iron. Cook until the waffle is well browned. Serve.

seasonal berry pancakes

VARIATIONS
Go crazy with the fruit on these all year. Citrus fruits wouldn't work, but try any other kind you like. Apples, pears, peaches, bananas, mangoes, papayas—you name it. If you can't drink cow's milk, you can use soy milk or rice milk here.

SUGGESTIONS
Buy a flat of berries, make a big batch of these pancakes, and freeze them. You'll have summer all winter long.

Go to the farmers' market in summer and you cannot resist buying berries. You'll carry home flats of blueberries and pints of fat raspberries that stain your hands with their juices and tart little wild huckleberries and tiny strawberries still on the stem. Sure, when you get home you can eat a pint in one sitting with your hands. But those other berries? Those could go into pancakes.

There are more steps involved here than making a mix from a bag. But the results will make you feel good. A warm morning, bare feet on the tile floor, a pot of coffee going, and you have time to mix flours and pull eggs from the refrigerator. And those berries, just as delicious as the day before, if not more. Your family will be happy. • *Makes 12 small pancakes*

BERRY COMPOTE
2 cups berries (whatever is in season)
½ cup sugar
1 cup (8 ounces) orange juice, fresh squeezed if possible
¼ teaspoon vanilla extract

PANCAKE BATTER
¾ cup (90g/3oz) tapioca flour
½ cup (57g/2oz) sorghum flour
½ cup (57g/2oz) oat flour (make sure it's certified gluten-free)
⅓ cup (29g/1oz) teff flour

2 teaspoons xanthan gum
½ teaspoon guar gum
1 tablespoon baking powder
1 teaspoon fine sea salt
3 tablespoons sugar
1½ cups (12 ounces) whole milk
2 large eggs
1 teaspoon vanilla extract
4 tablespoons (½ stick or 2 ounces) unsalted butter, melted and cooled
Canola oil, butter, nondairy spread, or bacon fat for greasing pan

Making the berry compote. Place everything into a medium saucepan and bring to a boil. Reduce the heat to low and simmer, stirring occasionally so the bottom does not burn, until the compote has reached the thickness of syrup. Remove the pan from the heat and set aside the compote.

Combining the dry ingredients. Sift the tapioca flour, sorghum flour, oat flour, and teff flour into a small bowl. Add the xanthan gum, guar gum, baking powder, salt and sugar. Stir and set aside.

Combining the liquids. Put the milk, eggs, and vanilla into a small bowl. Whisk together. Add the melted butter and stir again.

Finishing the batter. Make a well in the center of the dry ingredients. Pour in the liquids. Stir until combined.

Folding in the berries. Scoop a few tablespoons of the berry compote into the pancake batter and stir. This should turn the batter red or purple, depending on the berry.

Patience. Let the pancake batter stand for at least 1 hour before cooking the pancakes. (For best results, make the batter the night before you intend to eat them.)

Cooking the pancakes. Set a sauté pan over medium heat. When it is hot enough that you can feel the heat on your palm held a foot above it, add enough of your favorite grease—canola oil, butter, or nondairy spread—to coat the pan. (Bacon fat makes the crispest pancakes.) Dollop about ¼ cup of the pancake batter into the pan, from the height of a few inches. Allow the pancake to cook. Don't be overeager to turn it. When bubbles have formed and mostly popped on the surface of the pancake, turn it. The second side always takes half the time to cook as the first, so watch this carefully. Remove the pancake from the pan. Make the rest.

Have you ever noticed how each successive pancake cooks more quickly, so that the last ones burn easily? That's because the burner is getting hotter with each passing moment. Here's a trick: between each pancake, turn down the heat of the burner, just a touch. This way you won't have to suffer any burnt pancakes.

Serving the pancakes. When you and yours are ready to eat, top the pancakes with some of the berry compote. Enjoy.

homemade pork sausage

VARIATIONS
If the amount of fat in these sausages gives you pause, you might not want to make them—great sausages require fat. If you do not have a spice grinder for the fennel seeds, you can crush the fennel seeds by putting them on a cutting board and smashing down the seeds with the edge of a small skillet. If you do not have a sausage stuffing attachment or a stand mixer, you can make the ground meat into patties.

SUGGESTIONS
One of our favorite dinners is rice and sausages, with a bit of mustard. Have sausages and eggs for breakfast or sausage sandwiches for lunch. If you want a more complex meal, stuff chicken legs with sausages or make shepherd's pie.

We were inspired to start making this sausage by the folks at Skagit River Ranch, just outside of Seattle. Every Saturday, we bought a pound of their sweet Italian sausage and ate it happily throughout the week. After someone gave us a sausage stuffer attachment for our stand mixer as a wedding present, though, we decided to make our own, with Skagit River pork.

Fatback is a slab of fat that runs along the back of the pig. Most grocery stores don't sell it, but if you can find a good butcher shop, it should be readily available and fairly inexpensive. Unlike bacon, there's no meat in fatback. The fatback adds moisture to the sausages, making them spit their juices after you cook them, and helps to give them a consistent texture.

• *Makes about 20 sausages*

3 pounds pork shoulder, cut into 2-inch pieces
¾ pound fatback, cut into 1-inch pieces
3 tablespoons thinly sliced garlic
2 tablespoons finely chopped fresh rosemary
2 tablespoons toasted fennel seeds, crushed
2 teaspoons cracked black pepper

1 tablespoon smoked paprika (Pimentón de la Vera)
Pinch red pepper flakes
1½ tablespoons kosher salt
¾ cup fresh apple juice, chilled
3 tablespoons canola oil
10 feet hog casings, soaked in lukewarm water for at least 1 hour and rinsed through

Marinating the sausage meat. At least a day before you plan to serve the sausages, combine the pork, fatback, garlic, rosemary, fennel seeds, pepper, paprika, and red pepper flakes in a large bowl and toss to combine. Cover the bowl with plastic wrap and put it in the refrigerator overnight. Put the grinding attachment for your stand mixer in the freezer.

Freezing the meat the next day. Take the meat out of the refrigerator and put it in the freezer for 1 hour. It should be fairly frozen before you work with it, because this makes grinding much easier. Put the grinding attachment and metal bowl for your stand mixer in the freezer as well.

Grinding the meat. Pull the grinding attachment out of the freezer and attach it to your stand mixer. Pull the metal bowl and meat from the freezer. Push the meat through the grinder into the chilled bowl. Add the salt. With the mixer set on low, mix the meat together for 1 minute. (This develops the protein in the meat, makes the mixture sticky and coherent, and distributes the salt evenly.) Add the apple juice and mix for 1 minute.

Testing the flavors. Form a small patty of the meat. (Put the mixing bowl back into the refrigerator while you do this.) Set a small sauté pan over medium-high heat. Add 1 tablespoon of the oil. Fry up the sausage patty until the internal temperature reaches 150°F. Eat and see what you think. Adjust the seasonings accordingly with the remaining uncooked meat.

Stuffing the sausages. Attach the sausage stuffer to the end of the grinder. Take the meat out of the refrigerator. Affix one end of the casings to the stuffer. Turn on the mixer, push the sausage meat through the grinder again and watch it fill the casings. Keep pushing the casings forward as the sausage meat emerges, working with someone else, ideally, for the extra pair of hands. When you have run out of meat, turn off the grinder. Running your hands down the length of the stuffed casings, make a crimp and quick twist every 3 to 4 inches. (This will determine the size of your sausage links.) At the end of each link, crimp and twist a different way; this will keep the sausages from unraveling.

Blanching the sausages. Fill a large sauté pan with 3 cups of salted water (it should taste like the ocean) and bring it to a boil. Reduce the heat to a simmer. Starting with one end of the sausage length, twirl the sausages around each other until you form a giant spiral. Put the spiral

of sausages on a cutting board. Slide the sausage spiral into the simmering water and blanch until a meat thermometer inserted into the middle of one of the sausages registers an internal temperature of 160°F, about 5 minutes. Drain the water. Put the sausage spiral into the refrigerator for later use.

Cooking the sausages. When you are ready to cook individual sausages, preheat the oven to 450°F. Cut off as many links from the spiral of sausages as you wish to cook. Add the remaining 2 tablespoons of canola oil to a large oven-safe sauté pan over medium-high heat. When the oil is hot, add the sausages. Sear on one side until they are a nice crackling brown, about 3 minutes. Slide the pan into the oven. Bake until the sausages are spitting and snapping gently, about 10 minutes. Insert a thermometer into one of the sausages to make sure they have reached an internal temperature of 120°F. Eat.

Sweet rice flour

Teff flour

Tapioca flour

Oat flour

Amaranth flour

Mesquite flour

Millet flour

Potato starch

Sorghum flour

how to work with gluten-free flours

When you first start working with gluten-free flours, expect to be confused. I had grown used to baking with regular flour, with a few forays into cake flour, or tipo 00 flour for homemade pasta. Mostly, I just sifted white flour into a bowl and never thought about it. There are more gluten-free flours in the world than there are flours with gluten. At first, this may feel overwhelming. Eventually, you might feel like Shauna and I do—time to play.

The main difference between gluten-free baking and the more traditional kind is that you must combine flours to bake gluten-free. There are a few exceptions—chickpea flour for socca, sorghum flour for rotis—but for the most part, you will need at least three flours.

One of the three should be a whole-grain, a solid base: sorghum flour, brown rice flour, garfava flour. The next should be a starch, to lighten up the mixture, since gluten-free baked goods tend to be dense: potato starch, tapioca starch (also known as tapioca flour), cornstarch, or arrowroot powder. The third flour should have a particular personality you want to add to your baked goods. Amaranth flour has a soft texture and slight malt flavor. We like it in cookies and cinnamon rolls. Almond flour adds protein and a bit of fat for flavor. Coconut flour adds taste to baked goods, but it sucks up all the moisture around it, so you have to play with the amount of liquids in your treats. Millet flour makes a great crumb. Quinoa flour is savory and great in quiches. Teff flour is the finest-textured flour in the world, so during baking it almost melts, which helps to bind together muffins and quick breads. You can have more than three flours, but work with at least three.

Shauna has learned from years of experimenting and failed baking attempts, along with cookies and brownies everyone loves. However, if you are just starting your gluten-free life, you might find all of this overwhelming. If so, you can make a flour mix of equal parts sorghum flour, tapioca starch, potato starch, and sweet rice flour. You'll see that combination in some of the recipes in this book. Or, you could also try our other favorite all-purpose mix: forty percent superfine brown rice flour and sorghum flour, sixty percent potato starch, tapioca flour, sweet rice flour, and cornstarch.

Simply open bags of flours, or weigh them out, then dump them into a large container in your kitchen. (We buy food storage containers at a restaurant supply store, where they are surprisingly inexpensive.) Whisk the flours together until the flour mix is one even color. Now you can use this as the flour in your kitchen. Play with the flours and learn your favorites.

what's cooking today?

The morning passes in various habits and fashions, interrupted only by the turning of pages and the sipping of coffee. The pot sits empty. Our love for each other doesn't always involve memorable mouthfuls, meals that linger in the mind, and mâche salads. There are reminiscences of beloved childhood pets, imagined trips to Lake Powell, and the repetition of a thousand jokes that no one else could understand. We learn about each other in increments, every day, in stories that slip out and asides that surprise us.

However, food always starts to creep in. Our love of food is expansive and insatiable, the way we love each other.

Danny stretches his neck to look back over his arm, searching the sky. He turns toward me. "The weather is shifting. I think I'll roast some butternut squash today." Autumn has arrived. He's going to be bombarded by ideas.

He sits at the computer and starts searching the growing list of restaurant websites he visits for inspiration. Gramercy Tavern, Hearth, Daniel—what are they doing right now? "Almond-crusted foie gras terrine with prune napoleon? Are you kidding me?" He always looks at what his old chef in Colorado is doing. "Moules rustica with Thai basil, galangal, and Pinot Gris. Hmm." Chicago, Boston, Portland—they all intrigue him. "Grapefruit granita, avocado ice cream, and pistachio meringue crumbles." Most of the restaurants he watches are in California. They're a month ahead of us in season, so they give him ideas for his next menu. Chez Panisse, Lucques, and Zuni Café always inspire him. "Duck sausage with wilted cabbage, pancetta, honey, and balsamic over liver toast. Oh baby, we're having that for dinner tonight."

If he's horrified, then he shouts out to me. Mostly, he stares at the computer, silent save for some sighs. He's listening to the whistles and harmonies on the plates other people have put before him, picking out his own rhythms. Some men look up sports scores during the day, commenting on teams and decisions by coaches. Danny does this with other restaurants.

Sometimes we play a game. He reads me a menu and I guess the restaurant. I'm getting pretty good at it now—they all have voices. And hearing these flavor combinations and ingredients I had never encountered before teaches me.

"Sweet pea, where did you put the book?"

"The book" in our house is *Culinary Artistry*, written by Andrew Dornenburg and Karen Page, a book that nearly every chef in America owns and few home cooks know. Danny's copy was so beaten up—brûlée custard and mustard sauce on text, pages ripped, *G* to *H* falling out and stuffed back in again—that I bought him a clean copy and kept the old one at home. The new one was battered again soon.

The book collects the hard-won knowledge of people who work with food into one source. What goes well with lamb? What doesn't work with eggs? It does not contain recipes or headnotes, just alphabetical lists of foods. When you feel familiar with techniques and trust your ability to cook, then you arrive here.

"Oh God, it's a godsend. I look through it and find something new every day. I didn't know that melons went well with anise seed and lychees. That gives me an idea."

During one trip to Uwajimaya, I spied some shiso leaf among the herbs and asked Danny what it was. "It's good. It's mostly used in Asian cooking. It's for savory stuff."

Returning home, I grabbed our copy of the book. Cranberries were on the list. So were ginger and mint. Looking up, keeping my finger on the page, I said, "Hey, I want to make this into a sorbet today."

Danny looked at me, confused, but he didn't say no. We experiment in the mornings.

And the sorbet turned out great.

Once, when I was teaching a cooking class, I led the group through the store to show them how easily they could eat gluten-free. In the produce section, I started talking about the joys of eating in season. A young woman raised her hand and said, "If you've never tried to eat in season, and the grocery stores have everything available year-round, how are you supposed to know what's in season?"

It was a good question. It reminded me of something Danny had told me recently. "Colorado was such a landlocked place. We had tomatoes all year round. There aren't many farmers there. The specialty guy in Denver bought half his crap from California. I kind of knew there were seasons, but I didn't get the entire grasp of it until I moved to Seattle."

How had I learned about foods in season aside from Danny? I had started shopping at farmers' markets, but I couldn't tell that to my students in the grocery store, because the store was paying me to teach the class. Everyone in the group offered suggestions. "The fruit in season is the cheapest," one woman shouted out.

"It's always at the front section, near the door, because they want you to buy it first," said another.

I told them to check out Seasonal Cornucopia.

Every morning, Danny looks up something on our friend Becky Selenguts's website, Seasonal Cornucopia. Formerly a chef at the Herbfarm in Seattle, Becky researched every kind of produce, foraged foods, herbs, meat, and seafood available in the Pacific Northwest, then collated it all onto a website. So when Danny's thinking of the fish he wants to cook that night, he plugs in halibut and sees that it's still not in season. Three more weeks to wait. He spends a part of the morning deciding what to cook instead.

On Saturday mornings, we do something we never do on the weekdays: watch television.

Danny doesn't have much time for most television chefs. But he makes an exception for Jamie Oliver. *Jamie at Home* is broadcast at a maddeningly early nine thirty in the morning. We don't miss it. We grab another cup of coffee and settle into bed, cuddling, the remote control clutched in Danny's hand. We both sit staring at Jamie's humble kitchen, the wooden cutting boards scarred from so much use, the vegetables from the garden so enormous that people shopping at grocery stores can only dream of something that good.

Then our minds start racing.

Sometimes, Danny sends himself a text message, a squiggle of an idea that will develop through the day into a meal for the people who come in that evening. "Maybe leeks? Prosciutto? Pasta. How about balsamic vinegar?"

Danny starts dancing earlier on Saturdays than any day of the week.

And so the morning passes, with suggestions and inspirations, excited conversations about food from magazines and cookbooks, our favorite chefs on television. "Anything excites me about food. When we talk about it or walk through the market, my mind gets going." I grow excited about tackling new cooking projects between bursts of writing. "How about sloppy joes?" I ask.

"Make them with veal," Danny answers.

Hmm. There's an idea.

Danny bounces on his feet, a new idea brewing. When he runs it past me, and I say "Yes, please!" he knows he has to get going.

"I want to get my hands in the food."

roast turkey breast with kiwi salsa

VARIATIONS
If you want to
make this salsa
with fresh kiwi
berries in the
summer and fall,
substitute 2 cups
of kiwi berries for
the 10 kiwis. If
you want to add
more kick, throw in
some chipotles or
habaneros.

SUGGESTIONS
This would be
fantastic with
roasted duck
breast instead, or
duck confit and
wild rice.

When you think of turkey, you think of Thanksgiving. Turkey deserves better than being relegated to a few times a year. Roasting a turkey breast is much easier than wrestling with a giant bird on that long, agonizing day of cooking. It's easy and juicy. Turkey has darker meat than chicken and a more distinctive taste.

This kiwi salsa is different from the salsas you buy in a jar. We've grown accustomed to red-hot chiles and tomatoes, spices that threaten to burn off the roofs of our mouths. Here, you have the sweetness of the kiwi with only a little kick of the jalapeños. We were inspired to make this by the kiwi berries we found at the farmers' market in the summer. When you go to the farmers' market and find something you've never eaten before, take it home and figure out what to do with it. You can play. Look up recipes. Ask your friends. Think about the tastes that go with it and create something new. • *Feeds 4*

KIWI SALSA
10 kiwis, peeled and medium diced
2 navel oranges, cut into segments
  (see page 117)
2 tomatoes, peeled and seeded
½ cup sliced green onions
1 bunch fresh cilantro, chopped
1 red bell pepper, medium diced
1 jalapeño pepper, seeds removed
  and fine diced

2 tablespoons brown rice vinegar
1 teaspoon each kosher salt and
  cracked black pepper

ROAST TURKEY BREAST
One 3- to 4-pound turkey breast,
  skin on, bone in
Kosher salt and cracked black pepper
2 tablespoons extra-virgin olive oil

Making the salsa. Combine all the salsa ingredients in a large bowl and stir. Remove a quarter of the mixture and puree it briefly in a food processor. Add the pureed part back into the salsa and stir. Refrigerate for at least 1 hour before serving.

Preparing to roast the turkey. Turn the oven to 500°F. Place the turkey breast, skin side up, on a rack in a roasting pan. Season the breast with salt and pepper. Slather the turkey breast with the oil and rub it in with your hands.

Roasting the turkey. Slide the roasting pan into the oven. Let the turkey roast until the skin gets a little crisp, about 15 minutes. Turn the heat down to 375°F. Roast the turkey breast until the internal temperature reaches 155°F, about 40 minutes. Take the turkey breast out of the oven and let it rest for a few minutes.

To serve, carve up the turkey breast and place several slices of turkey on each plate. Top with a generous spoonful of the kiwi salsa.

shiso-cranberry sorbet

VARIATIONS
This flavor combination would also work with melons such as cantaloupe or honeydew.

SUGGESTIONS
You can also use simple syrup to sweeten drinks like lemonade, iced tea, and club soda. If you want to flavor your simple syrup, throw in herbs like basil or mint for flavored drinks, or if you are adventurous, try a black pepper, tarragon, or ginger simple syrup.

Shauna dreamed up this sorbet one day, after she had first learned about shiso leaf. Because she was new to creating food, she had the playful spirit to try anything that seemed like a good idea. I'm sometimes constrained by my training. I've always regarded shiso as a savory herb.

Shiso leaf is from the same family as mint and basil, and it marries well with crab and other seafood. Mostly, shiso is used in Japanese cuisine, added to sushi and tempura. Although shiso tastes nothing like fennel, it has the same qualities: clearly a vegetal taste with a faint sweetness behind it. Still, when Shauna suggested combining shiso and cranberries, I thought she was crazy.

She was right. Shiso and cranberry are unexpectedly good friends. The shiso goes great with the cranberry's puckery qualities, the kick of the cinnamon, and the tartness of the orange juice. The kaffir lime leaf keeps everything interesting.

Playing with your food pays off sometimes. • *Makes 2 pints of sorbet*

1 cup sugar
1 cup water
2 pints fresh cranberries
1 firm apple (Gala or Fuji), peeled, cored, and roughly chopped

1 cup orange juice, freshly squeezed, if possible
8 shiso leaves (available at Asian markets)
1 cinnamon stick
1 kaffir lime leaf (if you can find it)

Making the simple syrup. Combine the sugar and water in a small saucepan and bring to a gentle boil over medium heat. Keep a pastry brush with a bit of water next to the pan and wet down the sides of the saucepan if the sugar creeps up. When the sugar has completely dissolved, the syrup will be clear. Turn the heat down to the lowest setting, cover the pan, and allow the syrup to simmer for 5 minutes. Set aside to cool.

Making the sorbet base. Put half of the simple syrup, the cranberries, apple, orange juice, shiso leaves, and cinnamon stick in a saucepan. Bring to a boil. Simmer for 3 to 4 minutes, then turn off the heat and throw in the lime leaf. Allow the mixture to steep for 1 hour. Strain the mixture and chill it in the refrigerator until it is cold.

Making the sorbet. Pour the sorbet base into a blender and puree. Scoop the puree into your ice-cream maker. While the ice-cream maker is starting to turn, drizzle in the remaining simple syrup. Freeze according to your ice-cream maker's specifications.

pickled apples

Say you're at the farmers' market in early June. The first carrots of the year have arrived. Not the enormous tough carrots you can buy at the grocery store all year long, but the sweet little carrots, almost too tender to have been pulled from the earth. If you're like us, you buy too many, just because you're excited that carrots are back in season. At the end of the week, no matter how hard you have tried, you have a pile of carrots left over. Make up a jar of pickled carrots for eating later.

Pickling is a great way to preserve vegetables. And you can make a quick pickled dish, some in less than an hour, others in a day. Apples grow soft with too much brine for too long. They take on the puckery tastes of the vinegar mixture and cease to taste like apples. Some pickled things, however, require days before the flavors shimmer to the surface. Shauna and I made dill pickles from scratch, about a week before our wedding. All twelve jars were gone by the end of the family picnic that was our rehearsal dinner.

Shauna loves anything pickled: apricots, grapes, pearl onions. I have yet to make her pickled pig's feet, but I will. • *Makes two 1-pint jars*

1½ cups apple juice, freshly juiced, if possible
1½ cups apple cider vinegar
2 teaspoons kosher salt
2 apples, peeled, cored, and cut into 1-inch cubes
  (use a good firm apple with a bit of tartness,
  such as Gravenstein or Honeycrisp)

20 allspice berries
½ vanilla bean, split
1 cinnamon stick, broken in half

Making the brine. In a medium pot, combine the apple juice, vinegar, and salt and bring to a boil. Reduce the heat to a simmer while you fill the jars.

Filling the jars. Put the apples, equally divided, into two 1-pint jars. Add the allspice berries, vanilla bean, and cinnamon stick to the jars. Pour the pickling liquid over the apples and screw on the lids.

Infusing the flavors by waiting. Allow the jars to sit overnight before eating the apples. The pickling taste will intensify each day. After 1 week, the apples will probably be too acrid to eat.

pickled vegetables

VARIATIONS
You could use champagne vinegar in place of the white vinegar, if you happen to have a lot of it lying around. A raspberry vinegar would be good for pickling fruits. Try balsamic vinegar with pickled cherries.

You can borrow this basic template to pickle plenty of other vegetables. Try pickling pearl onions, cabbage, watermelon rind, grapes, sunchokes, gingerroot, rhubarb, red bell peppers, or apricots. Once you find your own pickling rhythm, you could probably pickle something from the farmers' market every week. • *Makes eight 1-pint jars (or four 1-quart jars)*

THE BRINE
2 quarts water
2 quarts white vinegar
4 tablespoons fine sea salt
2 tablespoons black peppercorns

PICKLED FENNEL
2 heads baby fennel, with tops attached
1 large carrot, peeled and julienned
3 cloves garlic, peeled
1 bay leaf
Pinch freshly ground black pepper

BABY GOLD BEETS
1 bunch gold beets, boiled until tender, then peeled,
3 sprigs fresh basil
3 cloves garlic, peeled

BABY TURNIPS
1 bunch baby turnips
3 cloves garlic, peeled
1 bay leaf
1 teaspoon chopped fresh dill
Pinch sugar

BABY RED BEETS
1 bunch baby red beets, boiled until tender, then peeled
1 small nub ginger (about the size of half a thumb), peeled
3 cloves garlic, peeled
1 teaspoon chopped fresh dill
3 sprigs fresh tarragon

Making the brine. In a large pot, combine the water, vinegar, salt, and peppercorns and bring to a boil. Strain the liquid of the peppercorns.

Filling the jars. Put the vegetables and other ingredients into eight 1-pint jars (or four 1-quart jars). Cover with the pickling liquid and screw on the lid.

Infusing the flavors by waiting. Allow the jars to sit for 3 days before eating the pickles. Eat within 1 month of opening.

veal sloppy joes

VARIATIONS
You can certainly make this entirely with ground beef, if you wish. You could use cayenne pepper or red pepper flakes to hit the meat with spice if you don't want to buy the Piment d'Espelette.

SUGGESTIONS
Eat this with a good potato salad and use a bib.

Shauna and I both ate sloppy joes as a kid. For me, they were a summer thing. Ground beef with the Lawry's seasoning packet and cheap, starchy hamburger buns. Sloppy joes live up to their name. I practically had to be hosed down after eating one of these. I feel sorry for the kid whose parents invented this sandwich. Being called Sloppy Joe for the rest of his life had to be no fun.

Tastes from childhood can still be great as long as you use good ingredients.

Here, we use Piment d'Espelette, a robust peppery spice from Espelette, in the Basque country. Not as smoky as smoked paprika, or as sweet as traditional paprika, Piment d'Espelette adds an unexpected kick to this dish, an interesting flavor that makes you want to keep taking bites to figure it out. Its heat will surprise you, so go easy if you sprinkle it on roasted chicken or use it in bean dishes. • *Feeds 4 to 6*

1 pound ground veal
½ pound ground beef
1 medium yellow onion, peeled and finely chopped
2 slices smoked bacon, finely diced
1 tablespoon finely chopped fresh rosemary
1 tablespoon thinly sliced garlic
Pinch Piment d'Espelette
5 dashes Worcestershire sauce

1 teaspoon each kosher salt and cracked black pepper
2 tablespoons extra-virgin olive oil
1 tablespoon tomato paste
2 cups veal stock (see page 148) or chicken stock
1 cup ketchup
Rosemary Rolls (recipe follows), for serving

Marinating the meat. Combine the veal, beef, a third of the onion, the bacon, rosemary, garlic, Piment d'Espelette, Worcestershire sauce, salt, and pepper. Mix with your hands to combine well. Cover the bowl with plastic wrap and let the meat sit for at least 1 hour, preferably overnight, in the refrigerator.

Cooking the meat. Set a large sauté pan over medium-high heat. Put half of the meat mixture into the pan and cook, stirring to break it up, until the meat is browned, 5 minutes. Drain the meat of its grease and set aside while you repeat with the other half of the meat mixture.

Sautéing the vegetables. Pour the oil into the empty sauté pan and cook the remaining onion, stirring, until it is softened and translucent, about 5 minutes. Place the browned meat back into the sauté pan.

Making the sauce and serving. Stir in the tomato paste until the onions and meat are coated. Pour in the stock and ketchup. Turn the heat down to low and simmer the mixture until the fragrance entices and everything bubbles, about 20 minutes. Taste the meat sauce and season with salt and pepper and another pinch of Piment d'Espelette, if necessary. Cook the sauce over low heat until the liquid is reduced to a consistency that is just a bit thinner than molasses, about 10 minutes. Serve on the rosemary rolls.

rosemary rolls

Use the recipe for gluten-free bread that appears on page 180. When you are letting the dough rise the first time, add in 1 tablespoon of finely chopped fresh rosemary. At the end of the process, instead of forming the dough into a loaf, make balls the size of softballs out of the dough. Be sure to wet your hands first. Allow the rolls to rise on a greased baking sheet for the final hour before baking them. Bake until the bottoms have a solid thump, the tops are browned, and the internal temperature reaches at least 200°F, about 25 minutes. • *Makes 8 rolls*

the chef dance

"I have to get the remouillage going. We're out of chocolate mousse. The rabbits need braising. The produce guys are coming in at one. I have to put away all the veg, butcher the meat, butcher the fish. Damn, we're booked tonight. It's going to be busy and I have to play catch-up. We have to stop at the market for ginger because it slipped my mind when I was putting in that order."

I can't hear any of this monologue, but I don't need to know the words. I know it from his jiggling legs, his hands fumbling in the air, the faraway gaze. Danny's dancing.

When we first fell in love, this daily flip confused me.

Sweet and solicitous all morning long, Danny switches at about eleven thirty in the morning into a jangling bundle of nerves and curt answers. I can see him looking outside, toward the car. After breakfast and talking about food while we sit on the couch, I suggest we pay the bills before we leave for work that day. That only makes it worse.

"Paying the bills would trigger it, because I thought about the bills unpaid at the restaurant. Doing the dishes triggered it, because I thought about Hortensia's medical situation and whether or not she was going to stay. Taking a shower started me, because that meant we were getting ready to leave the house."

When we took the bus the first few months of our relationship, I realized he knew every route in the city, and how long it took to get from point A to point B. At the first sign of traffic, he'd crane his neck and start jingling his keys. He had to reach the restaurant.

I didn't understand, at first, or for a long time, really. How could a man so composed and easygoing turn into such a twerp an hour before leaving for the restaurant? I remember driving the road that curved along Lake Union early one afternoon, the sun soft along the leaves that had turned golden on the emptying trees. Filled with happiness, I turned toward him to share the image and saw that he was hunched over a notepad, scribbling notes to himself. When I pointed toward the road, he glanced up quickly, grunted, and went back to the restaurant in his mind.

I just kept driving.

What most confused me was this: an hour after being at the restaurant, he'd call me, happier than the clams he was cleaning with his hands. When I asked him if he was still feeling anxious, he'd chatter: "Oh no. I'm fine. I just needed to get here."

Was it me? In a way—yes.

"Before I met you, there was nobody to see me. If I knew we were going to be busy at Papillon, and I usually showed up at noon, I'd get there at eleven to make sure we were ready. If I smelled bad from the night before, it didn't matter. I'd skip the shower. I didn't care what people thought. I just did what it took to get it all done."

But I wouldn't let us leave the house at 8:30 in the morning so he could start working at 9:00. I insisted he be more human with me. Eat breakfast. Drink the coffee slowly. Read the newspaper. Spend a few hours off each day doing something fun.

He loves those mornings, and slowly he has started to relax more. But the compromises of a relationship made him antsy, at first. "Before, it was just me. I didn't have to think of another person besides the people eating my food.

"People outside of the business just don't understand why I think about the restaurant all the time."

It took me months to understand this part of him. I had to work with him at the restaurant to really understand.

As small as his kitchen is, Danny manages to fit three people in it: himself, Hortensia the dishwasher, and someone working pantry. One day, his pantry person needed the night off, unexpectedly. He asked if I could help out. Of course.

When I walked into the kitchen at three, buttoning up my borrowed chef coat, I looked at the board to his left and gulped. My God, dinner service started in two hours, and we still had that long list to cross off before we could serve? When I had dinner parties before meeting Danny, I planned for days, shopping at all the right stores, prepping ahead, and then cooking all afternoon. That's for three or four dishes, at the most.

I started segmenting oranges, slowly, perhaps so slowly that it gave him pain. But he didn't say anything. He patted me on the shoulder and returned to his high-speed chopping. In the time it took me to segment ten oranges, he had made a curry mayonnaise, a tarragon vinaigrette, and thyme oil.

By the time dinner service began, I was in a sweat, my feet aching. He seemed to stand up straighter as the evening went on. And when the rush began—the board filled with orders, every burner working, meat resting on a plate behind him, servers nowhere to be seen when the dish went up, the kitchen five hundred degrees, and me moving as fast as I could—he was all grace, his face filled with calm. The anxious Danny I tried to coax into composure on the ride into the restaurant? That man was long gone. This one was in control, in his element.

After that, I stopped being confused when he started jiggling his leg and asking if we could go. In fact, sometimes I look at him and ask, "Don't you have a lot to do today? Should we get going?"

That always makes him laugh.

One Sunday afternoon, we met our friends Seis and Pia outside the bakery near our house. Pia walked into the bakery with the kids, who were skipping at the idea of cookies. Seis stood with us on the sidewalk, talking about the banquet he was organizing at the hotel restaurant where he was executive chef. As he ticked off all he had to do, I could read the prep list on his face. He moved his feet around in a stuttering waltz.

I pointed toward him, laughing. "Hey, that looks familiar!" I said.

Danny beamed. Finally, I saw it in someone else. We explained it to Seis, who broke into a smile that we understood. You never stop being a chef.

So now, when Danny starts getting antsy late in the morning, I just look at him and say, "You dancing?"

"Yep."

I grab the keys and we start moving toward the door.

watermelon gazpacho

VARIATIONS
You could prepare this without watermelon and make it a more traditional gazpacho. Play with the flavors. If you want, you can thicken this with a little soaked day-old gluten-free bread.

SUGGESTIONS
Throw in some red grapes to garnish. Top with slivered Marcona almonds.

Our friend Seis invited us to the opening of the grand hotel restaurant where he was the executive chef. We went with our good friend Meri, who had just been in Spain. It was early September, and the heat was settling into fall. The first dish placed before us was a watermelon gazpacho.

Watermelon is certainly not traditional for gazpacho, but everyone does gazpacho a slightly different way. Some insist there must be bread for it to be authentic, but Meri told us that she had eaten gazpacho across Spain with no bread in it. Some of the gazpachos she tried there had red peppers in them, and one was topped with red grapes. Watery or thick, spicy or mild, gazpacho is like bouillabaisse. There is no one recipe. Every country, every region of Spain, and every mama has a different way of making gazpacho. Recipes are really only guidelines. They are a call to action, an enticement to make food. Something in the words catches your fancy and you move toward the kitchen. Play with this and make it your own.

However, don't make this in January, or I will hunt you down and slap you. • *Feeds 4*

1 seedless watermelon (2 to 3 pounds),
  fruit removed and cubed
2 ripe beefsteak tomatoes, peeled
  (see page 239), seeded, and medium diced
½ large red onion, peeled and finely diced
½ cucumber, peeled, seeded, and finely
  diced

½ red or yellow bell pepper, finely diced
3 tablespoons finely chopped fresh cilantro
2 limes, zest grated and juiced
1 tablespoon sherry vinegar
Kosher salt and cracked black pepper
3 tablespoons extra-virgin olive oil
  (with a fruity flavor)

Combining the ingredients. In a large bowl, combine all the ingredients, including 2 tablespoons of the oil.

Pureeing the soup. Pour a quarter of the mixture into a blender and mix it into a fine puree.

Finishing the soup. Pour the puree back into the bowl and garnish with the remaining tablespoon of oil. Chill it well before serving.

seared sea scallops with boulangerie potatoes and bacon butter

VARIATIONS
There are some nondairy "buttery" sticks that might work for the compound butter. If you cannot eat scallops, try roasted duck breast with this dish.

SUGGESTIONS
The bacon compound butter is pretty amazing with eggs. Try it on toast for a new experience. The potatoes are great with anything.

The peak season for Maine scallops is from mid-fall to mid-spring, making this dish a treat for the middle of winter. Make sure the scallops are entirely dry before you sear them. (Frozen scallops are not the best, but if that's all you can get, make sure that you rinse them under cold water and pat them dry as a bone after defrosting.)

Take your time when making these potatoes, even in cutting them, because you want a good starch on the potatoes. That's what is going to hold the potatoes together. In France, when this potato dish was invented, the bakery (*boulangerie*) had one big oven for the town. That's where people went to bake their potatoes, after all the bread was made. Meats were roasted on the top rack, potatoes below. This is why we use chicken stock, to recreate that roasted taste.

And bacon? Who can go wrong with bacon? • *Feeds 4*

BACON COMPOUND BUTTER
4 slices bacon
16 tablespoons (2 sticks) unsalted butter, softened
1 tablespoon thinly sliced garlic
2 tablespoons finely chopped fresh chives
1 teaspoon finely chopped fresh rosemary

BOULANGERIE POTATOES
4 slices smoked bacon, large diced
1 medium yellow onion, peeled, sliced, and core removed (French cut)
1 teaspoon finely chopped fresh thyme
1 tablespoon finely chopped garlic
4 large russet potatoes, peeled
½ teaspoon each kosher salt and cracked black pepper
½ teaspoon finely chopped fresh rosemary
2 cups reduced chicken stock

SEARED SEA SCALLOPS
12 large sea scallops
3 teaspoons kosher salt
6 tablespoons canola oil
3 teaspoons unsalted butter

Crisping the bacon. Chop the bacon into the smallest pieces you can. Set a large sauté pan over medium-high heat and add the bacon pieces to the sauté pan. Cook until the bacon is crisp but not burnt, 7 to 10 minutes. Allow the bacon to cool to room temperature.

Making the butter. Place the softened butter, garlic, chives, rosemary, and crisped bacon in a food processor. Whirl them up until they are well combined. The chives will bleed a green color into the butter, so don't be alarmed.

Tasting the butter. Bring a small sauté pan to medium heat. Spoon a bit of the bacon butter into the sauté pan. Taste the butter when it has melted. Does it need more seasonings? Add those into the food processor.

Chilling the butter. Scoop the bacon butter out of the food processor. Plop it onto parchment paper and roll it into a log. Refrigerate for later use.

Preparing to cook the potatoes. Preheat the oven to 375°F.

Cooking the bacon. Bring a large sauté pan to high heat and put the diced smoked bacon in the hot pan. As the bacon begins to crisp, lower the heat to medium-high. Add the onion and cook until soft and translucent and the bacon is crisp but not burnt, about 10 minutes. Toss in the thyme and cook until it releases its fragrance, about 2 minutes. Stir in the garlic. Remove from the heat.

Slicing the potatoes. Cut the potatoes in half lengthwise, and then cut them into ½-inch-thick slices. Be as precise as possible.

Baking the potatoes. Spread the onion and bacon mixture in a baking dish. Layer the potatoes, sitting them upright in a long line. They should have a slight tilt, like dominoes as they begin to fall. Season the potatoes with salt and pepper. Sprinkle the rosemary on top.

Cover the potatoes with the chicken stock and cover the baking dish with aluminum foil. Slide the dish into the oven and bake until the smell is rich in the kitchen, the stock has started to reduce and thicken, and the potatoes are tender, about 1 hour.

Preparing to cook the scallops. Pat the scallops dry with a paper towel. You want them as dry as possible. Season the scallops with salt on one side, about ¼ teaspoon per scallop.

Searing the scallops. Bring a large sauté pan, preferably cast-iron, to high heat. Pour in 2 tablespoons of the oil. When the oil is starting to smoke, put in 1 teaspoon of the butter and stir. Place 4 of the scallops in the oil and butter. Sear the scallops until the bottoms have turned a brown, almost caramel, color and formed a crust, 2 minutes. Do not burn them.

Flip over the scallops. Let them sit for 1 minute. They should feel firm, with some give. Flex your fist and touch the middle of your forearm. That's what they should feel like. Allow the scallops to rest on a plate. Sear the remaining scallops in the same way.

To serve, place a line of the boulangerie potatoes on each plate and place the scallops nearby. Dot some of the bacon butter on the scallops and let it melt.

how to make sauces

Shauna tells me that sauces intimidate people. They are too hard to make. They take a lot of work. It's only restaurant chefs that know how to make sauces.

If you want to eat a piece of meat plain, that's fine. That's why God invented ketchup. But if you want the satisfaction of taking food from a raw state—bones and vegetables—to an elevated level of taste, sure to impress and sate your friends, well, as my friend Doug says, "It's time to shut up and put on your big-boy pants."

Go ahead. Learn how to make sauces.

I believe in the classics. If you learn the basic techniques, you can play all you want after that. But knowing the right way to make sauces keeps you humble and ensures that they will taste good.

In classical French cuisine, there are five mother sauces: sauce espagnole (brown stock thickened with roux), hollandaise (egg yolks and clarified butter), tomato sauce (mostly tomatoes thickened with roux), velouté (chicken stock thickened with roux), and béchamel (milk thickened with roux). Most of the sauces I make, and the ones in this book, are variations on sauce espagnole.

Traditionally, as you can see from the list above, chefs thicken sauces with roux, which is a combination of butter and flour. Does that make gluten-free sauces impossible? Not at all. I like sorghum flour for making a roux, because its texture is something like that of whole wheat pastry flour. However, after I made my restaurant gluten-free, I eased back on the roux and allowed the sauces to reduce slowly, instead. I find, to my surprise, that I like these sauces better. These sauces taste cleaner, more themselves, instead of tasting like the flours.

Reducing a stock-based sauce intensifies the flavor. (Don't reduce a hollandaise, or it will break. If you reduce a tomato sauce, it runs the risk of burning.) If you start off with an entire saucepan filled with liquid and simmer it down until it is reduced to a quarter cup, imagine all the condensed flavor you'll have.

As with every other technique, there is a template for making a meat-stock-based sauce:

- Caramelize the vegetables and herbs.
- Deglaze the pan with alcohol or another liquid.
- Reduce the liquid until the pan is almost dry, not Death Valley dry, but a couple miles west of there.
- Pour in stock. (We use veal stock most often.)
- Reduce the stock by half its volume.
- Strain the stock.
- Swirl in a bit of butter at the end to give richness.
- Season and serve.

Sauces make a great accompaniment to meats, grains, and vegetables. Making sauces will give you a sense of accomplishment, as well as providing a better eating experience for whoever you are feeding. If you are intimidated, you can start with pan sauces. Take the drippings from the pan after roasting meats, add vegetables and herbs, pour in stock, reduce it, swirl in butter, and serve. Once you can make pan sauces, you'll want to graduate to more difficult sauces.

apple-rosemary muffins

During the first autumn in our new home, we tried to figure out some way to make use of the windfall apples dotting our backyard. Whenever we forgot to collect ripe apples from the tree, we looked out the back window the next day to see dozens of apples on the grass. One weekend, we made quarts of applesauce and canned them for the winter. We had a thin layer of applesauce left on the bottom of the pan, so we made these muffins, flavored with the rosemary growing profusely by the back door.

We've been making this deliberately every fall since. And if Danny's really dancing, I can hand him some of these to eat in the car on the way to the restaurant. • *Makes 12 large muffins*

2 teaspoons canola oil for oiling large
  muffin tin
1½ large crisp apples, peeled and cored,
  cut into quarters
1 teaspoon finely chopped fresh rosemary
2 tablespoons mild honey
1 cup (85g/3.5oz) tapioca flour
½ cup (85g/3.5oz) teff flour
⅔ cup (85g/3.5oz) sweet rice flour
½ cup (48g/1.7oz) almond flour
¼ cup (28g/1oz) milk powder
1 teaspoon xanthan gum

½ teaspoon guar gum
1⅓ cup brown sugar
1 teaspoon baking powder
½ teaspoon fine sea salt
½ teaspoon ground cinnamon
2 large eggs
1 teaspoon vanilla extract
8 tablespoons (1 stick) butter, melted
  and cooled
½ large crisp apple, peeled, cored, and
  fine diced

Preparing to bake. Grease a large muffin pan with the oil. Preheat the oven to 325°F.

Making the apple puree. Put the quartered apples into a food processor with the rosemary and honey. Pulse until everything has combined into a pulp.

Combining the dry ingredients. Mix the tapioca flour, teff flour, sweet rice flour, almond flour, milk powder, xanthan gum, and guar gum together. Sift the mixture into another bowl. Add the brown sugar, baking powder, salt, and cinnamon and stir to combine.

Combining the wet ingredients. Mix the eggs and vanilla together. Stir in the apple pulp.

Making one mixture. Pour the wet ingredients into the dry ingredients and stir until just combined. Add the melted butter and stir. Mix in the diced apple.

Baking the muffins. Spoon the batter into the muffin pans. Bake until the tops are browned and a knife inserted into the middle comes out clean, about 30 minutes.

Let the muffins cool in the pan for 10 minutes before moving to a wire rack to cool. Eat when the muffins have cooled completely.

venison osso bucco with blackberry-port sauce

SUGGESTIONS
This dish goes well with mashed potatoes, which serve as a color contrast for the sauce.

Growing up in Colorado, we ate venison pretty regularly. My parents had friends who hunted, and sometimes they brought venison over for our fondue parties. I still remember that bite of venison dipped in melted cheese.

In Seattle, most people regard venison as an exotic meat. Shauna had her first taste a few years ago, in Alaska, at the home of friends who had a freezer full of meat on the back porch. I'd love for more people to try it. Venison has a slight gamey taste in the first chew, and then becomes mild in the back of the mouth.

You might expect this sauce to be sweet, but it's not. The venison and veal stock balance the port and blackberries. You get a hit of each flavor in a really complex taste, and the meat is suffused with that taste. • *Feeds 8*

BLACKBERRY-PORT MARINADE
One 750-ml bottle ruby red port
  (this can be inexpensive)
1 tablespoon roughly chopped fresh thyme
1 tablespoon roughly chopped fresh sage
1 teaspoon crushed fresh juniper berries
1 tablespoon cracked black pepper
1 cup blackberries, crushed (fresh are best)

VENISON OSSO BUCCO
8 venison shanks
Kosher salt and cracked black pepper

5 tablespoons extra-virgin olive oil
2 quarts veal stock (see page 148)
2 large carrots, peeled, quartered
  lengthwise, and chopped
2 large yellow onions, peeled and roughly
  chopped
4 stalks celery, roughly chopped
½ cup garlic cloves, smashed and peeled
5 large sprigs fresh thyme, roughly
  chopped
2 tablespoons butter

Making the marinade. The day before you plan to serve the venison, combine all the marinade ingredients (minus 1 cup of port set aside for later use) in a large bowl.

Marinating the venison. Smear the marinade over the venison shanks. Put the shanks in a bowl and pour the remaining liquid from the marinade over them. Cover the bowl with plastic wrap and marinate the meat in the refrigerator overnight.

Preparing to cook the next day. Preheat the oven to 375°F.

Searing the shanks. Wipe the shanks clean, reserving the marinade. Season the shanks with salt and pepper. Set a large sauté pan over medium-high heat. Pour in 3 tablespoons of the oil. Add the shanks to the hot oil in two batches. Sear the shanks until the bottoms are browned, then flip them over and sear the other side. Remove the shanks from the pan and sear the second batch. Set the sauté pan aside for later use.

Cooking the shanks. Transfer the seared shanks to a Dutch oven. Pour the veal stock over the shanks and place the Dutch oven on a back burner over high heat. Bring the liquid to a boil, then reduce the heat and allow the liquid to simmer while you prepare the vegetables.

Caramelizing the vegetables. Drain the fat from the sauté pan you used for searing the shanks and set the pan over medium-high heat. Pour in the remaining 2 tablespoons of oil. Add the carrots, onions, celery, and garlic and cook, stirring frequently, until the vegetables are browned and softened, about 10 minutes. Toss in the thyme and cook, stirring, until it releases its fragrance. Pour the reserved blackberry marinade into the sauté pan. Cook until the marinade coats the vegetables, 2 to 3 minutes.

Deglazing the pan. Pour the remaining 1 cup of port into the sauté pan, scraping up the goodness from the bottom. Allow the liquid to cook until it is reduced by half its volume, about 5 minutes.

Braising the shanks. Pour the blackberry-port liquid into the Dutch oven and bring the liquid to a boil. Cover the Dutch oven and slide it into the oven. Cook until the meat is tender enough that you can pull it away from the bone with a fork, 2 to 2½ hours.

Making the sauce. Remove the shanks from the sauce and set aside. Strain the liquid, discarding the vegetables. Pour the liquid back into the Dutch oven. Bring to a boil, then reduce the heat to medium and cook until the sauce is reduced enough to coat the back of a spoon, about 20 minutes. (The sauce should be reduced to about half or a quarter of its original volume.) Swirl in the butter. Taste the sauce, then season with salt and pepper, if necessary.

To serve, place a shank on each plate and spoon the sauce over it.

running food errands

A t just about noon every day, Danny and I go on a field trip.

When Danny worked at larger restaurants, he never stopped for food on his way to the restaurant. But the restaurant where he works is so intimate, and the kitchen so small, that he doesn't have the storage space for a week's worth of produce orders or a pantry full of oils and vinegars. Instead, he works with small amounts of food and replenishes his stock when needed. This means that we leave the house to walk around markets, sniff ginger, and try out different spices for the dishes he imagines.

It's not a bad way to spend part of the afternoon, especially when we're spending the restaurant's money.

At World Spice Market, glass jars line the wall, in vivid oranges, speckled peppercorns, and mustard browns. We could easily spend hours, opening every jar, taking deep whiffs, and then sharing the smells. "What is that? Sumac? I haven't worked with that in ages." I sometimes find it hard to tear myself away from the glossy vanilla beans, the earthy Madras curry powder, and the puckery-smelling star anise.

We still haven't tried the nineteen different types of chiles, but I'm eager to taste the smoked cherry and avocado leaf.

Danny calls to me from across the spice store and says, "Sweetie, try this." He dabs his finger in the powder he has just purchased, and then puts it on his lips. "Kiss me," he says. When I do, my lips dance, a wild sharpness and vivid sweetness mixing on my tongue to mingle and emerge, entirely unexpected. The spice tastes deeply familiar, but new. The sensation reminds me of when I was a kid, and I forced myself to walk around the house with my eyes closed to imagine what it might be like to be blind. When I opened my eyes, everything gleamed brightly, born again for a few seconds, new to my senses.

"What is that?" I ask him. He turns the little glass jar and points to the label. "Saigon cinnamon."

Walking in a daze through the Spanish Table, a shop in Seattle dedicated to foods from Spain, we come to the refrigerated cases in the back. Hanging there is the great prize: Jamón Ibérico. With fat like white satin ribboning the edges and threaded through the rich pink, this meat is relatively rare in the United States. The black pigs in Spain eat only acorns the last six weeks of their lives, and then the meat is cured for at least thirty-six months. Sadly, it is beyond our budget. I nudge Danny to buy a small amount for the next month's menu so I can sneak a taste, but he can't. So we buy the sherry vinegar for which we came in and leave with a sigh.

On rare occasions, we run to a big grocery store for some last-minute item. But mostly, we wander around Pike Place Market from October to May. During the summer, this working-man's market becomes a tourist attraction crammed with visitors, and filled with young men throwing whole salmon at the fish stall at the front of the market, so we avoid the place entirely.

DeLaurenti's looks like an old-fashioned grocery store, with a black-and-white tiled floor, but the shelves are filled with French Dijon mustards, demi-glace in jars, and chocolates from Venezuela. We can't afford to shop there for our staples, and neither can the restaurant, but the cheese case makes us look like orphans at the window for a long time. When I'm desperate for it, I sneak in and buy some oregano salami from Salumi.

When we go to Don and Joe's meat counter, Danny watches the butchers break down a side of lamb and says he wants to do that someday. At Sosio's, our favorite produce stand, Danny is silent, dumbfounded by all the choices. We duck into the dairy stall for cream, the truffle store for more honey, Beecher's for some cheese (that one's for home, so I pay for it), and stop at the pirozhki stand for Danny. We could spend three hours together at the market. In every place, I ask him questions about the food. "What's that?" I ask, as if I'm two years old.

We will never run out of new foods to try.

Before I met Danny, I would have thought most of these foods beyond me. Only restaurants served truly magnificent food. My humble kitchen could only produce decent meals. The year after I went gluten-free, I dipped my toes into the warm waters of good extra-virgin olive oils, tart vinegars, and meats that weren't plastic wrapped on a Styrofoam tray. (Okay, I didn't actually dip my toes into them.) With Danny, I slid all the way in and swam.

And what I discovered is that almost every food I began to love, including the rare and expensive, was not beyond my skill or the worth of my kitchen. Once, I had thought of those foods as "gourmet," the purview of "foodies." Danny hates the words *gourmet* (not the magazine, though) and *foodie*, the same way he laughs every time we go to a grocery store with an "ethnic foods" aisle.

"Food is food. If you cook, you don't think of ingredients as elitist. It's just that some of them make you sit up more and say, 'Well, hello to you.' Making food with great ingredients instead of the most convenient ones is like hav-ing sex that leaves you breathless, instead of wham bam thank you ma'am."

The fanciest foods, and the most expensive, start with humble beginnings in the earth. The folks who sell foraged mushrooms at our farmers' markets are ex-hippies with thrift-store clothes. Olives grow on gnarled trees in flat fields, and teams of farm workers are required to pick the fruit. Sea salt is gathered from the ocean. Most often, it's the snouts of pigs that touch the truffles first.

"Look at the fishermen. They have the shittiest job of all. Out on the crazy seas, getting salmon, days away from home, bilging out water, eating bad food that will survive the sea spray."

Before Danny and I started taking slow sniffing spins around small stores selling great food, I couldn't under-stand why I should spend money on saffron, when it costs something like thirty-five dollars an ounce. He helped me understand. We're paying for the labor, the dignity of human work. It requires the stigmas from over one hundred thou-sand crocus flowers to produce one pound of saffron threads.

"Saffron has such a beautiful scent. You can feel the weathered hands of the people who picked all the threads to fill that one-ounce jar we bought today. I have such re-spect for that spice, enough to use it sparingly. There are chefs who use it like it's going out of style just because it is expensive, and they think it makes them look good. But if you overpower a dish with saffron, it's going to be disgust-ing. You have to respect the ingredients."

We wander back to the car, laden down with bags and new ideas for cooking. We talk about the people who might have produced our food, the friends who sold it to us in the market. I love these food field trips. I really loved when my third-grade class visited McDonald's for the day, but these field trips with Danny are much better.

frisée salad with oranges, almonds, and garlic dressing

VARIATIONS

Marcona almonds would be a decadent pleasure here—they are a bit pricier, but oh my. If you use Marconas, watch the salt level in the dressing, since they are heavily salted.

SUGGESTIONS

The garlic dressing would be great on many other salads. The dressing does have raw eggs, so be sure to ask guests if they mind that, especially children and pregnant women.

Some of you might think you have never eaten frisée before, but you have. If you've ever bought spring mix in the plastic boxes, those curly white bits you ate were frisée, so don't be frightened by this new food.

We make a mistake of only thinking of taste when it comes to food. One of the reasons food is so satisfying is that one bite can be an interplay of sounds and textures, smells and sights, as well as taste. There are all sorts of components to this salad: the crunchiness of the almonds, the tart sweetness of the oranges, the garlicky kick of the dressing, and the slightly bitter crispness of the frisée. That's what makes it a good salad—everything balances out. • *Feeds 4*

1 large navel orange
1 large egg
1 large egg yolk
1 tablespoon chopped garlic
Kosher salt and cracked black pepper

1 cup canola oil
2 heads frisée, cleaned and chopped
　(wash under cold water, spin)
½ cup slivered almonds

Making the orange segments. Slice off both ends of the orange. With your knife, take off the outer layer of the skin. Don't dig in, the way you do when you peel an orange with your hands. Slice close to the flesh of the orange, removing the white pith. Take off any remaining pith with your knife, working closely.

Cut between the membranes of each fibrous white part. If you do this slowly, the segment of orange should simply pop out. (This is known as supreming the orange.)

Making the dressing. Blend the egg, egg yolk, and garlic in the food processor. Season the dressing with salt and pepper. With the food processor running, slowly drizzle in the oil. When the dressing has become a coherent mixture, turn off the food processor.

To serve, Dress the greens with 3 tablespoons of the garlic dressing, perhaps more, depending on your fancy. (Save the rest of the dressing in the refrigerator for other salads.)

Throw in the almonds and toss the salad. Place the orange segments on top, after you have plated it.

chicken stew with pistou manchego

VARIATIONS
You could add green or yellow bell peppers, mushrooms, or any vegetables of the season that would stand up to a stew. Rabbit leg would be good in the stew. Roasted pork tenderloin, with the pistou as a side dish, will knock your socks off.

SUGGESTIONS
If you want to kick up the heat, add some Spanish smoked paprika (Pimentón de la Vera). But not too much—Spanish food isn't super spicy, the way some people believe. You could also make a great breakfast by sautéing up a quick pistou and placing poached eggs on top.

Pistou manchego is not made with Manchego cheese. The servers at my restaurant made that mistake the first few days that this was on the menu. It's called *manchego* because the dish originates from La Mancha, in Spain.

The French have ratatouille. The Spanish have pistou. Whatever you call it, this is a great summer dish. All the vegetables vibrate with color and taste in July and August, and they don't need much cooking. With a few fat tomatoes and squat peppers, a plump eggplant, a long zucchini, and some stewing in a fruity extra-virgin olive oil, this dish makes the meal at the end of a summer evening. • *Feeds 4*

1 medium eggplant
Kosher salt
1 large zucchini
1 red bell pepper
1 large red onion
3 tablespoons thinly sliced garlic
2 tablespoons finely chopped fresh thyme
5 tablespoons extra-virgin olive oil
  (with a fruity flavor)

Kosher salt and cracked black pepper
4 chicken breast and thigh pieces,
  bones removed
2 medium tomatoes, peeled, seeded,
  and diced
4 cups chicken stock
1 tablespoon unsalted butter
3 tablespoons finely chopped fresh
  Italian parsley

Preparing the eggplant. Slice off the top and bottom of the eggplant. Cut it into large chunks, about 1 inch each. Season generously with about a tablespoon of salt, toss, and allow to sit for 1 hour.

Preheating the oven. Turn the oven to 425°F.

Cutting the vegetables. Slice the zucchini lengthwise and cut it into large half-moons. Open the pepper and remove the seeds and the pith. Cut the pepper into large chunks. Peel and thinly slice the onion. Drain the eggplant and pat the pieces dry.

Roasting the vegetables. Put the eggplant, zucchini, pepper, and onion in a roasting pan. Sprinkle with the garlic and thyme. Pour 3 tablespoons of the oil over the vegetables and toss together to coat. Season the vegetables with salt and pepper, about 2 teaspoons of each, and toss again. Slide the roasting pan in the oven and roast until the vegetables are a bit browned and sizzling, about 35 minutes.

Searing the chicken breast. Meanwhile, set a large oven-safe sauté pan over high heat. (You might need 2 sauté pans.) Pour in the remaining 2 tablespoons of oil. Place the chicken breasts and thighs, skin side down, in the pan. Cook the chicken until the bottoms turn golden brown, 3 to 4 minutes. Flip the chicken pieces.

Making the stew. When the roasted vegetables are done, turn the oven up to 450°F. Drain the grease from the sauté pan, leaving the chicken in the pan. Ladle in the roasted vegetables. Add the tomatoes. Pour in the chicken stock. Put the sauté pan back over high heat and bring the liquid to a boil. Slide the pan into the oven. Cook until the internal temperature of the meatiest part of the breast reaches 155°F, 20 to 25 minutes.

Finishing the sauce. Remove the chicken from the sauté pan. Bring the liquid to a boil over medium-high heat. Drop in the butter and cook the vegetables until the sauce starts to thicken, 3 to 5 minutes. Taste the stew and season with salt and pepper, if necessary. Just before serving, sprinkle the stew with the parsley.

To serve, make a mound of the saucy vegetables in a large bowl and arrange the chicken pieces on top.

smoked salmon profiteroles

VARIATIONS
If you cannot eat cow's milk dairy, try a nondairy butter substitute in the profiteroles and use a soft chèvre in place of the cream cheese for the filling. We worked with a lot of different flours in this recipe and this is the best combination we found.

The word *profiteroles* intimidates people. The food itself intimidates too. When you make profiteroles the first time and they don't work out entirely the way you expected, don't blame yourself or the recipe. Profiteroles require patience. If you are intimidated by the pastry bag, use two spoons. Go easy on yourself.

These gluten-free profiteroles will not rise as high as traditional profiteroles. That's the lack of gluten at work. Sometimes they might fall and falter a bit, or wobble down after you take them out of the oven. That's okay.

With the bite of smoked salmon in smooth cream cheese, the proof of these will be in your mouth. They're the perfect handheld appetizer, so many tastes in one. • *Makes 15 to 20 profiteroles*

SUGGESTIONS
You could fill the profiteroles with seared foie gras, chicken liver custard, tuna salad, egg salad, or chicken salad. If you are making the profiteroles ahead of time for a party, freeze them when they come to room temperature after baking. Pull them out of the freezer about 2 hours before the party.

PROFITEROLES
½ cup (56g/2oz) corn flour
¼ cup (51g/1.2oz) sweet rice flour
¼ cup (30g/1oz) tapioca flour
1 teaspoon baking powder
1 cup water
8 tablespoons (1 stick) unsalted butter
¼ teaspoon salt
2 large eggs
1 large egg yolk mixed with 2 tablespoons whole milk

SMOKED SALMON FILLING
8 ounces smoked salmon (buy the best kind you can)
8 ounces cream cheese, softened
1 shallot, peeled and thinly sliced
2 tablespoons finely chopped fresh dill
1 tablespoon finely chopped fresh chives or Italian parsley
1 medium lemon, zest finely chopped
1 teaspoon each kosher salt and cracked black pepper

Preparing to cook. Turn the oven to 400°F. Sift the corn flour, sweet rice flour, tapioca flour, and baking powder into one dry mixture.

Making the dough. In a medium saucepan, combine the water, butter, and salt. Set the pan over high heat and bring the mixture to a boil. As soon as the butter is melted, sift in the flour mixture. Stir and stir until the ingredients are incorporated together. When the mixture is complete and has become a ball of dough, keep stirring to cook the flours a touch more.

Finishing the dough. Move the ball of dough to a stand mixer. Using the paddle attachment and with the mixer running on medium speed, drop 1 egg into the pastry dough and mix until the egg has become incorporated. Drop the next egg into the dough and mix until incorporated. The dough will be soft and just a little runny.

Shaping the profiteroles. Ideally, spoon the dough into a pastry bag with a large star tip and plop small balls about the size of dollar coins onto a baking sheet lined with parchment paper. If you don't have a pastry bag, two spoons will also do: take a dollop of the dough in one spoon, then scoop under it with the other spoon, shaping and molding back and forth between the spoons until you have formed a soft, rounded ball. Drop it carefully onto a baking sheet.

Brushing the profiteroles. Brush the egg yolk and milk mixture over the tops of the profiterole dough.

Baking the profiteroles. Slide the baking sheet into the oven and bake the profiteroles until they have puffed up and out and the tops are golden brown, 20 to 25 minutes. Tap the bottom of one profiterole and listen for a hollow sound. Pull the baking sheet out of the oven and set the profiteroles aside to cool on a wire rack.

Making the filling. Put all the filling ingredients into a food processor. Whirl it up. Taste the filling and adjust the seasonings according to your preference.

saigon cinnamon crème brûlée

VARIATIONS
For a coffee brûlée, steep 1 tablespoon of ground coffee with the cream. For a mint crème brûlée, steep 1 teaspoon of minced fresh mint. For a chocolate hazel-nut brûlée, use ½ cup of ground hazelnuts and 1 tablespoon of good cocoa powder. Strain well before cooking.

SUGGESTIONS
Chefs have a macho ethic—they want to use the big blowtorches. Make it easy on yourself and buy a small blowtorch meant for cooks. Be patient and pay attention. If you are afraid of the blowtorch, you can put the ramekins under the broiler, on the highest rack, until the sugar melts and becomes caramel, 2 to 3 minutes.

A few days before my first date with Shauna, I burned my hand at the restaurant. As I shook a blowtorch over the sugar on top of a crème brûlée, I was sidetracked by one of the servers talking to me, and the caramel, which was about two hundred degrees, ran down the ramekin and over my little finger.

Damn.

The day of our date, which I had been looking forward to for over a week, the Band-Aid on my burn came off while I was walking to the coffee shop. The burn didn't look pretty. I considered walking back and covering it up. And then I thought, Oh, whatever. She has to see this is going to happen sometimes. Toward the end of our time together, Shauna put her hand on mine, circled my finger with hers, and said, "What's this?" All I could think was, She touched me. I think she likes me.

Turns out she did.

Chefs always have burns and scars on their arms. Someone who wants a pristine person with manicured hands has to look elsewhere. That Shauna could handle my nasty burn was a good sign. Thanks to the crème brûlée. • *Feeds 6*

1½ cups heavy cream
½ cup whole milk
Pinch salt
½ vanilla bean, split and scraped

1 teaspoon Saigon cinnamon (Vietnamese cassia cinnamon)
3 large eggs
1¼ cups sugar

Preparing to bake. Preheat the oven to 300°F. Put a large kettle of water on to boil.

Heating the cream. Pour the cream and milk into a large, heavy saucepan and add the salt and vanilla bean. Bring the mixture to a boil. Sprinkle in the cinnamon, then pull the saucepan from the burner. Allow the mixture to steep for 10 minutes.

Whisking the eggs. Whisk the eggs together. Whisk three-quarters of the sugar into the eggs.

Tempering the eggs. Pour ¼ cup of the hot cream mixture into the egg mixture, whisking continuously—slowly, slowly is the way to go. Afterwards, pour in the rest of the cream mixture until it is fully incorporated.

Pour the mixture through a strainer into a bowl.

Cooking the custards. Pour the creamy mixture into six 6-ounce ramekins, filling them three-quarters full, plus a smidge more.

Put all the custards into a roasting pan and slide the pan into the oven. Take the ramekin in the left front corner out of the pan. Pour the boiling water into that space, taking care not to spill water into the custards. When the water has come halfway up the ramekins, put the ramekin you removed back in the pan.

Bake until the custards are set, 60 to 70 minutes. Jiggle the pan a bit. The custards should not move. If they do, continue to bake them. (But do not let them brown.) Remove the pan from the oven, keeping it level.

Cooling the custards. Allow the brûlées to cool in the water bath for 30 minutes. Gently remove the ramekins, one by one from the water bath, taking care not to jostle them too much. Wipe the water away from the sides, cover the ramekins with plastic wrap, and put them in the refrigerator.

Let the custards chill for 2 to 3 hours, or overnight if possible.

Finishing the brûlées. Pour 1 tablespoon of the remaining sugar over each brûlée. Fire up your blowtorch, somewhere between a small flame and a blazing fire. Cup a ramekin in your palm with your fingers creating a bowl around it. Tilt the ramekin toward you slightly, at about a 15-degree angle. Very carefully work the blowtorch over the top half of the brûlée, working down. The caramel will start to drip.

Slowly, with control, turn the ramekin, letting the caramel drip down. Try not to burn the sugar or yourself. If you have to choose, burn the sugar.

When you are getting close, pull the blowtorch away and keep turning the ramekin, making sure the sugar is completely covered with caramel. (There might be a hole in the caramel that will spread open, revealing cold sugar. Don't touch it with your fingers. Use a spoon if you can't stand the hole.)

Set aside each ramekin as you finish. After 2 to 3 minutes of sitting, the caramel on top should be hard. (That's half the fun for people eating it—cracking the caramel.)

university seafood and poultry

"Hi Jeannette, it's Dan. I need five pounds of mussels, three fryers, and two sides of the ruby red. And what kind of fish do you have today?"

Every morning, at about 8:30, he makes the same call. University Seafood and Poultry. The day has begun.

After we run food errands, we always stop at U Sea (as we call it) for the fish of the day. In the evenings he leaves himself cryptic text messages as a reminder: "chix, muss, dk ft." (For the record, that's chickens, mussels, and duck fat.) Just after noon, our car slides up to the three-minute loading zone in front of the store.

"When I first came from Colorado, I was just amazed at the fish I'd get here. . . I never knew what smelt was, or razor clams. I never ate fresh albacore tuna, only the stuff from the can. When I worked at Papillon, we ordered our fish from a place in Denver that got its fish from a company on the East Coast, a business called Seattle Fish."

Now, we are buying fish in Seattle—the freshest fish available in a store—from Dale and Jeannette, who have been running the same business that Dale's father began sixty years ago. None of the decorations have changed in decades, save for a fresh coat of paint once in a while. There's a stuffed moose head on one wall, a fish tank full of squirming crabs, and a staff who has aged with the place. Martin, the one with the bushy mustache who tells us about his hunting trips, has been there for the fewest number of years: eighteen. Chuck has been there for thirty.

"These are just nice folks. I love the personal connection with them. The chain of command in a big company is so enormously long that the guy at the top is divorced from the reality of the customer. But at U Seafood, they know the customers. Some of them have been coming in for forty years. You can see from the way Dale talks to them. He leans across the counter, truly listens, and winks at the older ladies."

This is real seafood, old school. Because the place has been in business for sixty years, these folks know the fishermen and the best boats. They buy local, from Northern California to Alaska, sometimes extending to Hawaii. They're the best kind of businessmen, a dying breed in America.

When we walk in, everyone greets us with big smiles. "How you doing? How's the restaurant doing?" We ask Dale and Jeannette about their son, their vacation coming up, and the state of the economy. We chatter happily while one of the employees grabs Danny's boxes from the back, everything on ice. We wave good-bye and make our way to the car.

Danny has been buying his fish from U Seafood for years. Before he met me, he used to ride a city bus with a big box of fish on his lap.

When he worked at Cassis, the Seattle French bistro where he was the sous chef, U Seafood delivered. (Cassis was a bigger restaurant, so it could meet the minimum order charge for delivery.) Every day, Danny met the same driver at the door. "Where are you going for Thanksgiving?" He may have been just shooting the breeze with Mitch, but that relationship was vital to him. His relationship with every purveyor—the guys who deliver the produce, the cheese guys with the giant truck, his meat man, and the company with the pantry staples—is vital. Good connections with purveyors mean they look after him, finding him the best deals on high-quality ingredients.

Since deliveries usually don't happen on the weekends, Danny has taught me not to order fish at a restaurant on Sundays.

So our relationship with the folks at U Seafood is more than just a bright spot in our day. It's vital to Danny's work. "I get good fish because of my connection with them. I might have an idea for a fish special that day, and then I'll call and find out they got in fresh halibut that morning. I've learned to let them guide me."

Every afternoon, I sit on a cushion and meditate. Danny cleans and portions fish.

"You get the whole fish and find a little spot where you can open the belly. Take a sharp knife, cut down, and it all opens up. Take out all the guts and innards. For some fish, I have to do that. For salmon, I take the head off, clean the fish, remove all the pin bones, and then portion it out."

I have watched him. He looks at each piece of fish with full focus, his eyes intent, his entire body quiet while his hands caress the flesh and search for pin bones. In that moment, he cannot be distracted. And he's not thinking of anything else but that fish, with his hands.

Danny's focus on the fish is more than just his relaxed contemplation for the day. He has to pay attention for the benefit of the restaurant. "How can I do this carefully enough so that I'm not wasting anything? If you're bringing down an entire halibut, there are going to be some nice pieces of meat left on the bones that would make a great stock. But you want to butcher the fish well enough so that all the meat goes to the customer.

I need to run a 30 percent food cost. Take the cost of what you spend on food and divide it into the total food sales. You want to be able to make 30 percent more than you spent. If I throw some of that halibut away, carelessly, then I'm not going to make my food cost."

He never wastes a moment.

mussels with rosemary, cream, and mustard

VARIATIONS
If you cannot eat dairy, you can omit the cream and still have something delicious.

SUGGESTIONS
Other flavor combinations that work with mussels: garlic, lemon, and curry; saffron and tomatoes; orange zest, fennel, and Pernod.

I love these mussels. We made this dish at the French restaurant in Breckenridge, and I ate it all the time. After cooking for the night, if there was any sauce left in the bottom of the pan from the last order, I'd grab crusts of bread and sop them in this goodness. The smooth cream, the punch of mustard, and the sharp warm bite of rosemary—this classic flavor combination got me hooked. Everyone who eats them slurps up the sauce after the mussels are gone. Bowls come back dry.

For best results, avoid buying mussels at the grocery store, unless you find a store that has them in a display case on ice. Most grocery stores wrap plastic around the mussels, suffocating the shellfish. This could make you sick. Find a reputable seafood purveyor and buy mussels whose shells are completely shut.

The flat side of the mussel has a gangly string, almost like a tuft of hair, called the beard. You need to pull this off, because you don't want to eat it. Pull up from the bottom, which is the heaviest part of the beard, or else you might not grab it all. I use my hands, but I've debearded thousands of mussels at this point. You can use a knife. • *Feeds 4*

2 tablespoons extra-virgin olive oil
3 shallots, peeled and thinly sliced
2 teaspoons chopped garlic
1 teaspoon finely chopped fresh rosemary
¼ cup dry white wine
1 tablespoon Dijon mustard

2 pounds mussels, debearded and washed
½ cup heavy cream
2 teaspoons butter
Kosher salt and cracked black pepper
3 tablespoons chopped fresh chives

Sautéing the vegetables. Set a large sauté pan over medium heat and add the oil. Add the shallots and garlic to the hot oil and cook, stirring, for 1 minute. Throw in the rosemary and cook, stirring, until it is fragrant, about 1 minute.

Making the sauce for the mussels. Pour the wine into the pan, scraping up all the goodness from the bottom. Cook until the wine is reduced by about half its volume, about 1 minute. Stir in the mustard. When the mustard is fully incorporated and the liquid is bubbling, about 1 minute, throw in the mussels and cream and stir. When the cream is fully part of the sauce, 1 to 2 minutes, add the butter. Stir it all around.

Finishing the mussels. When the mussels have opened their shells, they are done. Pluck them from the pan and place them in bowls. Comb through all the mussels and throw away any mussels that did not open; you don't want to get sick off a bad mussel, believe me. Season the mussels with salt and pepper, about 4 little crunches of the fingers for each bowl. Sprinkle the chives on top.

pan-seared albacore tuna with black-eyed peas, mushrooms, and lime-mint vinaigrette

VARIATION
If you don't eat pork, this dish would still work without the bacon. Of course, it won't taste the same, but the beans will still be mighty good. Button mushrooms will work fine if shiitakes are not in season. Wild mushrooms in season are even better.

SUGGESTIONS
This tuna is great when grilled.

This entrée began as a daily fish special, invented around eleven thirty in the morning, when I heard that U Seafood had a good price on albacore that day. I love ahi tuna, but I can't always afford it, at the restaurant or at home. However, in Seattle, local albacore is environmentally sound, tasty, and relatively cheap.

You might think, at first, that these flavors wouldn't work together. But black-eyed peas have a meatiness that is matched by the mushrooms, echoed by the albacore. And the citrus works like little pokes to the palate. With all these flavors together, this dish is like a massage to the mouth.

That day, the special was so popular that I put it on the menu the next month. We have been eating it at home ever since. • *Feeds 4*

3 slices bacon, finely diced
2 cups stemmed and sliced shiitake
  mushrooms
Kosher salt and cracked black pepper
2 large cloves garlic, peeled and
  thinly sliced
1 medium yellow onion, peeled and
  finely chopped

1 cup dried black-eyed peas, soaked in
  water overnight
1 cup grapeseed oil
1 lime, zest grated
¼ cup fresh lime juice
1 tablespoon chopped fresh mint
4 albacore tuna steaks, about 6 ounces
  each, at least 1 inch thick

Cooking the beans. Place the bacon in a large saucepan over medium heat. When the bacon is approaching crispness, throw in the mushrooms. Season with salt and pepper (go easy on the salt—remember the bacon) and cook, stirring, until the mushrooms begin to soften, about 5 minutes. Add half of the garlic and cook for 1 minute. The bacon should be crisp now.

Remove the bacon and mushroom mixture, but leave the bacon fat in the pan. Add the onion to the pan and cook, stirring, until it is softened and translucent, about 5 minutes. Add the remaining garlic and cook until it is perfumey. Stir in the black-eyed peas. Pour in enough water to cover the peas by 1 inch and cook until the peas are fork-tender, about 15 minutes.

Strain the peas. Add the bacon and mushrooms back to the pan, add about 2 tablespoons of the grapeseed oil, and toss. Taste, then season the peas with salt and pepper. Keep the saucepan somewhere warm.

Making the mint-lime vinaigrette. Combine the lime zest, lime juice, and mint. Slowly drizzle in ¾ cup of the grapeseed oil, whisking continuously. Sprinkle in a bit of salt and pepper. Taste and let yourself enjoy the zing.

Searing the fish. Season the tuna steaks on both sides with salt and pepper. Bring 2 sauté pans to high heat. Add 1 tablespoon of the grapeseed oil to each pan. When the oil starts to smoke, place the tuna steaks in the pans. Sear the tuna until the bottom turns a golden brown color, about 1 minute. Flip the tuna steaks over and cook until the other side forms a golden crust and the middle is still pink, or until the internal temperature reaches 120°F, about 1 minute more. Remove them from the heat.

To serve, mound the peas on each plate. Place a tuna steak on top of each pile of peas. Drizzle the vinaigrette atop them all.

smoked duck breast ravioli

VARIATIONS
You could easily make this with smoked chicken breast. Think of a food you love and stuff it into ravioli: spring vegetables, mushrooms, smoked trout.

SUGGESTIONS
You can top this ravioli in any number of ways, fresh tomato sauce, light Alfredo sauce, or basil pesto. You can also make it simple with olive oil and good Parmesan.

NOTE
To toast the hazelnuts, put them in a small oven-safe nonstick pan and toast in a 400°F oven, stirring occasionally and taking care not to burn them, for 10 to 15 minutes.

Smoking the duck breast gives it an autumnal, foresty flavor. Besides, once you have set up your home smoker, you're going to want to smoke a lot of foods. You can buy duck breasts individually, but it's more economical to buy the entire duck. You can make a stock out of the carcass and use that as a broth for the ravioli.

Ravioli is a good recipe for smoked duck breast. Making homemade ravioli is a great way to impress someone. Once you have played with it enough that you feel dexterous, you can make a hundred different kinds of ravioli.

Gluten-free ravioli is definitely different than regular ravioli. It's a little tougher, not quite so supple. It will never be the angels of air that great traditional ravioli can be. But good gluten-free ravioli is still better than store-bought regular ravioli. And besides, what are you going to do? Go the rest of your life without eating ravioli? • *Feeds 4*

SMOKED DUCK BREAST

1 quart water
½ cup salt
¼ cup sugar
2 kaffir lime leaves (if you can find them)
1 lemon, zest grated and juiced
1 small piece lemongrass (1½ to 2 inches long) or ¼ cup freshly grated lemon zest
1 tablespoon black peppercorns
1 teaspoon coriander seeds
1 small nub ginger (about the size of half a thumb), peeled
2 duck breasts and 2 duck legs (break down a whole duck and save the rest for stock)
2 tablespoons canola oil
2 cups applewood chips, soaked in water for at least 1 hour

RAVIOLI

1 tablespoon extra-virgin olive oil
1 small yellow onion, peeled and finely diced
2 cloves garlic, peeled, smashed, and finely diced
1 tablespoon finely chopped fresh rosemary
2 tablespoons breadcrumbs
1 cup high-quality fresh ricotta cheese
4 ounces soft goat cheese (chèvre)
¼ cup hazelnuts, toasted (see Note) and ground into a chunky texture
Kosher salt and cracked black pepper
1 recipe fresh gluten-free pasta, rolled out for ravioli (see page 60)
3 large eggs, lightly beaten with 1 tablespoon of water

Brining the duck. Combine the water, salt, sugar, lime leaves, lemon zest and juice, lemongrass, peppercorns, coriander seeds, and ginger in a large saucepan and bring to a boil. Remove the pan from the heat and set the brining liquid aside to cool completely. Put the duck breasts and legs into a large pot. Cover them with the cooled brining liquid and marinate in the refrigerator overnight.

Preparing to cook the next day. Preheat the oven to 400°F.

(continued on next page)

Searing the duck. Remove the duck breasts and legs from the brine and pat them dry. Lightly score the skin on the duck breasts, being sure not to cut into the meat. Set a large sauté pan on medium-low heat and pour in the canola oil. Put the duck breasts, skin side down, into the hot oil. Sear the breasts until the fat renders out, about 10 minutes. When the breasts have crisped on the bottom, flip them and cook for 1 minute more. Take the breasts out of the sauté pan. Sear the duck legs the same way. Set aside the duck fat for other purposes.

Assembling your smoking center. Line a 4-inch, half hotel pan with aluminum foil. Put the soaked applewood chips on the aluminum foil and a 2-inch, perforated half hotel pan on top of that. (Hotel pans are stainless steel rectangular pans used in restaurants, available at restaurant supply stores.) Put the seared duck breasts and legs into the top pan and cover with aluminum foil.

Put the hotel pans directly onto a burner over medium heat. Turn on your hood fan or open a window because you will have smoke. Leave the duck to smoke until you have a lovely wood-smoke smell throughout the house, the duck achieves a smoky golden glow, and the internal temperature of the duck breast reaches 120°F, about 30 minutes. Remove the duck from the hotel pans.

Put the duck legs into an oven-safe sauté pan and slide the pan into the oven. Continue to roast them in the oven until the internal temperature reaches 185°F, about 30 minutes. When cool, pull the meat apart to shred it.

Making the ravioli. Set a small sauté pan over medium heat and add the olive oil. Add the onion and garlic and cook, stirring, until the onion is softened and translucent, 2 to 3 minutes. Add the rosemary and cook until it is fragrant, about 1 minute. Stir in the breadcrumbs until they are coated. Remove the mixture from the pan and spread out on a plate. Allow to cool to room temperature. Once the mixture has cooled, combine it with the ricotta cheese, goat cheese, hazelnuts, and shredded duck. Season with salt and pepper.

Cut the lengths of fresh pasta into 2-inch squares. Working with half of the pasta squares, dollop a small amount of filling in the middle of each. Brush the edges of the pasta with the egg and water mixture. Place another pasta square on top and press down, crimping the edges.

Bring a pot of salted water to a boil. Add the ravioli and cook until the ravioli feels soft and pliable, 4 to 5 minutes. Take one out of the water and test the edge with a fork; if it yields to the fork easily, the ravioli is ready to eat. Drain the remaining ravioli.

using fresh herbs

Do you want to make your food taste better immediately, with very little effort? Throw out your dried herbs, especially the ones that have been sitting on your pantry shelves since the 1980s. Dried herbs really don't taste like anything. And don't use the cheap stuff just because it's cheaper.

Fresh herbs are full of flavor. Every chef knows this. You will not find a single good restaurant with dried thyme in its kitchen. Instead, the last person to touch the plate before it leaves the kitchen has little bowls of perfectly chopped herbs for garnishes on the plates.

If you spend a bit of money in spring and plant your favorite herbs in pots on the back porch, you can avoid buying the herbs in plastic containers for six to nine months of the year. I need, at the least: thyme, basil, oregano, Italian parsley, chives, mint, sage, rosemary, lavender, and cilantro.

Some herbs require a chiffonade, which is when you roll large leaves into a cigar shape and slice them thin. Roughly chopped herbs go into sauces and soups, to be strained later. When a recipe calls for fine chop, pay attention. Remove the woody stems from rosemary, thyme, and sage—those will affect the taste. Chives need to be tiny, since they are mostly used to add color to the plate. Big chunks of chive really don't look that attractive. Take the time to do it right.

If you wrap a damp paper towel around fresh herbs, they last longer.

roasted chicken with apricot-corn relish and cilantro sauce

VARIATIONS
This dish is best with dried apricots, but if you come across some ripe apricots during the height of the season, toss ½ cup of them, chopped, into the relish. Do not puree them, however. Instead of cilantro, try basil.

SUGGESTIONS
This is fantastic at a summer picnic with potato salad or roasted fingerlings and coleslaw.

A good roast chicken is always lovely. If you can spice up the chicken with flavors in combinations new to you, you will be able to eat roast chicken the rest of your life.

This recipe works best when you cook bone-in chicken breasts with part of the wing still remaining, known in the culinary world as an "airline breast." You can find these at a good butcher's shop or ask the butcher at your grocery store to cut the breasts this way for you. Roasting the breast with the wing still attached means a juicier piece of chicken. Nobody likes a dried-out chicken breast.

Beware—some people are deeply opposed to cilantro (also known as coriander leaf). They claim it tastes like dish soap. I don't taste this soapy flavor myself, but if you're going to serve this to guests, you might want to suss out their feelings on this matter first. • *Feeds 4*

APRICOT-CORN RELISH
8 ounces dried apricots
1 teaspoon canola oil
1 medium yellow bell pepper
4 ears of corn, husks and hairs removed, kernels shaved off
1 medium yellow onion, peeled and minced
¼ cup extra-virgin olive oil
2 tablespoons champagne vinegar
1 teaspoon thinly sliced garlic
1 tablespoon chopped fresh Italian parsley

CILANTRO SAUCE
½ bunch fresh Italian parsley
2 bunches fresh cilantro
3 tablespoons pine nuts, toasted (see Note)
1 clove garlic, peeled and minced
1 lemon, zest grated and juiced
1 cup extra-virgin olive oil
Soda water, as needed
Kosher salt and cracked black pepper

ROASTED CHICKEN BREASTS
2 tablespoons extra-virgin olive oil
4 chicken breasts on the bone with half of wing still remaining

Soaking the apricots. Soak the dried apricots in a bowl of hot water for 10 minutes. Drain them and cut them into small slivers.

Roasting the pepper. Preheat the oven to 425°F. Rub the canola oil on the pepper. Put the pepper in a small oven-safe sauté pan and slide it into the oven. Roast, turning the pepper every 5 minutes, until the skin begins to blister, about 20 minutes. Put the pepper in a bowl and cover with plastic wrap. Let it sit until cool to the touch. Peel the skin and remove the seeds. Chop up the pepper.

Blanching the corn. Add the corn kernels to a pot of boiling salted water for 1 minute, then plunge them into ice water to stop the cooking. Drain the corn kernels once they are cooled.

Making the relish. Combine the onion, roasted pepper, olive oil, vinegar, and garlic and stir. Stir in the apricots and corn kernels. Puree a quarter of the mixture in a food processor. Add that back into the relish. Add the chopped parsley. Chill.

Preparing the cilantro sauce. Remove the leaves from the parsley and throw out the stems. Chop up the cilantro, including the stems. In a food processor, combine the parsley, cilantro, pine nuts, garlic, half of the lemon juice, and the lemon zest and process. With the machine still running, slowly drizzle in the olive oil, then the remaining lemon juice. The consistency should be like a runny pesto, not a thick paste. If the sauce is too thick, thin it out with soda water. Season with salt and pepper.

Preparing to roast the chicken breasts. Preheat the oven to 450°F.

Searing the chicken breasts. Set a large sauté pan over medium-high heat. Pour in the oil. Put the chicken breasts, skin side down, into the hot oil. Sear until the skin is golden brown, then flip the chicken breasts over and slide the sauté pan into the oven to cook until their internal temperature reaches 155°F, about 15 minutes.

To serve, drizzle and dart the cilantro sauce around each plate. Put the roasted chicken breast on top. Spoon ¼ cup of the apricot-corn relish on top of each breast.

Note: To toast the pine nuts, put them in a small oven-safe nonstick pan and toast in a 400°F oven, stirring occasionally and taking care not to burn them, for 5 to 10 minutes.

our saturday afternoon ritual

After we go to the seafood store on Saturdays, we make one stop before heading to the restaurant. Danny isn't dancing anymore, since we are doing the work that begins his day. In fact, at this point, he's nearly skipping down the sidewalk.

We're headed toward one of Seattle's best farmers' markets.

Every Saturday morning, Danny and I wake up early, thinking, "It's market day." Our languorous mornings are suddenly shortened. We're fine with that. There's so much to discover, and we're on the way to find it all.

"The first time I went to the farmers' market, I thought it was so cool. When I moved here, I was in my early twenties, and I wasn't as in tune with food as I am now. I did my first internship in a place that served yellow tomatoes in the middle of winter. What did I know? The head chef at Cassis asked me to pick something up one Saturday morning, so I stumbled into the farmers' market, early. I wanted to buy everything. My eyes were opened."

The first time I went to a farmers' market, I had just started feeling well after a lifetime of lousy. In that summer sunlight, I had mental clarity for the first time after years of fumbling through brain fog. My friend Meri and I walked into the Ballard Market. We met a bounty of berries and goat cheese, apricots so juicy that they dripped over our hands after we bit into them, fat bouquets of sun-warmed dahlias for ten dollars, and pungent arugula with dirt still clinging to the roots. The eggs barely fit into their cartons, the raspberries stained my fingers red, and the piles of sweet corn smiled like sunshine.

Separately, Danny and I started going to a farmers' market every week. Maybe he was squeezing melons on one end of the market while I was looking for zucchini on the other. Be forewarned, if you have never been to one before. Going to a farmers' market can change your life.

"I started paying more attention to food. When I lived in Colorado, I didn't get any seasonal food. Peaches in the summer from Grand Junction and melons from the western part of the state. That was it. Here, not only did every food have a season, but some of them had a two-week season. I didn't want to miss anything."

When I walk through the grocery store, I see the same food, all year long. Strawberries go up and down in price, but they are always in the produce section. However, after I ate my first tiny strawberry, locally grown, in June, I have not been able to buy them at the store again. From the farmers' market, the taste was a tart sweetness, almost liquid, filling my mouth so completely that I felt overwhelmed by the experience. Grocery store strawberries? Tasteless red forms with white insides.

So much grocery store food goes through a complex manufacturing and shipping process, passing through thousands of hands and miles before it reaches me. At the farmers' market, I accept the food from the hands that grew it.

"The stuff at the grocery store is all shiny from the hoses. But at the market, you see blemishes and vegetables with some dirt still on them. I know that this just came out of the ground. You can tell the farmers are tired, because they have been up since three in the morning, and they are still wearing the same jeans they were wearing yesterday when they were digging the food out of the field. I respect farmers so much."

Both of us feel like kids at the candy store on those Saturday afternoon forays through food stalls. In the summer, July through September, we enter on the southwest corner, and Billy Alstott's tomatoes, peppers, and basils perfume the entire area. We dip homemade corn chips into chunky salsa, made entirely of his produce, and we stop talking for a moment, look at each other, and grab two tubs for the week. In the middle of the market is our potato guy. He has a Rasputin beard, dirty overalls, and Russian fingerlings, purple roses, and blue Peruvians. Which to choose? Jeremy finally has chanterelles in again, and the restaurant gets a reduced rate, so Danny grabs big handfuls. The Hmong farmers always grow the most beautiful herbs we've ever seen, three times as long as the ones in a plastic package at the store, more sturdy, and bright green. All the food made after we go to the market is flavored with this day.

"It was because I started going to the farmers' markets that I decided I wanted to change the menu every month, based on the seasons. The thought of cooking the same dishes, again and again, when beautiful produce arrived every week, just killed me."

Danny goes to the farmers' market every Saturday for the restaurant, and I gather the produce we need for home. One of the gifts of working in such a small restaurant is that he can buy something that grabs his attention and use it in a special dish that night. He doesn't have to buy a case of anything, just a small amount. When he spotted a bunch of fresh Italian parsley, he started thinking about making a flavored oil. He could make a bright yellow coconut-curry sauce (apples, raisins, carrots) for a roasted pork tenderloin from Skagit River and garnish the sauce with dots of the spring green oil. Quickly, he ran around the market to gather all he could. I met him at the end, with my food in hand. Sadly, another Saturday at the market had come to an end.

The first time Danny and I went to the farmers' market together, we had only known each other for two weeks. I was being filmed for the Food Network. A tiny mic snaked down my shirt, a guy with a boom mic trailed me, and another guy with a huge camera followed my path, as I walked through the market and talked. I could have been intimidated or stilted, but I felt fine. Danny was with me. We talked about the quality of the pea vines and the dandelion greens. He bought me flowers. Talking with the farmers, with him by my side, I felt at ease.

"I was amazed that I had found a woman who wanted to go to the farmers' market with me. Meeting someone who shared my enthusiasm about food was my dream come true."

We haven't stopped going to the market together since. With Danny working nights, we don't have many traditional dates. But we have a standing date, every Saturday just past noon, at the University District farmers' market.

risotto with english peas, fava beans, and prosciutto

VARIATIONS
If you cannot eat dairy, you can use a good nondairy "butter" in place of the butter, and a hard goat's cheese in place of the Parmesan.

SUGGESTIONS
Use this recipe as the template for risotto and adjust the ingredients: seafood risotto, beet risotto, spinach risotto, artichoke risotto, and sweet corn risotto.

So many chefs consider May to be the first of the year. Everything in the world is growing again, and green vegetables are finally arriving in the markets again. Vegetables that aren't frozen! Or from Peru! Finally. Wait for spring to make this dish.

Fava beans are buttery, slightly bitter, and a little nutty. Unlike lima beans, which have a chalky texture, these slide right through your teeth. English peas simply taste like spring. Shauna hated peas all her life, because she grew up eating frozen peas. The first spring she ate fresh English peas, she changed her mind.

Creamy risotto is blended with these dots of spring color, and everyone is happy. This recipe may seem lengthy, but believe me, it's worth it. And what could be better than an afternoon in the kitchen, making up a risotto that could make someone you love feel lucky to know you? • *Feeds 4*

½ cup fava beans
1 cup English peas, shelled
5 tablespoons extra-virgin olive oil
5 tablespoons butter
1 medium yellow onion, peeled and
   finely diced
2 cloves garlic, peeled and chopped
1 tablespoon finely chopped fresh thyme

2 cups Arborio rice
½ cup dry white wine
1 quart chicken stock, brought to a boil
   and left warm on the back of the stove
Kosher salt and cracked black pepper
½ cup freshly grated Parmesan cheese
2 ounces prosciutto, thinly sliced

Blanching the fava beans and English peas. Bring a pot of salted water to a boil. Have a large bowl with ice water waiting. Pull the strings from the fava beans and shuck them from their shells. Plop the fava beans into the salted water. When they rise to the surface, remove one fava bean. The outside layer should peel away easily and the inside of the bean should be bright green. If so, remove the fava beans from the boiling water with a slotted spoon, plunge them in the ice water, and let them cool for 2 to 3 minutes. Remove from the ice water and peel away the waxy outer layer. Set aside.

Repeat this process with the English peas, which will not need peeling.

Sautéing the vegetables. Bring a large saucepan to medium heat. Add 1 tablespoon of the oil and 1 tablespoon of the butter. When the oil and butter run around the pan easily, add the onion and garlic and cook, stirring occasionally, until the onion is softened and translucent, about 10 minutes. Add the thyme and cook for 1 minute more.

Coating the rice. Toss in the Arborio rice and cook, stirring occasionally, until all the grains are entirely coated, about 2 minutes. Pour in the wine and cook until the liquid is reduced by half its volume, 2 to 3 minutes. While the wine is reducing, push the rice around in the pan, gently. (If you stir the rice too vigorously, it will release all its starches and turn the risotto glurby.)

Adding the stock. At this point, pour the chicken stock into the rice, 1 cup at a time, stirring continuously. (Imagine that you are trying to put a baby to sleep with your stirring.) When the liquid is absorbed, but not dry, add more stock. Continue this process until all the stock is absorbed.

Making the risotto creamy. Taste the rice. It should be chewy and soft, without being mushy. If it is crunchy, turn down the heat and keep adding liquid. Taste the risotto and season with salt and pepper. Toss in the remaining butter and the Parmesan cheese. Stir until everything is fully incorporated. Place the lid on the saucepan and allow the risotto to sit, covered, until the risotto is beautifully creamy, about 2 minutes.

Frying the prosciutto. Roll up the prosciutto slices and cut the slices into a large chiffonade. Fry up the prosciutto slices in a medium sauté pan until they are crisp.

Finishing the risotto. Spoon the fava beans and English peas into the risotto and stir gently.

To serve, scoop up the risotto and place it into large bowls for the eager guests. Drizzle each bowl of risotto with some of the remaining olive oil and top with the prosciutto slices.

spaghetti with chorizo, fresh clams, and oregano pesto

VARIATIONS
You can make this dish with basil pesto or cilantro pesto. Red bell peppers would be great to toss in as well.

SUGGESTIONS
You can mix and match in some mussels and shrimp. This sauce would also be great on top of rice or roasted potatoes.

Taylor Shellfish, a family business run in Washington State for over one hundred years, has some of the best oysters and shellfish in the country. Their seafood is farmed, but it's done with meticulous care and environmentally sound practices. Their seafood tastes briny, of the ocean and nothing else. Just one of their Kumamoto oysters—with a bit of lemon zest, a sliver of shallot, and a touch of sake—is enough sensory pleasure to fill an evening. And their clams, cooked for this spaghetti on a cold Seattle day, are just the right bite.

This is one of those dishes you could eat forever. Every bite is different, grows in intensity, and mellows at the same time. You just want to spoon more and more of this in your mouth. • *Feeds 4*

OREGANO PESTO
½ cup fresh oregano leaves
⅓ cup freshly grated Parmesan cheese
2 cloves garlic, peeled and chopped
1 tablespoon pine nuts
2 tablespoons finely chopped fresh Italian parsley
¾ cup extra-virgin olive oil
Kosher salt and cracked black pepper
1 lemon, juiced

CHORIZO AND CLAMS
1 pound chorizo links
2 tablespoons extra-virgin olive oil
3 large shallots, peeled and thinly sliced
2 cloves garlic, peeled and thinly sliced
2 pounds clams, washed
½ cup dry white wine
16 ounces gluten-free spaghetti (see page 60), cooked al dente, drained, and tossed with a little extra-virgin olive oil

Making the pesto. In the food processor, combine the oregano, Parmesan cheese, garlic, pine nuts, and parsley. Whirl it up. With the machine running, slowly drizzle in the oil. Taste the pesto and season with salt and pepper. Then mix in the lemon juice.

Cooking the chorizo. Bring a large saucepan of salted water to a boil over high heat. Drop the chorizo links in the water and cook until their internal temperature reaches 155°F. Pull the chorizo links out and allow them to cool. Slice them into ½-inch pieces on the bias.

Bring a large sauté pan to high heat. Pour in the oil. Put the chorizo slices in the hot oil. Sear the sausages on one side until browned and flip them over.

Sautéing the vegetables. Toss the shallots and garlic into the pan with the chorizo. Cook, stirring, until they release their fragrance, about 3 minutes. Add the clams to the pan. Pour in the white wine, scraping up the goodness from the bottom of the pan. Toss the ingredients around and place the cover on the pan.

Finishing the dish. When the clams have opened after 4 to 5 minutes, remove them from the pan. Throw away any clams that do not open. Stir in 4 tablespoons of the oregano pesto. Taste the sauce and season with salt and pepper, if necessary, or add more pesto. Drop the cooked pasta into the sauce and toss until everything is coated.

parsnip and celery root puree

VARIATIONS
If you cannot eat dairy, you can replace the cream and butter with chicken stock and extra-virgin olive oil. Sunchokes are a good replacement for the celery root or the parsnips, because you don't have to peel them.

SUGGESTIONS
This goes well with chicken, beef, pork, and some seafood, such as scallops or sturgeon.

Parsnips have a slight starchy sweetness. They're not candy sweet, but they have an earthy, vegetal sweetness. They need a full frost to develop their true sweetness, a honeyed mellow richness that adds something unexpected to grilled and roasted vegetable dishes. Popular in Great Britain, parsnips are underused in this country. They are wonderful in stews and soups.

Most people have never heard of celery root, much less cooked with it. There's a paradoxical peppery blandness to it, just like celery, but intensified. People think there's no produce available in the winter. But there are sharp tastes like these to cut through the cold.

This puree adds a new complexity to whatever you normally serve. The same old thing can get boring after awhile. Liven things up a bit. • *Feeds 4*

3 large Yukon gold potatoes, peeled and cut into 1-inch cubes
5 tablespoons salt
2 medium parsnips (about 4 inches long), peeled and cut into 1-inch cubes

1 large celery root, peeled and cut into 1-inch cubes
1 cup heavy cream
1 tablespoon unsalted butter
Kosher salt and cracked black pepper

Boiling the potatoes. Place the potatoes and 3 tablespoons of the salt into a large pot of cold water. Bring to a boil. Cook until the potatoes are fork-tender, about 30 minutes. Drain.

Cooking the parsnips and celery root. Simultaneously, bring another large pot of water with the remaining 2 tablespoons of salt to a boil. Throw in the parsnips and celery root and cook until they are fork-tender, 4 to 5 minutes. Drain the parsnips and celery root and put them in a food processor. Whirl until the puree is smooth. You might have to add a bit of water or a smidge of cream to allow the vegetables to puree fully.

Making the puree. Push the tender potatoes through a fine-mesh sieve with the back of a ramekin or a large wooden spoon. (If you own a ricer, use that here.) Combine the potatoes with the parsnip and celery root puree.

Finishing the puree. Bring the cream to a boil in a large saucepan on medium-high heat. Stir the butter into the puree, then the hot cream. Taste the puree, then season with salt and pepper.

petrale sole with mushroom duxelle and cilantro-mustard sauce

VARIATIONS
If you cannot eat eggs, you can make the sauce into a pesto instead.

SUGGESTIONS
You can put the mushroom duxelle into profiteroles for a savory pasty, or slip it into soups and sauces. You can stuff a pounded-out chicken breast with duxelle too. The cilantro-mustard sauce would work well with nearly every fish, with chicken, or with rabbit. It's great as a sauce for rice.

Mushroom duxelle was one of the first classic techniques I learned in culinary school. You should know how to do it too. It's a slow process. It's all about dicing fine, sautéing, adding the mushrooms, deglazing with alcohol, and slowly reducing. Most of the fundamental techniques of cooking are in there. If you are relatively new to cooking, this is a good recipe to practice on. (Plus, the name makes it sound impressive.)

Petrale sole is classified as sole, but it's really from the flounder family. Caught up and down the Pacific coast, petrale sole is almost always available in Seattle, although its best season is the summer. This light, meaty fish is thin enough to roll.

The mushrooms go well with the meatiness of the flounder, and the cilantro-mustard sauce, which has a nice little kick to it, marries well with the mushrooms. • *Feeds 4*

MUSHROOM DUXELLE
3 tablespoons extra-virgin olive oil
½ medium yellow onion, peeled and minced
5 cloves garlic, finely chopped
1 tablespoon finely chopped fresh thyme
2 pounds chanterelle or button mushrooms, finely chopped
½ cup dry white wine
Kosher salt and cracked black pepper

CILANTRO-MUSTARD SAUCE
1 large egg
1 large egg yolk

2 teaspoons chopped garlic
½ lemon, juiced
2 tablespoons Dijon mustard (or more, depending on your taste)
1 cup canola oil
1 bunch chopped fresh cilantro, stems and all
Soda water, as needed
Kosher salt and cracked black pepper

PAN-SEARED PETRALE SOLE
4 fillets petrale sole, about 6 ounces each
Kosher salt and cracked black pepper

Sautéing the vegetables for the duxelle. Set a large sauté pan over medium-high heat. Pour in the olive oil. Add the onion and garlic and cook, stirring, until the onion is softened and translucent, about 5 minutes. Toss in the thyme and cook until it releases its fragrance, about 1 minute. Throw in the mushrooms and cook, stirring frequently, until they have released their juices and softened, about 5 minutes.

Deglazing the pan. Pour in the wine, scraping up the goodness from the bottom. Cook until the wine has evaporated, being careful not to burn the vegetables, about 7 minutes; this is the stage at which you must pay attention. Taste the duxelle and season with salt and pepper and remove from the heat.

Making the cilantro-mustard sauce. Blend the egg, egg yolk, garlic, lemon juice, and mustard in a food processor. With the machine running, slowly drizzle in the canola oil; you don't want the sauce to separate. Toss in the cilantro. If the sauce feels thicker than you want for a sauce, thin it out with some soda water. Taste the sauce. Season with salt and pepper.

Preparing the fish. Preheat the oven to 450°F. Season both sides of the sole fillets with salt and pepper. Place the fillets, skin side up, on a cutting board. (If you bought the fish with the skin already removed, look for the darkish seam running down the fillet. That's where the skin was.)

Stuffing the fish. Place 2 tablespoons of the mushroom duxelle about a third of the way up from the end of the fillet closest to you. Going slowly, roll the fish around the stuffing, pulling it tight with each turn. When you finish, place the seam side down.

Baking the dish. Place the 4 stuffed fillets in a baking dish. Slide the baking dish into the oven and bake until the fish is firm and the internal temperature reaches 120°F, 7 to 8 minutes.

To serve, spoon the sauce on the bottom of the plate. Place the baked fish on top.

pork campagne

SUGGESTIONS
Mustard is essential for campagne. I love to eat pâté with good pickled vegetables. Little dabs on crackers satisfy me.

I started making campagne at Cassis, the French country bistro in Seattle. True, I made one in culinary school, but you have to cook for years before you really know a dish. At Cassis, we made a different pâté every week, ground pork or duck. As long as it wasn't expensive, the head chef let us make whatever we wanted. One week I made a fish pâté, and the next a vegetable terrine. And really, we started making pâtés to use up leftover meats. That's why it's pretty funny when people think of pâté as a snooty gourmet thing. It really isn't.

Campagne is country-style pâté, coarsely textured and spreadable. You can use a variety of meats, based on whatever you have on hand. It is really rich. Eat too much and you'll roll out the door. So a good campagne can last in your refrigerator for at least a week, and it freezes well too. My head chef, Pierre, always called pork campagne the French meatloaf. That's how I think of it too. This is more accessible than people believe.

2½ pounds ground pork
3 large eggs
2 tablespoons chopped garlic
1 tablespoon finely chopped fresh rosemary and fresh thyme mixed together
1 tablespoon brandy

1 teaspoon each kosher salt and cracked black pepper
1 tablespoon canola oil
10 to 12 strips of bacon (fatty bacon works well)

Preparing to cook. Preheat the oven to 375°F.

Mixing the campagne. In a bowl, combine the pork, eggs, garlic, herbs, brandy, salt, and pepper with your hands. (Don't use a food processor, because the texture will become too fine that way.)

Making a taster. Form a little patty of the campagne. Bring a small sauté pan to medium-high heat. Pour in some oil and fry up the patty. Taste the campagne patty to see if it's seasoned well for you: it should have a hit of rosemary, a hint of brandy, and the warm feel of pork. Add more of the ingredient you are missing and season the meat mixture with salt and pepper, if necessary.

Forming the campagne. Line a terrine pan or 9 x 11-inch loaf pan with plastic wrap, using a big enough piece to have the edges spill over the sides. Place the bacon in the pan, with the edges hanging over the sides. Pat the pork mixture into the pan. Wrap the bacon pieces, tenderly, over the top of the campagne, and fold the plastic wrap over the top. Cover with aluminum foil.

Cooking the campagne. Transfer the loaf pan to the oven and cook the campagne until the edges have shrunk away from the sides and the fat has settled in the crevices, 1½ to 2 hours. The internal temperature should be at least 150°F.

Cooling the campagne. Remove the pan from the oven and put a 2-pound weight of some kind (a brick or thick book) on top of the campagne. Let it remain until the campagne has cooled to room temperature, then transfer to the refrigerator to chill overnight.

To serve, slice the campagne and serve. I like it with capers, cornichons, mustard, and gluten-free crackers.

fig chutney

VARIATIONS
You can make a kumquat chutney like this one, but use white wine or white port in place of the ruby red port.

SUGGESTIONS
This chutney is delicious with grilled chicken or pork. Spoon it over roasted duck or quail. Use it as a spread for sandwiches or as a topping for ice cream.

I learned to make this from Tom Colicchio, the head chef at Gramercy Tavern when I worked there. In the tavern, the fig chutney was slathered on a grilled prosciutto sandwich with fontina cheese. I still like that sandwich.

I've played with this recipe since and made it my own. You can too.

Figs go especially well with cheese because the rich sweetness complements the tangy complexities, especially of blue cheeses. Figs are fleshy and sensuous, just like the best cheeses can be.

• *Makes about 2 cups*

3 pints fresh figs (the chutney looks best if you mix different types)
1 tablespoon olive oil
2 large shallots, peeled and thinly sliced
1 teaspoon fresh thyme, chopped

½ teaspoon Saigon cinnamon (Vietnamese cassia cinnamon)
¼ teaspoon freshly grated nutmeg
1 cup ruby red port

Preparing the figs. Remove the stems from the figs. Quarter them and set them aside.

Sautéing the vegetables. Set a large sauté pan over low heat and pour in the oil. Add the shallots and cook, stirring, until they are softened and translucent, about 5 minutes. Add the thyme, cinnamon, and nutmeg and cook until the herb and spices are fragrant in the kitchen.

Making the chutney. Add three-quarters of the fresh figs. Pour in the port and stir. Raise the heat to medium and cook the chutney, stirring frequently to prevent burning, until it is reduced and starts to thicken, 15 to 20 minutes; however, do not overstir the chutney, because you want the figs somewhat chunky. Stir in the remaining figs and cook for another 3 to 4 minutes.

Chilling the chutney. Chill the chutney in a long, shallow casserole dish, so it can chill evenly; if you put it in a deep container, it will keep warm and continue cooking, and the bottom will be hot and turn sour faster.

his first hours alone

We have driven and talked, laughed and slapped each other on the arm, listened to the radio, and kissed. Some days, there is sunlight through the trees as we wind our way through the Arboretum, holding hands. As soon as we drive down Madison and we can see the lake, I know that he's leaving for work soon.

The man loves his job. He loves me more. But when it's time to work, it's time.

He clambers out of the car, grabs the boxes of fish, and flings on his backpack. He leans in the window and kisses me, deeply. And then, he walks into the restaurant, doing

his little Charlie Chaplin walk. (Sometimes, I comment on his physique, but we'll leave that alone.)

I wander down to the coffee shop on the corner, to buy him a large coffee, with an enormous amount of sugar. And then I walk back again, slowly, stalling the good-bye.

Back at the restaurant, I know he's in the kitchen. So I shout, "Hey, Chef!" (I really do call him "Chef "in that moment. He's in his kitchen. It's a sign of respect.)

He comes around the corner, and smiles. "Hey, pumpkin." He kisses me as he reaches for the coffee. But there's a tightness in his smile, a little tapping in his toes. He's in his domain. And from that moment until dinner service starts, he will be back there chopping and searing, starting stocks and reducing them, preparing apple crisps and cutting down lamb. He has not a moment to waste.

And so I throw my arms around him, hold him close, kiss him on his now-sugary lips, and walk out the door, trailing "I love you" behind me. I drive away.

His work begins.

Even though he is the sole chef at the restaurant for much of the day, Danny's workday now is far easier than when he was the sous chef at Papillon in Denver.

"I walked in at seven in the morning; I was the sous chef for lunches, Monday through Friday, and I hit the ground running. Mondays and Tuesdays I worked at night too. Those were long days. So, it's seven in the morning and I have to cook off one hundred pounds of potatoes. The guys at night would peel the potatoes, toss them in the sink, put them into buckets, and run water over them. I'd boil them all in two big pots, about an arm's width around, and add a bunch of salt and turmeric for color. I'd cook them in the back part of the back kitchen. Every time I'd walk by to do something else, I'd put a knife through them to check for doneness. If they were done, I'd tell the dishwashers to get them out and run them through the ricer. On to the next task.

Just the thought of pouring one hundred pounds of potatoes into pots gives me the itches.

"I was in charge of all the sauces. I started them all from scratch, every day. A butter sauce. A saffron-butter-ginger sauce. Madeira sauce. Lobster thermidor sauce (capers, brown sauce, cream, white wine). There were eight to ten sauces every day. Once I made each one, I'd hold them in the bain marie on the steam table. That damned thing was hot. During the summer in Denver, I'd sweat through a T-shirt standing there. I always brought an extra shirt to work."

Ten sauces from scratch every day? Before I met Danny, I had never made a sauce.

"Frank, the chef de cuisine, came in about nine. When he came on the line, he tasted every one of my sauces. 'You need more of this,' he'd say. 'This is too thick. This is too thin.' He was quite the perfectionist with sauces, and he had an amazing palate. He made me work my ass off. It made my sauces good."

Seriously, the thought of this makes me a little terrified. Lecture to one hundred teenagers about the early history of film? No problem. Sit down to write an essay? Let me have the computer. But making sauces from scratch and being judged that way?

"On New Year's Eve my first year there, I came in early and so did Frank. We were going to be slammed that night, and Frank told me, 'I want every one of those sauces fuck-ing perfect.' I worked and worked at them, and when he tasted them, he went down the line and pointed: 'Perfect. Perfect. Perfect.' Damn, I was proud."

Danny's sauces are fantastic. He won't tell you that. I can.

"And then I had to make crab cakes. Make the ravioli. The red curry sauce for the prawn satay (coconut milk, shrimp, garlic, lemon juice, red curry paste, and cream). Prep cooks put it in a pastry bag. Two prawns on each skewer, a little squirt on the prawns, and roll them in breadcrumbs. On the days we had braised lamb shanks as a special, I'd get in at six thirty, because those take time to do right. On Fridays we had a carrot puree for which I was responsible too: a bucket of peeled and chopped potatoes and one of carrots, curry powder, turmeric, and salt. A giant pot of it."

I'm a little dizzy, thinking of it.

"Orders came in at about ten. If the truck wasn't there, I had to get on the phone and ask the rep why. When it did come, I had to go through every box with the invoice, to make sure we weren't missing anything. If the snow peas were shitty, I had to send those back and ask for more."

Certainly, it was far more stressful than our little jaunts around the farmers' market. But he loved it. He thrived on it.

"By eleven, I had my station set up, and had created a lunch special and fish special. And then I'd run my ass for four hours. At the end, even though I was on salary, I'd stay around for a while, cleaning and helping to prep for dinner. I hated leaving, thinking those guys were going to get screwed. I made sure that I wasn't the one who got the call saying, 'We got fucked because you didn't do enough.'"

He was only twenty-seven years old when he was in charge of the 130-seat restaurant for lunch. He stayed at Papillon until he was thirty-two, and the last three years he was the head sous chef at night, far more stressful than lunch. "I learned so much at that job."

Afternoons at his current restaurant are calm by com-parison. But still, I respect his work enough to let him get to it. Danny has a work ethic like no one I have ever met. He never stops working. He never stops enjoying the work.

"Some days I have to scrub the hoods before I can work. Grease has a way of occupying the kitchen, and that small space means the hoods get coated with a film of grease."

There was the executive chef, reaching into the hood with a wire scrub brush, grease running down his arms.

"That's what I love about being a chef. It's not about the glory. It's about the food."

veal stock

SUGGESTIONS
Once the final stock has cooled down to room temperature, you can pour it into ice cube trays so you will have good veal stock on hand when you need it.

VARIATION
Some recipes might call for light veal stock, which means the first batch of simmering. Some call for veal stock, and that means the light veal stock and remouillage have been married and reduced.

Somehow, people feel like restaurant-quality food is beyond their reach. It's just not true. One of the main differences between most home cooks and chefs is that chefs have veal stock at their disposal. It's so much easier to make than you think.

If you learn how to make veal stock, your food will be instantly better. A mustard sauce for steak. Gravy for pot roast on a Sunday afternoon. A port-balsamic sauce for halibut. An endless number of stews. Honestly, if you want to elevate the level of your food and transform every familiar dish so that friends and family look at you with astonishment, start making veal stock.

Veal stock is incredible. It's an amazing, amazing thing. The flavor is so intense. Rich. Dark. Meaty. Veal stock adds depth to what you are making, because it brings forward the other flavors of a dish without stomping on them. Veal stock enhances, instead of dominating.

And you don't have to worry about your kid's college fund with this. Veal stock requires five pounds of bones, some vegetables, and herbs. You will have to go to a butcher for veal bones, but this is a good chance for you to meet your butcher anyway.

The length of this process might prevent you from making it. But once you have made stock once, you'll find this process quite easy and enjoyable. You don't have to take this through the remouillage stage, either. Light veal stock, which is what you get after the first six to eight hours of simmering, is still great.

Spend part of a weekend doing this. It doesn't have to be scary. • *Makes about 3 quarts*

5 pounds veal bones (good soup bones from the butcher, thick with knuckles)	**2 tablespoons black peppercorns**
2 tablespoons extra-virgin olive oil	**2 bay leaves**
1 large yellow onion, peeled and chopped	**3 tablespoons tomato paste**
1 large carrot, peeled and roughly chopped	**5 large sprigs fresh thyme**
3 stalks celery, roughly chopped	**5 large sprigs fresh Italian parsley**
1 large head garlic, cut in half	**3 large sprigs fresh rosemary**

Blanching the bones. Place half of the bones in a 10-quart stockpot. Cover with enough water so that there is twice as much water as bones. Bring the water to a gentle simmer over medium heat and simmer, never allowing the water to boil; do not rush this. Skim the scum from the surface of the water throughout this process, about every 10 minutes. Allow the water to simmer, continuing to skim the scum, for 1½ hours.

Straining the bones. Strain the water so you are left with the bones. Run the bones under cold water to clean them of any gunk. Clean out the stockpot and start fresh.

Roasting the bones. While you are blanching the bones, preheat the oven to 400°F. Place the other half of the veal bones in a roasting pan. Coat the veal bones in the oil. Roast the bones until they are golden brown and start to fill the house with the lovely roasting smell, about 1 hour. Toss

VARIATION
Demi-glace is the richest version of veal stock and it makes any sauce spectacular. To make demi-glace, reduce the final veal stock by another half its volume on a very low simmer, about 1 hour. Put ¼ cup of this reduced stock in the freezer for 15 minutes. If you shake the bowl and the stock moves like gelatin, you have demi-glace. If not, keep reducing.

in the onion, carrot, celery, and garlic. Allow them to roast, making sure that nothing burns, for another 20 minutes.

Starting the stock. When the bones and vegetables have finished roasting, remove them from the roasting pan. Drain all the fat from the bones and vegetables. Pour 1 cup of hot water into the roasting pan and scrape up all the goodness from the bottom.

Combine all the bones and vegetables together in the cleaned stockpot. Add the peppercorns, bay leaves, tomato paste, thyme, parsley, and rosemary, and cover with enough cold water so there is twice as much water as bones. Pour in the scraped bits from the roasting pan. Bring the stock to a gentle simmer, with one lone bubble coming to the surface once in a while. Cook, skimming the scum intermittently throughout the process, for 6 to 8 hours.

Straining the stock. Fill your sink with ice cubes. Strain the stock into a smaller pot, throwing away the vegetables. Place the smaller pot full of stock in the ice and allow the temperature to come down. When the stock has cooled completely, place the stock in the refrigerator. Place the bones in the refrigerator. (If you simmer the stock overnight, you can work with the bones in the morning, without refrigerating them.)

Making the remouillage. The next day, place the bones back in the stockpot. Cover them with enough cold water so that there is twice as much water as bones. Place the stockpot over medium heat and bring the water to a gentle simmer. Allow the liquid to simmer, skimming the scum as you go, for 4 hours. This allows you get as much flavor out of the bones as possible.

Marrying the two stocks. Take the cooled stock out of the refrigerator. Skim the solidified fat off the top. Combine the two stocks together in the stockpot and bring them to a gentle simmer over medium heat. Cook, skimming all the scum that rises from the stock, until the stock is reduced by half its volume, about 3 hours.

Pour ¼ cup of the stock into a large bowl and put it in the freezer for 15 minutes. If the stock has the consistency of a runny gravy, you are done. If the stock is still watery and loose, pour it back into the pot. Bring the stock to a boil, then simmer it on low heat until it is reduced by a quarter of its volume, another 30 minutes.

Strain the stock into a smaller pot. Place the stock on ice until completely cooled. You can start using the stock at this point, or refrigerate it overnight.

crab, avocado, and cucumber salad with tarragon vinaigrette

VARIATIONS
You could use mango instead of papaya. Lobster would certainly work here, as would crayfish. Play with the herbs, because a basil or chervil vinaigrette would be delightful here.

SUGGESTIONS
Cut all the ingredients for the salad into same-size bites, because that will heighten the sensuality of the salad.

June has been lovely, but not that warm. It's the first week of July, and summer is finally beginning in Seattle. No one is complaining of being too hot yet. Bounty is appearing at the farmers' market, and fresh king crab from Alaska is on ice at the seafood store. It's time for crab and avocado salad.

The fleshiness of the crab melts into the creaminess of the avocado and dissolves into the soft yield of the papaya. The tarragon dressing dances with everything. There are some dishes you have to actively chew. This one you can put in your mouth and let it sit there for a moment, savoring.

Shauna so loves this salad that she's willing to bend her rules about eating in season for another round of it in January, when the Dungeness crab is cheapest in our area. • *Feeds 4*

TARRAGON VINAIGRETTE
1 bunch fresh tarragon, stems removed
¼ cup champagne vinegar
1 large shallot, peeled and thinly sliced
1 teaspoon Dijon mustard
½ teaspoon each kosher salt and cracked black pepper
¾ cup olive and canola oil mixed

SALAD
½ pound king or Dungeness crabmeat, shells carefully removed, in chunks
2 large ripe Hass avocados (tender yet firm to the touch), cut into cubes
1 large ripe papaya, peeled, seeded, and diced
1 medium cucumber, peeled, seeded, and julienned
3 tablespoons finely chopped fresh chives

Making the vinaigrette. In a blender, combine the tarragon, vinegar, shallot, mustard, salt, and pepper. Puree the mixture and then transfer it to a bowl. Slowly whisk in the oils; this will give the vinaigrette a broken look, making the tarragon visible in the dressing.

Making and serving the salad. In a bowl, mix the crabmeat, avocados, papaya, and cucumber with 4 tablespoons of the vinaigrette. For each serving, put a handful of the salad on a medium plate. Drizzle additional vinaigrette and sprinkle the chives around each salad.

asian pear tart

VARIATIONS
It's hard to replicate the texture and taste of an Asian pear. This fruit stands alone. You could try an apple butter on the bottom of the tart instead of the apricot jam.

SUGGESTIONS
This goes well with ice cream or pear sorbet.

Asian pears surprise you. They look like yellowing apples, with freckles. The skin is crisp, the flesh firm to the touch. Eat an unyielding Bartlett pear and you'll be disappointed. Eat an Asian pear and the juice will drip down your chin.

Asian pears, ubiquitous across the Northwest, are perfect for early-autumn tarts. They keep their shape in heat, not falling into mush the way a Comice might. They have a pear perfume, with a hint of early-summer melons. And the taste only intensifies when baked.

Shauna once watched our French friend Francoise make an apple galette while they talked. With deft movements, Francoise spread apricot jam on the bottom of the tart shell, and then placed sliced apples in overlapping concentric circles. The jam bubbles up into the pear slices, keeping the tart juicy. That moment inspired this tart. • *Feeds 10 to 12*

TART SHELL
½ cup (63.5g/2.2oz) sorghum flour
½ cup (60g/2 oz) tapioca flour
½ cup (96g/3.4 oz) potato starch
½ cup (102g/3.4 oz) sweet rice flour
2 tablespoons sugar
¼ teaspoon salt
¼ teaspoon ground cinnamon
8 tablespoons (1 stick) frozen butter
1 large egg

¼ cup ice-cold water
Butter for greasing pan

ASIAN PEAR FILLING
6 to 7 medium, firm Asian pears,
  cored and sliced ½ inch thick
⅓ cup sugar
½ vanilla bean, split and scraped
⅓ cup apricot jam

Combining the flours for the tart shell. Sift the sorghum flour, tapioca flour, potato starch, and sweet rice flour into a large bowl. Stir in the sugar, salt, and cinnamon. Sift into another bowl.

Grating the butter. Grate the frozen butter directly into the dry ingredients. The butter will fall into the flours in soft swirls and start to melt in as soon as you stir. (Hint: this works well with traditional tart doughs too.) Work with your hands to mix everything, until the dough feels like cornmeal or large pieces of sand.

Finishing the dough. In a small bowl, whisk the egg and water together with a fork. Make a well in the center of the flours. Stir in the liquid, working from the inside out. Feel the dough for soft suppleness, instead of stiffness or sogginess. Feel free to use your hands at the end.

Chilling the dough. Refrigerate for at least 1 hour, or overnight if possible.

Preparing to bake the tart shell. Preheat the oven to 375°F. Butter and flour an 11-inch tart shell. (We like sweet rice flour for this.) Pull the dough from the refrigerator and let it come to room temperature, about 1 hour.

Rolling out the dough. Roll out the dough between 2 pieces of parchment paper, to the approximate shape of the tart pan. (This saves you flouring the countertop, and thus adding more flour to the dough.) If the dough breaks apart a bit, do not worry—there's no danger of the crust becoming tough by overworking it, which could happen in a gluten dough. Press the dough into the pie pan and repair it that way.

Freezing the tart shell. Place the tart shell in the freezer until the crust is frozen, about 1 hour.

Blind baking the tart shell. Butter a piece of aluminum foil approximately the size of the pie crust. Place it, butter side down, onto the tart crust and fit snugly against the sides. Bake, pressing down any puffed-up portions with a spoon, until the shell has a good color, about 15 minutes. The tart should feel flaky, rather than sticky.

Preparing the filling. Toss the pear slices with the sugar and vanilla bean scrapings, coating them well.

Filling the tart. Spread the apricot jam generously across the bottom of the tart shell. Place the pear slices on top of the jam in concentric circles (or as close as you can get). Once you have finished the outside circle, start again in the middle. Make as many circles as you need.

Baking the tart. Bake until the pears take on a pale brown color and the juices drip down into the jam, creating something like caramel, 35 to 40 minutes.

Let the tart cool in the refrigerator for at least 1 hour, then slice it up.

cheese plate

As Danny and I round the corner toward the restaurant, we are deep in conversation. In the middle of murmuring, Danny switches to six-year-old, Christmas-morning excited: "The Peterson truck is here!"

He nearly jumps out of the car before I can bring it to a stop. "Go! Go!" I exhort.

Not much can interrupt us from our eyes-locked-in-love-with-each-other talking. But a giant semitrailer truck full of cheese? That will do it every time. (That, and the perfectly placed smart-ass comment.)

Oh god, I love cheese. About a decade ago, I decided

to give up cheese, in an attempt to lose weight. Walking down the aisles of the grocery store, I felt a bit like a drug addict trying to be good, desperate for a fix. Everything I wanted to eat contained cheese. I checked the labels. (Actually, I realize now, that was pretty good preparation for going gluten-free. It was the first time I examined labels on food.) Six weeks later, I gave up. I shaved a small slice of Irish cheddar off a creamy white block, and I was done. I have never looked back.

What is life without cheese?

(I'm so sorry, those of you who cannot eat dairy. Look away.)

"The worst experience I had with cheese happened in Fairplay, Colorado, at this historic hotel. My best friend's mother had just driven us over the Boreas Pass, in autumn, with all those aspens turning color. She treated us to lunch. The food was good, so I ordered cheesecake for dessert. Oh god, it tasted like it had been made with American cheese, like plain slices off the plastic. I finished the cheesecake, to be polite, but I have never been able to eat American cheese since."

American cheese is a swear word.

"Cassis in Seattle was the first place I worked that asked me to put together cheese plates. In some of the bigger places, the garde-manger did cheese plates with the desserts, so I never touched them.

"Every night we had five different cheeses on the plate: a sheep's, a goat's, a cow's, a blue, and one surprise cheese. We had them already portioned out for dinner service, so I started snacking on them instead of stopping for dinner. That's where I first tasted Taleggio, this beautiful creamy cow's cheese. I'd try cheeses I had read about but never eaten.

"And then I saw the Peterson's truck for the first time. They were our purveyor, so they sent us catalogs. They were like porn. I just stared at them, studying the Irish cheeses, Spanish cheeses, the cheeses of the Pacific Northwest. I started ordering different ones for the restaurant, just so I could taste them, gobbling up knowledge."

Danny has introduced me to dozens of cheeses I had not known existed, like pecorino fresco, the soft sheep's cheese only available in the spring. Or Bûch Maître Seguin, a goat's cheese with a crumbly outer edge and a creamy inner circle. I loved the Peterson catalog's description of Saint Nectaire, a cow's milk cheese made in the mountains of Auvergne, in France: "a wonderful combination of a summer pasture and sweet, fruity milk flavors." Once I tasted it, I liked the cheese more than the description.

Eating cheese that had not been mass-produced in a cheese factory always makes me think: how many hands have touched this before it reached mine? Where did this food begin? On a small farm in Spain? In the mountains of France? In the udder of a cow or a goat? Every bite of food we eat comes with stories.

Putting together a cheese plate means combining those stories, so that everyone is heard and no voice shouts over another.

"Start with something familiar and branch out from there. If you like brie, look for other cheeses that have that consistency. Pierre Robert looks a little like brie. Try a bite. Oh, that's much better than brie, let me have some of that.

"For a dinner party, try doing all cheeses from Spain. Serve them with Marcona almonds, some quince paste, vegetables you pickled with sherry vinegar, some good olives, or some preserved lemons.

"Or, if you know that one of your guests can't have cow's milk, try goat's milk cheeses. Push yourself to try kinds you have never eaten before. Go to a store, or market, with a good cheese section. Ask questions. Try different goat cheeses, of different textures. What do you think? What do you want to eat more of?

"Serve a smidge of cheese for each person. Just a little taste. A four-ounce piece of cheese at the end of a good meal would be too rich.

"And bring the cheese up to room temperature before you serve it. If you put cold cheese on a cold plate, the flavor will remain trapped inside the cold.

"Different seasons mean different garnishes. Chutney made with fresh figs in the fall, or slivers of apples. Grainy mustard and small sausages for the winter, or shaved fennel salad. During the summer, strawberries and fresh cherries are enough to complement some cheeses. There are so many choices. Fresh honeycomb. A bit of pâté. Bite-size grilled sandwiches made out of one of the cheeses. Olives are always good. Pay attention to the tastes in the cheese, and find small bites with textures, smells, and tastes to match.

"Really, there is no end to the choice of cheeses. Thank heavens. There's so much left to discover."

Those of us who are gluten-free once worked under the erroneous assumption that we could not discover the joys of blue cheese. Most artisanal blue cheeses are started with mold that is made from bread. It was believed, for decades, that even that small amount would make a celiac sick. However, in 2009 the Canadian Celiac Association conducted stringent tests to detect any detectable gluten in blue cheeses from around the world, including Roquefort and Saint Benoît from France. The researchers never detected any gluten. And so, whether it's Point Reyes from California or Cashel Blue, a soft blue cheese from Ireland, you can eat your blue cheese.

Let me tell you, Danny and I have no criminal tendencies. (Well, I may have borrowed a copy of *Gourmet* magazine from the dentist's office once.) But if we were to ever take up a life of crime? We would never, like Bonnie and Clyde, go on a fast ride through the United States, stylish and savvy, robbing banks. Instead, we'd be far more likely to hijack a Peterson's cheese truck, throw the driver a pound of Roquefort Vieux Berger, and ride off into the sunset, nibbling on goat cheese as we go.

gluten-free crackers (and pizza dough)

VARIATIONS
Play with the flavors of these crackers. You could try oregano or tomato-basil. Anise seed. Garlic. Black pepper. If you like crackery-thin pizza crust, this dough makes 2 pizzas. If you like far chewier, doughier crust, use the entire dough to make your pizza.

SUGGESTIONS
If you don't already own a pizza stone, you might want to buy one for these crackers, this pizza, and the bread recipe in this book.

Shauna couldn't eat traditional flatbread crackers anymore, so she set out to make gluten-free versions. These delicate crackers taste like a rustic flatbread, with a crisp crunch and a little give. Feel free to play with the flavors you might like on top: fresh rosemary, sea salt, a little cracked black pepper.

Here's a secret we discovered after creating this dough: this also makes a great pizza crust. Roll it into a large oval, put it in as hot an oven as you can (at least 500°F), and you'll have thin-crust pizza with air bubbles. Hallelujah. • *Makes 20 to 40 cracker shards, or enough dough to make 2 thin-crust pizzas depending on the size*

1 cup (125g/4.4oz) cornstarch
¾ cup plus 2 tablespoons (125g/4.4oz) corn flour
¾ cup (125g/4.4oz) potato starch
¾ cup (125g/4.4oz) sweet rice flour or an equal amount of psyllium husks
1 tablespoon xanthan gum
1 teaspoon guar gum or an equal amount of psyllium husks
1½ teaspoons kosher salt
1¾ cups (375g/13.2oz) warm water, about 110°F

¼ cup (50g/1.75oz) extra-virgin olive oil
4 teaspoons (15g/.5oz) fresh cake yeast (or active dry yeast)
Gluten-free cornmeal for sprinkling on pan (not all are gluten-free due to manufacturing practices)
Olive oil, for brushing
Fresh rosemary (optional)
Coarse sea salt and cracked black pepper (optional)

Combining the dry ingredients. Sift the cornstarch, corn flour, potato starch, and sweet rice flours into a large bowl. Toss in the xanthan gum, guar gum, and salt. Sift the mixture into the bowl of a stand mixer. (You can also mix this by hand. It just means more bicep work.)

Activating the yeast. Put the warm water, olive oil, and yeast into a small bowl. Stir gently. Let sit for a minute.

Making the dough. Pour the yeasty water into the dry ingredients. With the mixer on medium, whirl for a few minutes, until the dough comes together and feels soft and pliable. Set the dough aside in a warm place and let it rise for 1 hour.

Preparing to bake. Preheat the oven to 450°F. If you have a pizza stone, make sure it is in the oven. If not, sprinkle a pizza tray or baking sheet with cornmeal.

Rolling out the dough. Grab ½ of the dough and place it between 2 pieces of parchment paper. Through the paper, roll out the dough as thin as you can make it. Gluten-free dough does not have the elasticity of regular dough, but if you go slowly you can roll it pretty thin.

Baking the dough. Transfer the dough to the pizza stone or prepared pizza tray. Brush the top with olive oil and press fresh rosemary, sea salt, and cracked black pepper lightly into the top. Bake until the dough has crisped up and browned at the edges, about 10 to 15 minutes.

chunky tapenade

VARIATIONS
If you can't eat fish, you can make this tapenade without the anchovies.

SUGGESTIONS
This makes a great sauce for lamb, if you thin it out with chicken stock or soda water. It's fabulous with a crusty bread, with deviled eggs, or in a tuna salad.

We love olives so much in our house that it's rare that the bowl stays full for long. However, it's worth buying more olives to make tapenade. We love tapenade with cheese, on top of gluten-free bread, or as a dip for pretzels or baby carrots. Since it's so easy to make, why not have some around?

You might be tempted to buy only pitted olives, since they seem more convenient, but the best flavors really lie in the olives sold with the pits. Alfonso olives—purple Chilean beauties cured in red wine. Picholine—green with a lemon zest echo. Niçoise—tiny French olives with a slightly bitter bite. Oh, and then there are Lucques, Cerignola, Sicilian oil cured, kalamata . . .

Pit the best olives by tapping a meat pounder on the top of the olive, which will break it open. You can also put the olives in a big zip-top plastic bag and smash them open with a rolling pin. You're going to be pureeing these, so don't worry about the appearance.

Once you start making this salty tapenade, you won't be able to stop eating olives either.

• *Makes 2½ cups*

1 cup pitted niçoise olives
1 cup pitted Picholine olives
2 oil-packed anchovy fillets
1 teaspoon thinly sliced garlic
½ teaspoon chopped fresh rosemary
½ teaspoon chopped fresh thyme
1 teaspoon capers

2 large basil leaves
1 cup extra-virgin olive oil (with a peppery kick)
Soda water, as needed
1 teaspoon fresh lemon juice
Kosher salt and cracked black pepper

Chopping the olives. Roughly chop a quarter of the olives, with abandon. Set them aside.

Pureeing the tapenade. Place the unchopped olives in a food processor. Toss in the anchovies, garlic, rosemary, thyme, capers, and basil. Whirl the ingredients up into a paste. With the machine still running, slowly drizzle in the oil until the tapenade has become a medium-thick paste. If the tapenade is too thick for your taste, you can thin it out with soda water.

Finishing the tapenade. Scoop the tapenade from the food processor. Fold in the reserved roughly chopped olives. Squeeze in the lemon juice. Taste the tapenade—it is likely to be salty enough, with the anchovies and capers. Season with salt and pepper, if necessary.

spiced walnuts

VARIATIONS
This spice combination works well with pecans and cashews—pistachios are good too, but they are generally already salted, so adjust your seasoning accordingly. If you cannot eat eggs, and have to skip the egg white, try making a simple syrup (see page 98) with the brown sugar, which will help the spices stick to the walnuts.

SUGGESTIONS
Leave these nuts around the house for guests. Take them to the office, where the people will love you. Make them for your kids who live away from home. They'll all make friends. These help gluten-free folks to feel that life is still rich.

Go back to Mom. Mom rocks.

These spiced walnuts are based on the ones my mother makes for Christmas every year. For over a decade, she has been sending out little tins of candied pecans to all five of us kids. She started sending them to me when I worked at Papillon in Denver. They disappeared by the end of the day I received them. After a couple of years of this, my head chef kept his eye out for the arrival of the box and tried to rifle through it before I even saw it! One of the best chefs in Colorado was a fiend for these nuts.

We added a little kick to these to make them reminiscent of the bar nuts at Gramercy Tavern. (Those were saltier, as were the earlier renditions of these. Make them salty and people will order more drinks.) We wanted nuts we could eat beyond Christmas, and to eat with cheese. Everyone who visits our house takes one walnut, proclaims it good, and then leans forward, over and over, to take more. • *Makes 4 cups*

4 cups walnuts
2 large egg whites
1 cup packed dark brown sugar
2 teaspoons kosher salt
2 teaspoons ground cinnamon, preferably
  Saigon (Vietnamese cassia cinnamon)

½ teaspoon smoked paprika
  (Pimentón de la Vera)
¼ teaspoon cayenne pepper

Toasting the walnuts. Preheat the oven to 375°F. Place the walnuts in an oven-safe sauté pan and slide the pan into the oven. Toast the walnuts, moving them around the pan intermittently throughout the process. Sniff for a rich walnut smell and look for a dark walnut color. There's a fine line in toasting nuts—a few minutes too long and they are burnt—so pay attention and roast about 7 minutes.

Preparing to bake. Turn down the oven to 300°F. Line a baking sheet with parchment paper or a silicone mat.

Coating the walnuts. Whisk the egg whites in a large bowl with 1 teaspoon of cold water. Add the brown sugar, salt, cinnamon, paprika, and cayenne pepper and stir. Add the nuts to the egg white mixture and stir until the nuts are coated.

Baking the walnuts. Spread the walnuts in a single layer on the baking sheet. Slide the baking sheet into the oven and bake the walnuts, tossing them occasionally, until they are crackling brown and hot, about 25 minutes. Allow the walnuts to cool on the baking sheet. Break up any sticky clumps with a spatula. Put them into a bowl and serve.

how to make stocks

Stocks require patience. Stocks require time. You simply cannot rush them. However, for most of the time that a stock requires to simmer and build in flavor, you do not have to be in front of the stove. Make this a Sunday afternoon project, and walk into the kitchen to skim once in a while. If you don't mind having the stove on all night, you can leave a veal stock on the back burner, on a low consistent temperature. The magic happens while you sleep.

Chefs have good stock at their constant disposal. Most home cooks have never made it. That's one of the big differences in taste between restaurant food and home cooking. For some reason, many of the people I have met seem to think that stock is a luxury item, too rich for their budgets. But all a stock requires is bones, some vegetables, and water. Really, this is one of the least expensive ways to build rich flavor into your food.

Use the best ingredients, since there are so few. Herbs that are wilting but still have taste? Those are okay. But if you can use the freshest herbs, just cut, you'll notice a difference in flavor.

Stocks are not garbage pots. Don't go through your refrigerator looking for a way to get rid of leftovers. And don't use the dirty carrot peels. That's disgusting. Would you put those on top of a risotto?

how to make a meat stock

- Clean and trim the bones.
- Blanch the bones. Cover the bones with water by 2 inches. Bring the water to a boil and turn it down to a simmer. Let it cook for 30 minutes.
- Skim the scum. Even when you think you have all the scum, there's still going to be more. Have a ladle next to your pot, in another container. Skim in a circular motion.
- Or roast the bones. This depends on your taste. Roasting intensifies the flavor, but you might not want the roasted taste in your stock. Your stock is not going to get dark if you roast the bones. Roast the bones and drain off all the grease. This skips the blanching process.
- Strain the bones from the water.
- Put the bones in a stockpot and cover with cold, cold water by a couple of inches. If you put too many bones in the pot, you won't have enough liquid, and it will burn the pot. If you have too much water, you will have to reduce the stock more.
- Add mirepoix (carrots, celery, and onions), peppercorns, bay leaf, and herbs to all stocks, and tomato paste, if you are going for a dark stock.
- Cook gently. Do not boil. Bring the stock up slowly to a gentle simmer, one bubble escaping at a time.
- Skim the scum. If you cook the stock overnight, you won't be able to do this. Skim when you wake up.
- Taste it. You should be able to taste the meat and the vegetables.
- Finish cooking. Chicken stock? 2 to 3 hours. Duck stock? 4 to 5 hours. Pork stock? 4 to 5 hours. (If you have a pig's foot, add it.) Veal stock? 10 to 12 hours.
- Strain the stuff. You have stock. If you want more flavor, reduce the stock.

If you take the time to make a stock on the weekend, every dish you cook during the week will be filled with flavor. In fact, the better your stock, the simpler your dishes can be. Have fun with the process. Don't rush it. You will find, after your first attempt, that homemade stock is better than the boxed stuff, every time.

Once you learn how to make stock, the gates are open to even better food.

soup's on

When Danny was in Buffet Banquet class at New England Culinary Institute, he was responsible for making a massive vat of watermelon-strawberry soup for the Taste of Vermont. He had to puree ten gallons of watermelon and strawberries, to start. "I was covered in it by the time I was done. If I hadn't been so shy, I would have asked a girl to lick it off me." Mixed with cream, and topped with crème fraîche and mint, the soup was wildly popular on that warm summer day. "I still liked that soup after making it, and I'd make it again."

Preparing soup is rarely that dramatic now, but it's one of Danny's favorite tasks in the afternoon.

Soup is one of the humblest foods on a restaurant menu. People talk about the flashy entrées, the surprising flavor combinations, and oh the desserts. Rarely does the soup inspire conversations. But if a soup at the beginning of the meal is oversalted, lacks flavor, or sits thin on the spoon, dinner will probably disappoint. "This is a good restaurant, but they can't make soup?" It sets the tone for the rest of the night. A great soup is memorable, like a chowder with fresh-caught clams, or a curried red lentil soup in the winter, with a dash of smoked paprika.

"I have to get it right."

For Danny, soup is more than a food. Making soup is his barometer for the seasons.

There's that little certain something in the air, a hint of coldness and wood-smoke fires. Danny starts thinking about pumpkins and roasting their seeds. "Hearty mushroom soups. Cabernet beef and vegetable soup." He slips in parsnips for creaminess and a faint note of sweetness. He actually grows excited about using celery root again.

"The first couple of winters in Seattle were tough. There was no snow. My immediate family was in Colorado. A good bowl of soup could be soothing. Potatoes and leeks. Black beans. Lentils, turnips, and roasted pork. Think about when it's cold, and hot soup first goes down your throat. It warms you up. Everything feels more manageable."

Spring brings light bouncing through green leaves still young enough that we appreciate them. "You want a soup with a bit of body to it, but something light as well. The soups from winter can be really heavy, cream based." Baby carrots. English peas. Yogurt for the depth. And mint, that light, nearly sweet taste, like that satisfaction of layers being shed, warm sun on the skin. "That's what makes spring so exciting. We still remember the winter."

During the summer, Danny's kitchen heats up to about 128°F. A lousy ventilation system, cramped space, a stove and oven that are constantly working, a dishwashing machine—they all conspire to make him sweat. Before dinner service, during heat waves, he ducks into the restroom, changes into his swim trunks, and dunks himself in the chilly waters of Lake Washington, just to prepare for the scorching service. "No way on the hot soups. Sweet corn. Heirloom tomatoes. Fresh basil. You want to take advantage of all that bounty. Gazpacho. This is the only time of the year for gazpacho."

One summer, I watched him chopping vegetables for a vichyssoise, and he took a few extra minutes to cut everything to a fine dice, the same size. At the time, I was confused. Wasn't he going to puree it anyway? What did it matter if the vegetables were the same precise proportions? "If you cut everything to the same specifics, then the soup is going to look so good you won't need to puree it. Strain everything after cooking, take the liquid, and reduce it. Add the cream and butter. Put the vegetables back in. That soup is going to look more refined. Plus, reducing adds layers of taste."

It's not that he's entirely against pureed soups. He makes them at the restaurant some of the time, more often at home. Although it's easy to put everything in a pot, boil it, and throw it in the blender, he has a different approach. "Take your time and think about what you want the soup to look like before you make it. If you are throwing some potatoes in the soup, make some fine dices and set them aside. Roast them separately, and when you are ready to serve, garnish the soup with a small parcel of the potatoes. Or make some homemade potato chips and pour the vichyssoise on top of them in a bowl."

When I make black bean soup now, I puree part of the soup, for the smoothness, and pour it back into the whole beans, for the bite. Danny taught me that.

When I first started cooking for Danny, he appreciated the meals I made us. It took him a while to trust me enough to tell me that I oversalted our food. (His palate was waking up, too, because he had quit smoking. So many chefs smoke, and I don't know how they can taste their dishes properly. Danny's senses came alive when he was no longer clouded with the smoke around his head.) Mostly, I salted my soups too early in the cooking process.

"Season the soup after you have cooked it. When you pull it off the heat and you're ready to eat it, that's when you season it. If you are making a mushroom soup, you should taste the mushrooms, not the salt. There should be a gentle nudge of thyme, basil, and bay leaf, a spot of the chicken stock. The mirepoix should be in there too, deep underneath. But you shouldn't really taste the salt. Salt is just a way of bringing the flavors forward."

Danny has taught me, repeatedly, to slow down and enjoy cooking, and to think about the effect the food will have on the people who eat it. "You can't just throw soups together. They have to be made with care. It's like a relationship. Everything needs to harmonize. If one part is out of balance, fix it."

He's teaching me about more than soups.

pumpkin soup

VARIATIONS
If you go to farmers' markets, ask the farmers what their favorite kinds of pumpkins for soup are. Experiment. You can use vegetable stock here if you wish.

SUGGESTIONS
Serve this for Halloween lunch.

One October at Cassis, I got this mad idea for the soup special that night. I roasted off fifteen baby pumpkins, hollowed them out, and made pumpkin soup. I placed each pumpkin in a bowl, the warm spiced soup in the baby pumpkins, and then garnished them with roasted pumpkin seeds. The owner of the restaurant kept giving me a hard time. "How Martha Stewart of you!" he kept whispering. But the diners thought it was really cool.

I would not recommend doing this every time you make this soup, or at all. The presentation was a big pain in the neck. But you can think about presentation when you are serving this. You could dust cinnamon and curry powder through a tiny strainer and sprinkle it over the top of the soup and on the sides of the bowl. A tiny dollop of crème fraîche, a swirl of roasted pumpkin seed oil—it doesn't take much to make your food look appealing. Your family and guests will love this soup no matter how you serve it, but they'll appreciate it more if you are thoughtful about how it looks. • *Feeds 4*

One 5-pound sugar or pie pumpkin
    (such as Autumn Gold)
6 tablespoons extra-virgin olive oil
Kosher salt and cracked black pepper
1 large carrot, peeled and large diced
1 red onion, peeled and diced
2 stalks celery, large diced
5 cloves garlic, smashed and peeled
1 tablespoon chopped fresh sage

1 medium sweet potato, peeled, quartered,
    and medium diced
½ teaspoon freshly grated nutmeg
1 small bay leaf
2 quarts chicken stock
½ cup heavy cream
2 tablespoons butter
2 teaspoons pumpkin seed oil (if you can't
    find it, you can use olive oil)

Preparing the pumpkin and seeds. Preheat the oven to 450°F. Cut the top off the pumpkin. Quarter the pumpkin. Remove the seeds and the guts and set aside the seeds. Toss the pumpkin quarters in 2 tablespoons of the olive oil. Season the pieces with salt and pepper and put in a baking dish. Bake the pumpkin in the oven until it is soft enough to scoop out with a spoon, about 30 minutes. Allow it to come to room temperature.

Spread the pumpkin seeds on a baking sheet and lightly coat the pumpkin seeds in 2 tablespoons of the olive oil. Transfer them to the oven while the pumpkin cooks, and bake until they start to brown, 5 to 10 minutes. Remove from the oven and season with salt.

Scoop all the flesh from the pumpkin. Set it aside.

Sautéing the vegetables. Set a medium stockpot over medium heat and add the remaining 2 tablespoons of olive oil. Add the carrot, onion, celery, and garlic to the hot oil and cook, stirring occasionally, until they are softened and the onion is translucent, about 10 minutes. Add the sage and cook until you can smell the herb.

Making the soup. Toss the sweet potato into the stockpot. Throw in the nutmeg and bay leaf. Pour in the chicken stock and add the pumpkin flesh. Bring the liquid to a boil, then reduce the heat to low and simmer until you can run a knife through the sweet potato, about 15 minutes.

Finishing the soup. Fish out the bay leaf. Puree three-quarters of the soup in batches in a blender and push through a strainer. Taste the soup and season with salt and pepper.

Add the cream and butter. Bring to a boil, then reduce the heat to low and simmer, stirring to prevent burning, until the soup is reduced and thickened to your liking, about 10 minutes.

To serve, ladle the soup into bowls. Garnish with the pumpkin seeds and ½ teaspoon of the pumpkin seed oil per bowl.

black bean soup with red pepper relish

VARIATIONS
If you do want this soup spicier, bump up the red pepper flakes to 1 teaspoon and add a touch of cayenne pepper.

SUGGESTIONS
Soups are always better the next day. This soup is great with grilled cheese sandwiches, made with a sharp Irish white Cheddar.

NOTE
To toast the cumin seeds, put them in a small sauté pan over medium-high heat. Toast, tossing occasionally, until the seeds are fragrant, 1 to 2 minutes.

Black bean soups taste like autumn and winter. You could make this in the summer, but it would be too heavy. Black beans have heft to them.

The first time I made black bean soup as a chef was when I worked at Café Sport, outside of Seattle. Tom Douglas had been the head chef at the Café Sport downtown. After Douglas left, the owner kept using all of Douglas's recipes. So I started making his black bean soup and ate it nearly every day for lunch. I've played with it a lot since—chefs are always messing with ingredients and proportions.

This is not a particularly spicy soup. I understand that some people like fiery-hot bites, but I think that takes away from the nuances and flavors of the food. I want the food to taste like itself, not just heat. It should have a little kick, but not too much. I don't want a soup to punch me in the mouth. • *Feeds 4*

RED PEPPER RELISH
1 large red bell pepper, roasted
  (see page 179)
1 tablespoon chopped fresh cilantro
1 tablespoon finely chopped green onion
2 teaspoons grated lime zest
2 teaspoons sherry vinegar
1 teaspoon thinly sliced garlic
1 teaspoon chopped fresh chives

SOUP
2 tablespoons canola oil
1 large yellow onion, peeled and large diced
1 medium carrot, peeled and large diced
2 stalks celery, large diced
2 tablespoons chopped garlic
2 teaspoons cumin seeds, toasted
  (see Note)
½ teaspoon red pepper flakes
1 dried chipotle pepper, stemmed
2 tablespoons tomato paste
4 cups chicken stock
1 cup dried black beans, soaked overnight
  in water to cover
1 small smoked ham hock, thawed
Kosher salt and cracked black pepper
4 tablespoons sour cream

Making the relish. Peel the roasted pepper and cut it into a small dice. Add the diced pepper to a bowl and combine with the cilantro, green onion, lime zest, vinegar, garlic, and chives. Transfer a quarter of the mixture to a food processor and pulse; it should feel chunky, not entirely pureed. Add the chunky part back into the relish and stir.

Sautéing the vegetables for the soup. Add the oil to a medium stockpot over medium heat. Add the onion, carrot, and celery and cook, stirring occasionally, for 1 minute. Add the garlic and cook, stirring occasionally, until the onion is softened and translucent, about 10 minutes. Stir in the cumin seeds and red pepper flakes and cook until they are fragrant.

Spicing it up. Add the entire chipotle pepper to the pot. Stir in the tomato paste. When it coats everything, add 3 cups of the chicken stock.

Cooking the soup. Drain the beans from the water they have been soaking in. Add them to the soup along with the ham hock. Cook over medium heat until the beans are completely tender

and the ham hock has started to peel away from the bone, 25 to 30 minutes.

    Finishing the soup. Remove the ham hock from the soup. Peel all the meat away from the bone and chop it up into bite-size pieces.

    Transfer the soup to a food processor or blender in small batches and puree; the final consistency should be just a touch thinner than a smoothie. If the soup feels too thick, thin it out with the remaining chicken stock.

carrot-mint soup with english peas and yogurt

VARIATIONS
You could use chicken stock for a heartier taste. If you have to avoid cow's milk dairy, try goat's milk yogurt instead.

SUGGESTIONS
Don't boil the soup for longer than a moment or the colors will fade away entirely.

Fresh peas in spring are worth the winter's wait. After frozen puddles, perpetual parkas, and weeks on end of long johns under the jeans, there is the first pile of English peas at the farmers' market. These have the crisp bite of a green vegetable that no wintertime morsel can ever provide.

And then there are the first carrots of the season, spindly and crooked, small with tendrils still trailing from the end. Nothing that orange has been here for months. Add a little mint to your basket to calm that spring frenzy and you're on your way to soup. • *Feeds 4*

2 cups English peas, shelled
1 cup loosely packed spinach
1 cup full-fat plain yogurt
3 large sprigs fresh mint, finely chopped
1 teaspoon grated lemon zest
Kosher salt and cracked black pepper
¼ cup extra-virgin olive oil, plus extra
  for pureeing soup
1 medium onion, peeled and large diced
2 stalks celery, large diced

5 large carrots (as fresh as you can find),
  peeled and sliced into thin coins
4 cloves garlic, smashed and peeled
2 sprigs fresh Italian parsley
3 tablespoons long-grain white rice
  (we like jasmine rice here)
1½ quarts vegetable stock
2 cups fresh carrot juice
2 tablespoons butter

Blanching the peas. Leave a bowl of ice water by the sink. Bring a large saucepan of salted water to a boil. Throw in the English peas and spinach. Cook the vegetables until the peas are tender with a nice bite, but still a vivid green, 2 to 3 minutes. Drain the peas and spinach and then plunge them into the ice-water bath. Remove them when they are cold.

Pureeing the peas. Puree the peas and spinach with the yogurt, along with 1 teaspoon of the chopped mint. Season with the lemon zest, then salt and pepper.

Sautéing the vegetables. Add the ¼ cup of olive oil to a large sauté pan over medium heat. Add the onion, celery, carrots, and garlic and cook, stirring, until the onion is softened and translucent, 5 to 6 minutes. Throw in 1 tablespoon of the chopped mint and the 2 sprigs of parsley and cook until they are fragrant, about 1 minute. Stir in the rice until it is coated. Add the vegetable stock. Simmer the liquid until the rice is tender and the flavors have mingled, about 10 minutes.

Pureeing the soup. Transfer the soup to a food processor and blend in batches. Drizzle in 1 tablespoon of olive oil per batch. Push the soup through a sieve and into a large bowl. When you have pureed all the soup, put it back into the pot and thin it out with the carrot juice.

Finishing the soup. Bring the soup to a boil for a moment and reduce the heat to low. Toss in the butter. Stir until the butter is incorporated. Taste the soup and season with more salt and pepper, if necessary.

To serve, ladle the soup into bowls. Dollop some of the pureed peas and yogurt on top and garnish with the remaining chopped mint.

creamless corn chowder

VARIATIONS
If you want this soup spicier, you could use a habanero instead of a poblano.

SUGGESTIONS
Take the time to make the corn husk stock. It really does make a difference.

NOTE
To toast the cumin seeds, put them in a small sauté pan over medium-high heat. Toast, tossing occasionally, until the seeds are fragrant, 1 to 2 minutes.

Think of summer and sweet corn rises to the mind. Shuck it just after picking and sit down to start chewing. The sweet flavor, the milkiness, the starchiness that sticks in your teeth—these are some of the joys of summer. Frozen corn just doesn't cut it.

This soup is an attempt to capture the intense flavors of fresh corn in every bite. Certainly, you could make a nice soup with fresh corn and chicken stock, but we wanted something more heightened, a soup to match the experience of plucking the corn from the stalk and putting it in the pot right away. Roasting the corn and using the husks to make a sweet corn stock are two of the secrets.

The body has a way of telling you what to eat in season. In August, you don't want anything heavy. Braised short ribs would just drag you down. This is a hearty soup, but not heavy, perfect for those summer evenings when the blue lingers in the sky until 10 p.m. • *Feeds 4*

5 ears corn
3 tablespoons olive oil
½ medium yellow onion, peeled and roughly chopped
3 to 4 cloves garlic, smashed and peeled
6 large sprigs fresh thyme
2 tablespoons olive oil
1 medium yellow onion, peeled and large diced
1 large carrot, peeled and large diced
1 stalk celery, peeled and large diced
1 red bell pepper, large diced

1 fresh poblano chile, ends and seeds removed, large diced
2 tablespoons sliced garlic
2 teaspoons cumin seeds, toasted and ground (see Note)
1 teaspoon chili powder
1 large russet potato, peeled and large diced
3 tablespoons cornstarch
Kosher salt and cracked black pepper
Dash Tabasco
2 tablespoons finely chopped fresh cilantro
1 lime, juiced

Roasting the corn. Roast the corn on the grill. (If you don't have a barbecue, you can roast these in the oven at 400°F.) Let the corncobs roast in their husks, turning them occasionally. When the husks have blackened and the corn is not burned, you are done. Peel back a husk and taste the corn. It should be as tender as corn on the cob, sweet and soft.

Shucking the corn. Remove the husks and hair from the corncobs, but do not discard the husks. Slice the kernels from the corncobs, but do not discard the cobs.

Making the stock. Set a large saucepan over medium-high heat and pour in the oil. Add the onion and garlic to the oil and cook, stirring, until the onion is softened and translucent, about 5 minutes. Add the grilled corn husks and the thyme. Cover with 2 quarts of water. Bring to a boil, then reduce the heat and simmer for 30 minutes. Strain the stock.

Sautéing the vegetables for the chowder. Meanwhile, set a medium stockpot over medium heat and add the oil. Add the onion, carrot, celery, red pepper, poblano, and garlic and cook, stirring, until they are softened and the onion is translucent, 4 to 5 minutes. Toss in the corn kernels.

Making the chowder. Add the cumin seeds and chili powder and cook until they are fragrant,

1 to 2 minutes. Toss in the potato and the corncobs. Cover with the strained stock. Bring to a boil, then turn down the heat to low and simmer until the potato is fork-tender, 15 to 20 minutes. Fish out the corncobs and throw them away.

Thickening the chowder. In a small bowl, mix the cornstarch with about 3 tablespoons of water until you have a nice little slurry paste. Stir a bit of the slurry into the soup and let it cook for 1 minute. Stir in more slurry and cook some more. (You have to let the starches of the slurry blend with the soup before it will thicken.) Simmer the soup until it reaches the consistency of very thin gravy.

Finishing the chowder. Taste the soup and season it with salt and pepper, as well as Tabasco. Toss in the cilantro, just at the end. Add the lime juice, stir, and serve.

honey, remember to eat

In the middle of the afternoon, as I go about my day's business away from Danny, I send him a text message: "Honey, remember to eat." If I didn't prompt him, the chef would go all day without a meal.

You might think I'm nagging him. Really, I'm not. "Thank god you remind me. I never think of it otherwise." If he doesn't eat, he's grumpy and exhausted by the time dinner service starts. If he does eat, his food will taste better for the rest of us.

Before we met, Danny never ate. "I might get a muffin at the coffee shop half a block from me." On Tuesdays, the first day of the week, he sometimes took the time to grab some takeout from the Thai place down the street. How-

ever, Wednesday began the busy days, and he never had the time to think about what to order. "Mostly, I just ate a lot of the bread we served at the restaurant, all day long." The year before we met each other, we ate opposite diets: I avoided anything with gluten and he ate nothing but.

Why didn't he just eat at the restaurant? I asked him this for months. Every day, he made incredible food—crisp pork belly with wild rice, curried red lentil puree, arugula-fig salad—for which other people paid a chunk of change. Why not plate up a dish and sit down to eat when he was hungry?

He always makes a face when I ask him this, particularly during the last two weeks of the month. "I'm tired of that food. It's just easier to go somewhere else and have someone else cook it." He spends all afternoon prepping for those dinners. Eating it would be like me eating the paper out of the printer. All right, but why not order Thai from down the street? We could find room in the budget for everyday takeout. He deserves it. "There have maybe been a few days when I could sit down for half an hour to savor my meal, and then saunter back to my station. But not many. I'm pretty much always eating on the run. The only time I ate regularly is when I worked in restaurants with staff meals. Even then, most of the time, I took my plate back to my station and ate my staff meal standing up."

I only worked in one restaurant in my life, as a waitress at a family-owned brunch and wedding place. The family was not so much close as crazy, throwing pots and pans at each other when flustered and in the weeds. My first day of being a waitress took place on Father's Day, during brunch. I was assigned the station on the second floor. Desperately behind on delivering orders, I walked up the stairs tentatively, with a large tray of egg dishes. Out of nowhere, a small child ran up the stairs, laughed devilishly, and poked his fists into the back of my knees, then ran away. The breakfasts flew across the room, the soft-boiled eggs smearing across the floor. That was my first day. It went downhill from there.

I was never offered a staff meal.

"When I reached the kitchen at Pierre's in the afternoon, I'd look in the walk-in. What was left? Beef tenderloin was on the menu, but nine times out of ten the scrap trimmed from the tenderloin wasn't being used. I'd think, hmm, how about boeuf bourguignon for staff meal?"

The chef or sous chef makes staff meal—also known as family meal—at larger restaurants. Certainly, part of the intent is to feed the staff. The gathering allows the chef to explain the day's specials, or go over any situations that need to be discussed. And whoever is cooking has a chance to play with flavors, experiment with ingredients, or throw together a meal with abandon. "If it didn't work out well, it was no skin off my teeth. Sometimes, if staff meal was really good, I could turn it into a special that night. That was pretty rare, however. Most of the time, staff meals meant burgers, enchiladas, beef with fried rice. Sometimes Pierre would go to Costco and buy big boxes of premade lasagna. Actually, I enjoyed those quite a bit."

But the biggest reason for staff meal, from the restaurant's point of view, is to get rid of product. "My friends and I have joked so many times about writing a cookbook called *What to Do with Chicken*. There's always chicken left over. If the ingredients were cheap, and that dish wasn't moving, the staff ate it. Sundays were the worst, because that was the last night of the week, and Pierre didn't want stuff lying around on Monday. I used lots of tomatoes going soft, onions turning green, battered zucchini." Danny swears that at some of the best restaurants he has ever worked in, some of the staff meals tasted like Hamburger Helper. "Did I want to make the staff decent food? Yes. Did I want to impress them with my skills? No. If I had spent two hours cooking a meal to wow the staff, I would have gotten my ass chewed."

But at least the food was placed before him and he ate. It took me months of knowing him to realize why he rarely eats at the restaurant. "Once I arrive, I never really look at food with hunger."

One summer, I worked as a coffee puller at an espresso shop. The first day there, I couldn't believe my luck—all the free lattes I wanted. By the end of the summer, I couldn't look at another cup of coffee. The next summer, I worked briefly at an ice-cream shop. I gained great biceps and lost my appetite for butter pecan and rocky road. (A year later, I regained the ice cream and lost the biceps.) Working with those foods made them simply part of the day, a means to an end, something I had to do.

Luckily, for Danny, the food he creates means more to him than the lattes did to me. A different hunger takes over, a hunger to make the food on the plate taste and look appealing. "I love thinking about presentation and texture, and how to build a plate. But the most important thing about being a chef is that you are a cook first. Weird wild garnishes and fancy foams? Some chefs can do them and have the food still burst with flavor in the mouth. Most chefs who are following that as a trend? They're turning out lousy food. The first rule is that the food has to taste good. If the plate looks good, but the diner spits the food out in her napkin, what's the point? The whole point of being a chef is making people happy in the belly."

Danny doesn't call himself an artist. I won't either, because it's such a loaded term. But he creates. He thinks about the food all day, letting ideas brew while he lies in bed or drinks coffee. And when he starts his work, he is all focused intensity, nothing intruding, placing everything he has in the service of each plate. "I want the flavors to dance together. I want people to look at the plate set down before them and be amazed, and have their stomachs start grumbling. I want them to have the full sensory pleasure in every bite, from the first anticipation until the last satisfaction."

When I'm writing, and I have finally found the focused awareness that allows me to push my ego away and work, I go hours without eating, or even thinking about food.

It makes sense that he's not hungry at the restaurant. At the end of the evening, however, he's ravenous.

boeuf bourguignon

I've never been to Burgundy, but I imagine the place would taste like this dish. Rich red-wine sauce. Lovely braised beef. Mushrooms, onion, bacon. So flavorful.

This is a great family meal. In fact, I have made it dozens of times for staff meals in various restaurants where I have worked. Start off with big pieces of beef. Marinate them one night, and sear them off the next. Roast the vegetables, work with the mirepoix, and pour in the wine. Wait for hours. Take a fork and rake it down the meat and the fork will fall. The tenderness slides down your throat.

When I was a kid, my mom made beef stew, which was probably the American version of this. But my mother never added a good bottle of wine or used strong stock. She just threw everything in the Crock-Pot. Her beef stew is amazing, but this goes one step further. • *Feeds 4*

3 pounds beef short ribs, bone in
4 large carrots, peeled and chopped
2 stalks celery, chopped
2 large yellow onions, peeled and chopped
5 large cloves garlic, peeled
One 750-ml bottle medium-bodied
   red wine (nothing expensive,
   but not cheap box wine)
Kosher salt and cracked black pepper
4 tablespoons extra-virgin olive oil
1 sprig fresh rosemary

3 sprigs fresh sage
1 bay leaf
1 tablespoon tomato paste
2 tablespoons sorghum flour
3 quarts veal stock (see page 148)
4 slices smoked bacon, finely diced
1 cup peeled pearl onions
2 cups quartered button mushrooms
2 tablespoons cold unsalted butter
2 tablespoons finely chopped fresh
   thyme

Preparing the night before. Cut the beef ribs into a Dutch oven. Cover the meat with the carrots, celery, onions, garlic, and wine. Allow the mixture to sit overnight in the refrigerator.

Preparing the next day. Pull the beef pieces out with tongs. Put them on a large plate covered with paper towels and pat dry. Season with salt and pepper.

Straining the marinade. Strain the vegetables from the wine, draining the liquid into a large saucepan. Put the saucepan over medium heat. Simmer the wine, skimming any scum off the top, until the liquid is reduced by half its volume, 30 to 45 minutes.

Searing the beef. Set a large sauté pan over high heat and add 2 tablespoons of the oil. Cook the short ribs, making sure they don't burn from all the sugars in the wine, until they are seared on all sides, about 15 minutes. Return the beef to the Dutch oven, pouring off all the grease.

Sautéing the vegetables. Add the remaining 2 tablespoons of oil to the sauté pan and put the strained vegetables in the pan. Cook over medium-high heat, stirring occasionally, until they begin to caramelize, about 15 minutes. Add the rosemary, sage, and bay leaf and cook until they are fragrant. Stir in the tomato paste until the vegetables are well coated. Add the sorghum flour and stir until everything is well coated.

VARIATIONS
You can use chicken stock instead of veal stock, but you will probably need to make a cornstarch slurry (a few tablespoons of cornstarch mixed with an equal amount of water) to thicken up the sauce at the end, since chicken stock usually doesn't have the same gelatinous quality as veal stock.

SUGGESTIONS
This works well in a slow cooker too. Serve with boiled potatoes, mashed potatoes, or rice. Use any leftovers as a sauce for pasta.

Reducing the wine. Pour the reduced wine, about 1½ cups, into the sauté pan. Cook over medium heat, scraping all the goodness off the bottom of the pan, until the liquid is reduced by half its volume, about 10 minutes.

Reducing the veal stock. Meanwhile, pour the veal stock into the Dutch oven with the seared beef and bring to a boil. When the stock has boiled for 5 minutes, add the contents of the sauté pan to the Dutch oven. Bring to a boil, then reduce the heat to low and simmer until the beef is very much fork-tender, 2½ to 3 hours.

Rendering the bacon. About 30 minutes before the beef is done braising, put the bacon slices in a large sauté pan over medium heat. Cook until the bacon is crisp and has exuded fat, about 10 minutes. Remove the bacon slices and dice them finely. Add the pearl onions to the sauté pan with the bacon fat and cook over medium heat, stirring occasionally, until they begin to caramelize, about 15 minutes. Add the mushrooms and cook, stirring, until the mushrooms are softened, about 7 minutes. Season with salt and pepper.

Finishing the dish. Remove the braised beef from the Dutch oven. Strain the liquid and throw away the vegetables and herbs. Drop the beef into the onion mixture in the sauté pan. Pour the strained liquid goodness back into the Dutch oven, followed by the beef and onion mixture. Bring to a boil. Add the butter and cook until the sauce is reduced by about half its volume, about 5 minutes. Throw in the thyme at the end. Garnish with the diced bacon.

don't be intimidated by french names

If you say the word *soufflé*, some people are going to be intimidated immediately. If there's an accent mark in the word, people feel they can't make that food.

Don't be intimidated by French names. The word *sauté* simply means "jumped," as in the vegetables jumped around the pan with the heat. You want the pan hot enough so that the vegetables jump in the thin layer of oil as you cook them. Cook and stir, fast—that's a sauté. Mirepoix is just carrots, celery, and onion, in equal parts. Blanch means to cook briefly in boiling salted water and stop the cooking process by shocking the vegetables in ice water. Monter au beurre means to finish a sauce with butter, swirling it in at the end to make the fat stick to all the parts of the sauce.

Classical French technique is still the basis for much of the world's cooking. There are, of course, so many ways of preparing food. However, the French method had its influences in many cultures, so it's a good place to start.

At my culinary school, the French teachers were intimidating. They could make you feel big in one second and two feet tall in the next. If you messed up in your station, they'd say, "That's wrong. Start over."

But I learned. That's why I went to school. All that training gave me a way of being with food in confidence. If you learn the structure of how to cook food properly, you have a skeleton upon which you can put flesh.

And sure, you could say that a julienned vegetable is cut into matchstick pieces, or that a chiffonade is "rolled up like a cigar and sliced." But there's something to be said for using the correct terms, for being respectful. You come to understand that there's a history to food, and you are becoming part of it by stepping up to the stove.

smoked salmon and tomato napoleon with horseradish sour cream

VARIATIONS
You could use the House-Cured Salmon (see page 194) in this recipe.

SUGGESTIONS
Do not make this in January. The tomatoes are from Mexico and Peru, and they taste like softballs. Wait until tomato season to enjoy this.

I first had smoked salmon on pizza at Beano's Cabin, a private club in Beaver Creek in Colorado, where I did my internship during culinary school. Jiminy Cricket, that was good. And now, smoked salmon is still a wow for me. I used to eat smoked salmon, mashed potatoes, and red pepper aioli sandwiches. It's making my mouth water right now to think about it.

When heirloom tomatoes are in season, we eat several every day: squat ones and long striped ones, tiny green ones, five-pound Buddha belly tomatoes. The afternoon before our wedding, my dad (who grew up in Iowa) stood at the sink in our kitchen and salted slices of heirloom tomatoes we had bought him at the farmers' market. The look of peaceful joy on his face has stayed with me ever since. Food does not have to be complicated to be memorable.

Shauna's brother doesn't really care what we serve for Christmas dinner, as long as horseradish sour cream is involved. Fresh horseradish has a surprising zing, and the prepared horseradish has a kick to it. Combine both and you'll enjoy this sauce.

Smoked salmon, heirloom tomatoes, and horseradish all have distinct tastes. Put them together and you have something else entirely. • *Feeds 4*

½ cup sour cream
1 tablespoon prepared horseradish
1 tablespoon finely grated fresh horseradish
1 teaspoon fresh lemon juice

2 tablespoons finely chopped fresh chives
Kosher salt and cracked black pepper
4 large ripe heirloom tomatoes (in season)
8 ounces sliced smoked salmon

Making the horseradish sour cream. In a food processor, combine the sour cream, prepared horseradish, grated horseradish, and lemon juice. Puree until smooth and then stir in the chives by hand. Season with salt and pepper.

Preparing the tomatoes. Slice the tomatoes to roughly ¼-inch thickness. Season with salt.

Stacking the napoleon. Start with a slice of tomato. Dollop some horseradish sour cream on top. Nestle a piece of smoked salmon in it. Repeat, going all the way up until you cannot eat any higher.

If you are presenting these on a platter, drizzle the sour cream sauce around the plate.

warm polenta with goat cheese

VARIATIONS
If you cannot eat dairy, you can substitute soy milk for the milk. If you don't have good Parmesan on hand, Manchego, Romano, or any stiff, crumbly cheese will do.

SUGGESTIONS
If you set the polenta aside to cool in a baking dish, you can slice it and grill or panfry the pieces later. You can use cookie cutters to cut decorative pieces, if you want to be cute. Instead of pasta, serve the creamy polenta topped with tomato sauce and roasted pork. Anything you would top pasta with will work on polenta.

The first time I ate polenta was at Café Sport in Bellevue. There, we grilled bread cubes with a little olive oil, lifted up the skin of chicken breasts and stuffed them with the cubes, then roasted the chicken until it was crispy. The chicken was served on top of creamy polenta, with gravy made from the roast drippings. The first time I ate it, I thought I would never be able to eat enough.

I love cooking polenta now. It's a great thing. You can eat it warm and as soft as baby food. Or you can chill the cooked polenta, cut it out, and grill it. Polenta is filling and comforting, and relatively inexpensive.

When we stood in the central piazza in Foligno, we heard two grandmothers arguing over the best way to make polenta. You might have your own way too. Just pay attention and take your time. This isn't instant food. • *Feeds 4*

2 tablespoons extra-virgin olive oil
2 large shallots, peeled and thinly sliced
1 teaspoon thinly sliced garlic
1 teaspoon finely chopped fresh rosemary
2½ cups whole milk
1½ cups water
1 cup gluten-free fine yellow cornmeal (not all are gluten-free because of manufacturing practices)

1 tablespoon butter
¼ cup freshly grated Parmesan cheese
1 teaspoon each kosher salt and cracked black pepper
2 ounces soft goat cheese (chèvre)

Sautéing the vegetables. Set a large sauté pan over medium-high heat and pour in the oil. Add the shallots and garlic to the hot oil and cook, stirring, until the shallots are softened and translucent, 3 to 4 minutes. Toss in the rosemary and cook until it is fragrant.

Making the polenta. Add the milk and water. As soon as the liquids come to a boil, pour in the cornmeal and turn the heat down to medium. Stir the mixture with a steady hand until the polenta becomes one mass and pulls away from the sides of the pan, 15 to 20 minutes.

Finishing the polenta. When the polenta is ready, stir in the butter until it is incorporated. Toss in the Parmesan cheese. Taste the polenta and season with salt and pepper.

To serve, scoop the polenta into bowls and dollop on the goat cheese.

prosciutto, pesto, and red pepper sandwich

SUGGESTIONS
Roasted peppers and pesto are great in pasta dishes and fish dishes. Blend roasted peppers with olives to make another kind of tapenade. I love roasted peppers and pesto in omelets.

NOTE
To toast the pine nuts, put them in a small oven-safe nonstick pan and toast in a 400°F oven, stirring occasionally and taking care not to burn them, for 5 to 10 minutes.

After we visited Italy, we wanted to have a slab of prosciutto in our home. Nearly every family there has one—a stand with a wooden base and a metal clamp to hold the whole cured ham in place while slicing off thin pieces with a sharp knife. Someday, we intend to make our own. But in the meantime, we have access to decent prosciutto here in the U.S., and it needs to be eaten.

The combination of good melt-into-the-pig-tasting prosciutto, tender roasted peppers, and familiar-but-still-good pesto makes me happy in the middle of a long afternoon of prepping.
• *Feeds 2*

PESTO
1 cup packed fresh basil leaves
2 tablespoons pine nuts, toasted (see Note)
1 tablespoon thinly sliced garlic
1 tablespoon fresh lemon juice
1 teaspoon each kosher salt and cracked black pepper
¾ cup extra-virgin olive oil
2 tablespoons freshly grated Parmesan cheese

ROASTED PEPPER
1 large red bell pepper
1 tablespoon extra-virgin olive oil

SANDWICH
4 slices crusty gluten-free bread (see page 180)
4 ounces thinly sliced prosciutto
4 ounces fresh mozzarella cheese (optional)
Kosher salt and cracked black pepper

Preparing to roast the pepper. Preheat the oven to 450°F.

Making the pesto. In a food processor, combine the basil, pine nuts, garlic, lemon juice, salt, and pepper. Whirl it up. With the machine running, slowly drizzle in the oil until it is vivid green and has the thick consistency of a slightly runny paste. Add the Parmesan cheese and pulse again until it is blended in. (The pesto should keep in the refrigerator for 4 to 5 days. The oxygen hitting the top of the pesto will darken it, over time. If you care about the color, scrape away the dark parts and serve.)

Roasting the pepper. Put the whole pepper in a roasting pan and coat it with the oil. Slide the roasting pan into the oven. Roast the pepper, turning it every 10 to 15 minutes with tongs, until it is mostly black and the skin starts to separate like an air pocket, about 30 minutes. The skin should blister, but don't let the pepper burn. Remove the pepper from the oven, put it in a large bowl, and tightly cover with plastic wrap.

Preparing the pepper. When the pepper has cooled, peel it with your fingers. Remove the stem and seeds and cut the pepper up. Do not rinse the pepper under water, as tempting as that is, because the water will wash away the flavors of the oil and pepper.

Assembling the sandwich. Slather the pesto like mayonnaise onto one side of the bread slices. Pile the prosciutto and peppers on 2 of the bread slices. If you can eat dairy, try some fresh mozzarella cheese as well. Season with salt and pepper. Close up the sandwiches with the other 2 bread slices and eat.

crusty bread that even those who eat gluten might like

VARIATION
Make this once with this combination of flours before you begin changing in other flours. Some you might like: amaranth, quinoa, or flaxseed meal. However, if you change the flours too much, you will change the composition of the bread so go easy. Substitute flours by weight, rather than volume.

VARIATION
You can also use this recipe to make a loaf of sandwich bread. Put the dough into a greased loaf pan before you let it rise for the last hour. Bake at 375°F, with an egg wash on top of the loaf, for 45 minutes or so, or until the internal temperature has reached 180°F and the thermometer comes out dry.

Gluten-free bread is the great quest of those who cannot eat the protein. It can be done, but here's the key: don't expect gluten-free bread to be the familiar gluten bread. Without gluten, bread is always going to be a bit less pliable, a little drier, and more of an unexpected texture than you wish. But once you get past the stubborn notion that everything should be the way it always was, you can have bread again.

There is gluten-free bread that you buy from the refrigerated section of the grocery store, just to make a quick piece of toast. It's more like a soggy bagel texture, but it does the job fine. And then there's bread that even someone who can eat gluten can enjoy. That's this bread.

When Shauna could eat bread, she was a snob about it; she only ate artisanal loaves from the best bakeries. That's why she experimented for years, making loaves she liked, and then loaves she loved, until she found this one. This bread has air pockets, a crisp crust, and an earthy, warm taste. When our friend Booth—who had not eaten good bread for a year after his celiac diagnosis—ate this for the first time, his happy gratitude told us to put it in this book. • *Yields 2 small loaves*

1¼ cups (227g/8oz) potato starch
1¼ cups (100g/3.5oz) almond flour
⅔ cup (85g/3oz) oat flour (make sure it's certified gluten-free)
½ cup (85g/3oz) millet flour
1 tablespoon active dry yeast
2 teaspoons xanthan gum or an equal amount of psyllium husks

1 teaspoon guar gum or an equal amount of psyllium husks
1½ teaspoons kosher salt
1⅓ cups warm water (about 110°F)
2 large eggs
⅛ cup canola oil
1 tablespoon honey

Mixing the dry ingredients. Put the potato starch, almond flour, oat flour, and millet flour into the bowl of a stand mixer. Whirl them up together for a moment. (If you don't have a stand mixer, sift the flours together into a large bowl.) Add the yeast, xanthan gum, guar gum, and salt. Stir to combine.

Adding the wet ingredients. Pour the warm water, eggs, canola oil, and honey into the dry ingredients. Mix with the paddle attachment (of with a large spoon if you are mixing by hand) for a few moments until the dough has fully come together. It will be soft. It will sort of slump off the paddle. Don't worry. That's the right texture.

Letting the bread dough rise. Put the dough into a large, oiled bowl. Cover the bowl with a clean cloth, then set in a warm place in the kitchen. Let the dough rise until it has doubled in size, about 2 hours. The risen dough will have a texture closer to traditional bread dough than the unrisen dough had.

Preparing to bake. At the end of the rising time, turn the oven to 500°F. Or, put a cast-iron Dutch oven into the hot oven to come to heat. Cut the dough in half and form two small boules

SUGGESTIONS
You can make rosemary bread by chopping a sprig of rosemary fine and throwing it into the dough during the first rise. The same is true for any flavor you want to try. Top the bread with a glug of olive oil and a few pinches of finishing sea salt for another taste.

(rustic-looking oval loaves). Make three ¼-inch deep cuts with a serrated knife on the top of the dough.

Baking the bread. If you have a pizza stone, put the loaves directly onto the pizza stone. When the Dutch oven has been heating for 30 minutes, take it out of the oven, carefully. Put a piece of parchment paper, wider than the Dutch oven, over the edges. Flour your hands to coax the bread dough into a coherent mass. Plop it onto the parchment paper, which will settle down into the Dutch oven. Tuck the edges of the paper into the pot, cover, and slip it back into the hot oven. Bake for at least 30 minutes, or until the bottom of the bread is brown and has a good thump to it. The internal temperature should be at least 180°F, and the thermometer should come out of the bread dry.

Allow the bread to cool for at least 30 minutes before slicing it up.

special food

"My cousin and I were out the door at four thirty or five in the morning. We walked to the pond in Breckenridge and caught a rainbow trout. I was eight years old, with a hunting knife, in the mountains of Colorado, cutting into something. That was cool. My mom filleted it and cooked it for us, with lemon and tartar sauce. I saw it from the beginning to on my plate. I've never forgotten it.

"The first time I ate shrimp bisque was the night of homecoming. My buddy had a date and I didn't, but I had a car, so I was their chauffeur. My friend wanted me

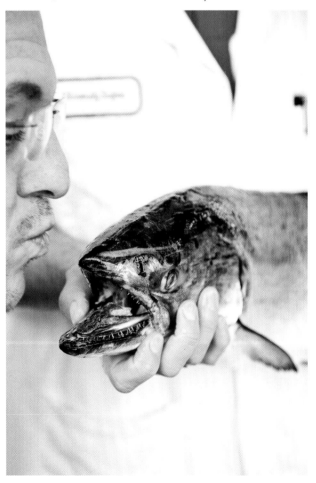

to eat dinner with them, which felt a little weird, but he bought my dinner, so why not? Thinking back to that bisque, I can still taste everything. I could taste the shrimp stock, the shrimp, the brandy they flamed it with, and the creaminess of the butter they used to finish the soup."

If it's done right, fish can be astonishing. The taste of it can stay with you the rest of your life, as those experiences stayed with Danny and made it into his hands, where he crafts the fish specials each night for the restaurant.

When Danny calls at the end of the night, and his voice jumps gleefully, I know he's bringing home the fish special for dinner. Petrale sole with shrimp and crab mousse and a cilantro-mustard sauce. Pan-roasted halibut, oven-dried tomatoes, saffron millet pilaf, and wilted arugula. Grilled sea scallops with a morel mushroom risotto and a watercress sauce. (Yes, I am spoiled, and I admit it.)

"That is one of my favorite things in the world to do, to craft a really nice fish special. When we go to the farmers' markets, I'm mostly thinking about the fish. Fish in Seattle is so incredible that it's easy to become inspired. I want to do it justice. I love fish. Fish is good."

I have to agree with him.

Danny made up his first fish dish at a restaurant in Seattle, when he was twenty-two. Café Cielo. "I paired grilled scallops with a lemon-thyme risotto. That was good."

In every restaurant where he worked afterward, he picked up something, a little trick or two. Frank, his head chef at Papillon, spent hours coming up with elaborate fish specials. He taught Danny exactly what should be on a plate and how to put flavors together. Mostly, Frank gave Danny many pointed pieces of advice, and then he gave him freedom. "There, I had the time for trial and error, to try different foods with different fish. Frank always wanted me to use grouper in the winter. Anything I wanted to do with grouper was fine. We'd get these big, beautiful scallops. I loved to play with those. It's just being on the line, cooking for hours, that gave me the confidence."

His time at the current restaurant in Seattle has been the amalgam of all the other places. Here he is in charge and can order what he wants and can finalize the fish specials late in the afternoon, just before dinner service begins. "I want something appealing, with good, clean flavors. I think about taste, to be sure, but also texture and smell, what the plate as a whole suggests."

If Danny had to work in a restaurant that never changed its menu, I think he might go insane. He thrives on the daily detective work of what works well with dill or acorn squash. If, however, something happened that meant he'd have to work on the line of a staid place, at least he would have the fish special to keep him creating.

Pasta specials too. Sometimes in restaurants, pasta is a great way to get rid of food, especially on Sundays and toward the end of the week. "If it's not too busy a night, you might go out of your way to make an outstanding pasta special. But sometimes you throw in beef scraps or parts of the dish from the night before that didn't sell. It still tastes good. People don't look at the pasta special and think, They're getting rid of stuff. They just hear the special and go ooooh. You make money that way."

At his current restaurant, however, because it is such a small place, Danny could craft something extraordinary out of the pasta special. Capellini with anchovies, fresh clams, bacon, and oregano—I loved that one. He brewed pasta specials in the back of his mind all day, the same way he worked on fish specials.

And he always kept gluten-free pasta in the kitchen, for the gluten-free customers who came in droves. He wanted them to feel included.

All of this intimidated me when I first started cooking for Danny. After a lifetime of following recipes, how could I create something he would like?

"Start with not being afraid," he told me. "Start with the fish that interests you and what would go well with that fish."

Cooking is about accepting trial and error, I have learned from him. Experiment. Some foods work together when you would never suspect it. "One time, Frank misread one of the plastic containers that we had at the walk-in at Papillon. Instead of grabbing the port wine sauce, he picked up balsamic vinaigrette. He made a gallon of sauce. He couldn't just throw it away. He used it in the fish special and it sold like crazy."

Sometimes, dishes turn out to be something no one wants to eat. "Once at Papillon I created a fish special with braised fennel. No one ordered it."

That story helped me to feel okay when I played with halibut poached with ginger and grapefruit and it turned out a little strange. I had hoped to write it up for the blog, but the tart tang of it made me think no one else but Danny would eat it. He enjoyed it enough that I found the courage to play again. I sautéed halibut cheeks with basil and sorrel, and squeezed a little lemon juice on top at the end. Danny gobbled it, rapidly, not saying a word. And then he looked up at me and said, "Great fish, sweetie."

I never knew fish could give me such joy.

halibut with millet, carrot-fennel salad, and golden raisin sauce

VARIATIONS
You could easily use quinoa in place of the millet. Currants would be good in the sauce. Black cod would work well too.

SUGGESTIONS
Please allow yourself to eat fish done medium-rare. This is how fish should be cooked, so it's still juicy. Too many of us were raised to think that fish should be flaky and overdone. That will ruin the taste of this dish.

Halibut had just come into season and I wanted to do something different. Spring had come along again, but it was just starting to warm up. I wanted something light, but not too light. If Shauna could have eaten wheat, I would have made couscous. Instead, I made millet, an excellent substitute.

The different layers of this dish give you the heartiness of the millet, the delicate flavor of the halibut, the earthiness of the carrots and fennel, and the sweetness of the golden raisin sauce, with the final punch of the vinegar.

This was just what I wanted. • *Feeds 4*

COOKED MILLET
2¼ cups vegetable stock
2 teaspoons extra-virgin olive oil
¼ teaspoon salt
1 cup millet

CARROT-FENNEL SALAD
3 large carrots, peeled
1 fennel bulb, cut in half through the
   bulb, root removed, thinly sliced
2 tablespoons champagne vinegar
Kosher salt and cracked black pepper

GOLDEN RAISIN SAUCE
1 cup golden raisins
½ cup sweet wine (such as Sauterne)
⅓ cup chicken stock
¼ cup soda water
3 tablespoons grapeseed or canola oil
1 tablespoon Champagne vinegar
Kosher salt and cracked black pepper

SEARED HALIBUT
4 tablespoons grapeseed or canola oil
4 fillets halibut, about 6 ounces each,
   at least 1½ inches thick

Cooking the millet. Set a large saucepan over high heat. Pour in the vegetable stock, olive oil, and salt. Bring to a boil, add the millet, and reduce the heat to medium-low. Cook until the millet is tender to the bite, 10 to 15 minutes. (If the liquid evaporates before the millet has finished cooking, add more stock.) Strain the millet and set it aside.

Blanching the carrots. Bring a large saucepan filled with salted water to a boil. Set a large bowl of ice water in the sink. Split the carrots in half lengthwise. Turn each piece cut side down and slice it in half lengthwise again, diagonally. Cook the carrots in the boiling water until they are starting to turn tender but still have a little crunch, 2 to 3 minutes. Remove the carrots from the hot water and shock them in the ice water. Drain them when they are cold.

Making the salad. In a large bowl, mix the carrots and fennel together. Toss with the vinegar. Taste the salad and season with salt and pepper. Set aside.

Making the golden raisin sauce. In a bowl, soak the raisins for 30 minutes in the wine. Afterwards, transfer half of the soaked raisins to a blender. Add the chicken stock and blend until pureed. Blend in the soda water to thin out the mixture, a bit at a time. Blend in the grapeseed or canola oil and the vinegar. Season the sauce with salt and pepper.

Add this puree to the remaining soaked raisins and stir.

Preheating the oven. Turn the oven to 450°F.

Searing the halibut. Set 2 large oven-safe sauté pans over high heat and add the grapeseed or canola oil. (You do not want to crowd the halibut fillets, so use 2 pans to give yourself plenty of space.) Put the halibut fillets, non-skin side down, into the hot oil. Sear them until they have a nice brown crust on the bottom, 2 to 3 minutes.

Roasting the halibut. Flip over the fillets. Slide the pans into the oven and roast the halibut until the internal temperature reaches 120°F, about 5 to 7 minutes.

To serve, make a little mound of the millet on each plate. Arrange the carrot-fennel salad on the millet. Perch the halibut fillet on top. Drizzle the sauce around the plate.

umbrian lentils with duck confit, sun-dried tomatoes, and cabernet sauce

VARIATIONS
French du Puy lentils or brown lentils will work too, as Castelluccio lentils can be hard to obtain. Put this over pasta—that's what this recipe was going to be first.

SUGGESTIONS
Don't undercook the duck. It will be hard as a rock, and you'll wonder why people always talk about duck confit. Duck confit is great in salads, in omelets, in duck hash, and on top of pasta. We always roast potatoes in duck fat for Christmas.

When we were in Umbria for our honeymoon, we fell in love with Norcia. The small town, the clean air of the Sibillini Mountains, the smell of truffles in the streets. Every other shop was a butcher's shop, with stuffed wild boars mounted on the walls outside, and whole prosciuttos hanging inside. I wish we had bought the wild boar and truffle salami we saw in one shop.

Strangely, what we remember best about the food is the lentils. Castelluccio lentils have been grown on the plains outside the town, without any chemicals, for centuries. These tiny brown lentils don't look like enough to celebrate; green du Puy lentils from France are much more striking. But the Umbrian lentils cook up tender and taste of the earth around Norcia.

Here I've paired them with a classic French technique: duck confit. Duck confit, when it is done right, is heaven on earth. The saltiness of the duck, the fattiness that it's cooked in, the way the meat falls off the bone—this dish has been made for centuries, and I hope it always is.

Since the folks at University Seafood sell poultry too, I was inspired to make this dish when I was picking up fish for a special one day and saw Dale pulling duck legs out of the walk-in.

• *Feeds 4*

DUCK CONFIT
10 large cloves garlic, smashed and peeled
1 bunch fresh sage
1 bunch fresh rosemary
1 bunch fresh thyme
¾ cup kosher salt
¼ cup lightly cracked black peppercorns
6 duck legs
4 cups duck fat (find this at your butcher's shop or online; see Resources, page 283)

WINE REDUCTION SAUCE
½ cup Madeira
½ cup Marsala
½ cup port

LENTILS AND CONFIT
⅛ cup julienned sun-dried tomatoes
2 tablespoons extra-virgin olive oil
1 large yellow onion, peeled and medium diced
1 large carrot, peeled and medium diced
1 large parsnip, peeled and medium diced
2 tablespoons finely chopped garlic
3 tablespoons chiffonade fresh basil
2 cups Castelluccio lentils (see Variations)
1 quart chicken stock
1 cup Cabernet
1 large shallot, peeled and chopped
2 cups veal stock (see page 148) or chicken stock
2 tablespoons butter
2 tablespoons cornstarch (if you are using chicken stock in place of the veal stock)
Kosher salt and cracked black pepper

Marinating the duck legs. The day before you plan to serve this, mix together the garlic, sage, rosemary, thyme, salt, and peppercorns in a large bowl. Mound a quarter of the mixture onto a baking sheet. Put the duck legs on top of the mound and cover with the rest of the mixture. Wrap the baking sheet tightly in plastic wrap. Put the baking sheet in the refrigerator and marinate the duck legs overnight.

Preparing to cook the next day. Preheat the oven to 350°F.

Preparing the duck fat. Set a large saucepan over medium-high heat. Add the duck fat and heat it until it melts, about 2 minutes.

Searing the duck legs. Remove the plastic wrap from the duck legs and wipe off the salt mixture. Set a large sauté pan over medium-high heat and pour in 1 tablespoon of the melted duck fat. Put the duck legs, 3 at a time, into the sauté pan. Cook until the duck legs are browned on the bottom, then turn them over, about 3 minutes. When the duck legs are browned on all sides, transfer them to a plate and sear the next batch.

Cooking the duck legs. Put the seared duck legs into a large baking dish. Pour in the melted duck fat to cover the duck legs. Cover the dish with aluminum foil. Slide the baking dish into the oven. Cook until the skin at the ankle starts to slide away from the bone, 2½ to 3 hours, depending on the size of the legs. Stick in your tongs and pull a bit of meat off the thigh. You should not have to chew the meat. It should melt in your mouth.

Remove the duck from the pan with a slotted spoon. Be careful, because you'll be dealing with hot oil, and the duck will be fragile. Let the fat drip off the leg for a bit, then place it on a wire rack with a baking sheet underneath to catch the duck fat.

Set aside the duck fat in the pan. Allow it to cool down and save it for later. It's gold.

Making the wine reduction sauce. Pour the Madeira, Marsala, and port into a large saucepan and set it over medium heat. Simmer until the liquids are reduced to ¼ cup, about 20 minutes; the sauce will grow thicker as it reduces, so be sure not to burn it.

Take the sauce off the burner to cool, and then refrigerate it. (This will keep in the refrigerator for up to a month.)

Preparing to cook. If the sun-dried tomatoes are packed in oil, drain them. If they are dry, rehydrate them with ¼ cup of hot water. Preheat the oven to 450°F.

Caramelizing the vegetables. Set a large sauté pan over medium-high heat and pour in the oil. Add the onion, carrot, and parsnip to the hot oil and cook, stirring, until the vegetables are warm, brown, softened, about 15 minutes. Toss in the garlic and cook until it is fragrant. Stir in the basil and cook until it is fragrant.

(continued on page 189)

Cooking the lentils. Put the lentils into the pan. Pour in the 1 quart of chicken stock. Bring to a boil, then reduce the heat to medium and cook until the lentils are tender, about 10 minutes.

Making the Cabernet sauce. Pour the Cabernet into a large saucepan over medium-high heat. Add the shallot and then simmer the wine until the pan is almost dry, 15 to 20 minutes. Pour in the 2 cups of veal or chicken stock and bring to a boil. Reduce the temperature to low and allow the sauce to simmer until it is reduced to a quarter of its volume, 10 to 15 minutes.

Finishing the Cabernet sauce. Remove the wine reduction sauce from the refrigerator and pour it into the Cabernet sauce. Turn the heat up to medium and simmer to meld the flavors, stirring occasionally, for another 2 to 3 minutes. If you are using veal stock, whisk in the butter and stir until the butter has swirled in entirely.

(If you are using chicken stock instead of veal stock, make a slurry with the cornstarch and 2 tablespoons of water. Mix them together well, then slowly add the slurry to the reducing sauce while whisking constantly. Once the sauce has thickened, add the butter.)

Heating the duck confit. If you are working with cold duck confit you made the day before, set a large oven-safe sauté pan over high heat. Scoop in 2 tablespoons of the duck fat and allow it to melt in the pan. Place the duck legs, skin side down, into the hot duck fat. Sear the duck legs until the bottoms are browned, about 3 minutes.

Slide the sauté pan into the oven. Cook until the duck is crisp and the internal temperature reaches 120°F, about 10 minutes.

Finishing the lentils. Nestle the sun-dried tomatoes into the cooked lentils. Shred the meat off 2 of the duck legs and mix it into the lentils. Taste the lentils and season with salt and pepper, if necessary.

To serve, swirl some sauce on the plate, place a small pile of lentils on the sauce, and perch a duck leg on top.

fettuccine with braised oxtail

VARIATIONS
You could replace the oxtail with veal or venison shanks for osso buco, or with braised chicken legs. You could use any hearty pasta that will retain its shape in this dish.

SUGGESTIONS
You could serve this over rice or mashed potatoes. If you want to make a stock with oxtail instead, that stock would make a hearty soup.

Don't be afraid of oxtail. Just knowing that it comes from the tail of a cow (it used to be the ox, but most oxtail sold in butcher's shops is from cow now) puts some people off. Have a sense of adventure and try it. Don't just stick with the same old foods. This recipe may sound intimidating, but this is really just great peasant food.

There's not a lot of meat on oxtail bones, so you might think it's not worth your time to make it. However, oxtail has a lot of muscle on it, which gets broken down when you braise it. The meat that is there falls apart and becomes gelatinous. That makes this oxtail so damned good. You only need a small amount to feel satisfied, so it's a dish rich in taste for not much price.

Plus, when you braise the oxtail, you can braise it in water or chicken stock and have a flavorful stock left over for other dishes. At Papillon, our wild mushroom raviolis bobbed in oxtail broth.

Making this recipe will take time, but that's where flavor is born. It's worth your time. • *Feeds 4*

4 oxtails, thawed
Kosher salt and cracked black pepper
4 tablespoons canola oil
1 large yellow onion, peeled and chopped
3 stalks celery, roughly chopped
1 large carrot, peeled, quartered lengthwise, and roughly chopped
5 cloves garlic, smashed and peeled
2 sprigs fresh rosemary
5 sprigs fresh thyme
2 cups full-bodied red wine

1 quart chicken stock
16 ounces uncooked gluten-free fettuccine (use store-bought pasta or the recipe for fresh gluten-free pasta on page 60)
1 large parsnip, peeled
3 tablespoons extra-virgin olive oil
2 cups quartered button mushrooms
5 large shallots, peeled and quartered
2 teaspoons finely chopped fresh rosemary
1 tablespoon butter
Parmesan cheese, for serving

Preparing to braise. Preheat the oven to 375°F. Season the oxtails with salt and pepper.

Searing the oxtail. Set a large sauté pan over medium-high heat and pour in 2 tablespoons of the canola oil. Put the oxtails in the hot oil and cook until they are browned on one side, about 5 minutes. Flip them and get some color on the other side, about 5 minutes. Place the browned oxtails in a Dutch oven.

Sautéing the vegetables. Drain the fat from the sauté pan. Pour in the remaining 2 tablespoons of canola oil. Add the onion, celery, carrot, and garlic and cook, stirring occasionally, until they have browned and softened, 10 to 15 minutes. Toss in the sprigs of rosemary and thyme and cook until they are fragrant.

Making the braising liquid. Pour in the wine to deglaze the pan, scraping up the goodness from the bottom. Cook until the wine is reduced by three-quarters of its volume, 7 to 8 minutes. Pour in the chicken stock. Bring to a boil, then reduce the heat to low and simmer for about 5 minutes. Pour the braising liquid over the oxtail in the Dutch oven. Cover the Dutch oven and slide it into the oven. Braise until the meat starts to fall of the bone, 2 to 2½ hours. Taste a piece of the meat. Do you want more? You're done.

Cooking the fettuccine. Bring a large pot of salted water to a boil. Toss in the fettuccine and cook until it is a little less than al dente so that it will hold its shape. (Gluten-free pasta usually takes less time to cook than you think, especially when you are going by the manufacturer's directions on the box.)

Preparing to make the sauce. Remove the oxtails from the sauce and set them aside. Strain the sauce into a large saucepan. Put the saucepan over medium heat and begin reducing the liquid.

Cutting the parsnips. Meanwhile, slice the parsnips into small coins, starting from the thin end. When you reach halfway up the parsnip, slice it in half lengthwise. Continue cutting coins from the parsnip, the same size as those from the first half.

Sautéing the vegetables. Set a small sauté pan over medium-high heat and pour in the olive oil. Toss in the mushrooms and cook, stirring, until softened and wilted. Throw in the parsnips and cook, stirring occasionally, until the mushrooms are browned and the parsnips are softened, 5 to 6 minutes. Toss in the shallots and cook, stirring, until they are softened, about 5 minutes. Add the chopped rosemary and cook until it is fragrant.

Making the sauce. Spoon the sautéed vegetables into the stock in the saucepan. Bring to a boil, then reduce the heat to low and simmer the sauce until it has thickened, 4 to 5 minutes. Stir in the butter until it is incorporated into the sauce.

Finishing the dish. Add the cooked pasta to the sauce. Pick the meat off the oxtails and drop it into the sauce. Taste the sauce and season it with salt and pepper.

To serve, spoon the pasta into large bowls and grate the Parmesan cheese over the top.

the opening act

There's something sturdy and dependable about the traditional dinner: a daily plate laid before us, meat at six o'clock, starch at ten o'clock, vegetables at two o'clock. But how many of those meals do you actually remember? Don't they begin to meld into one?

What I remember are tiny bites, singular experiences that stand out from the rest. Curlicues of pancetta, with a Campari and soda, on the piazza in Foligno as the sun began to set. "The first taste of crab fondue I ever ate, at Gramercy." A bowl of steaming edamame, sea salt flaked on top. The first oyster with Danny, in a ramshackle fish house on the Washington Coast. Those little cocktail wieners, wrapped in biscuits from a can—nothing better than pigs in a blanket when I was a kid. "My first bite of seared foie gras, in a tiny tart shell, with poached pear and apple butter." A long slice from a big block of Cheddar at a Vermont cheese shop. "Baked brie, so cheesy '80s, but it was my first time working at the Horseshoe with the new knives I ordered for school, and I sliced apples thin and fanned them out, and everyone was impressed." Guacamole, made to order at the table in a volcanic ash mortar, at a Mexican restaurant in Manhattan. A wedge of Cambozola at a neighborhood New Year's Eve party, with a glass of homemade eggnog. Even the Ruffles and onion dip made from a packet my brother and I ate at midnight on New Year's Eve, clinking them together and saying "Chip dip hooray!"

Little bites are sometimes the best.

Danny works hard on his appetizers for the menu. "They're a good way to stimulate the appetite, with just a few bites, and get the ball rolling. People who order appetizers, instead of simply an entrée, signal that they are settling in for the evening, for the entire experience of dining."

That's why, as opposed to my cheese and crackers or shrimp cocktail for parties, Danny puts together appetizers that have the complexity of full meals in only a few bites.

In the winter, lamb meatballs wrapped in purple Savoy cabbage with a red wine sauce. In the spring, seared sardines dusted in fennel pollen with pickled fennel and lemon zest. In the summer, butter-poached spot prawns with sweet corn and green beans. "It's simple. It's summer. You don't need much more." And in the autumn, when we are starting to long for more complex flavors, grilled quail with pancetta-wrapped figs and balsamic syrup.

I think I'll keep him.

Before I met Danny, I made appetizers for dinner parties by following recipes, meticulously. If a recipe worked once, I hewed to it for life. But watching Danny has taught me that no one ever makes a dish the same way twice. "That's one of the joys of tasting food at good restaurants—unexpected tastes buzz in my mouth, and land as ideas in the kitchen. At Pierre's, we made tuna carpaccio by wrapping the tuna loin in plastic wrap and freezing it. The next day, we sliced it on the meat slicer, super thin, and covered it with lemon juice, mustard and vinegar, extra-virgin olive oil, salt and pepper, shallots, chives, red peppers, and hearts of palm. But at Papillon, we'd hand cut the tuna loin, about two ounces each, pound the pieces out really thin, and then roll them out in plastic wrap, with a rolling pin, as thin as paper. We kept them in the cooler until an order came up. And then we'd dress them with daikon sprouts, wasabi, Thai dressing, and tomatoes. Both dishes were delightful."

Whenever I experiment with an ingredient I have never used before, I'm much more likely to play with it first in an appetizer, like chicken wings marinated overnight in yogurt, fenugreek, and cardamom, and then barbecuing with it the next day. If it's too strange, I haven't ruined dinner. (That one was good, though.)

"Making appetizers teaches you how to do the basics. Making appetizers is where you really learn how to pay attention to the food."

Danny shocked me when he told me this: nine times out

of ten, the kid making the appetizers—the pantry person or garde-manger—in a big restaurant is the least experienced.

"Working the appetizer line teaches you how to be organized. It teaches you consistency. You have to have your station set up tight because that's the first place that gets hit. You have to be ready for a good, busy night. And you have to get good at it, fast. If the restaurant gets hit at five, just when it opens, and the rest of the kitchen is helping to bail out the pantry, then once things get rolling, and orders for the hot side come in, it's going to screw everything up. Even

if the other people are totally prepared, that might throw them completely behind. You don't want to be the pantry guy at the end of that night."

In some restaurants, the pantry person has to do the dessert orders too, and make all the little garnishes, like lemon crowns and tomato roses, for the head chef to finish the dishes. That is one damned stressful job.

"That's just the beginning, sweetie. If you find you can't hack it at pantry, you're not cut out for the business."

house-cured salmon

VARIATIONS
You can change up the flavors of this salmon. Dill is only the classic choice. Play with it. You could use chervil; basil; chile peppers, to give it a kick; fennel seeds; ginger; horseradish; wasabi powder; or lemon zest. You can also do a wet cure with vodka. Mix about ½ cup of vodka with the sugar, lemon, and dill, and then coat the mixture on the salmon.

SUGGESTIONS
This goes great with scrambled eggs, works with cream cheese in a dip, or could liven up a potato hash. Anything with cured salmon and avocado is going to be fantastic. Slice the salmon as thin as possible. Put it between plastic wrap and lightly pound it out, or use a rolling pin, if you need it paper-thin.

Gravlax—the name intimidates but the food rewards the work. People think of this as a luxury food, something beyond their reach. But it's so easy. I learned to make it at culinary school, and I have been curing it ever since.

The most important ingredient in this dish is good-quality salmon. Great salmon tastes like the ocean, with a real meaty bite to it. People in the Pacific Northwest are particular about their salmon. Some of them are willing to pay thirty-four dollars a pound for Copper River salmon the six weeks it is available in Seattle. (I prefer Yukon River salmon, actually.) You want the taste of the salmon to be the strongest sensation, and the taste of salt, dill, and sugar to follow.

If you are concerned about the price of this, remember that buying a big piece of salmon from a seafood purveyor and curing it yourself is far more economical than buying vacuum-packed pieces at the grocery store. This will keep a couple of weeks in the refrigerator, and much longer if you freeze it.

Please buy wild salmon. Just say no to farm-raised fish. • *Feeds 4 (plus more, if you want)*

2 pounds wild Alaskan salmon, skin on
2 lemons, zest grated
½ cup sugar
½ cup kosher salt

2 tablespoons finely chopped fresh dill
Crackers, capers, and grated lemon zest, for serving

Removing the pinbones. The day before you plan to serve it, place the salmon on a cutting board, skin side down. Run your fingers down the flesh, rubbing as you go. The pinbones should appear at the surface of the fish. Grab each bone with needle-nose pliers. Caress the flesh of the salmon. Go slowly. Be gentle. Pull. Repeat the process, at least a few more times.

Mixing the curing ingredients. Combine the lemon zest, sugar, salt, and dill in a small bowl.

Curing the fish. Place the salmon, skin side down, on a length of plastic wrap. Cover the flesh with the salt and sugar mixture. Make sure the entire piece is covered well. (You might have some mixture left over, depending on the size of your fish. Do not use it all, because the fish will be too salty.)

Marinating the salmon. Fold the plastic wrap over the salmon, pulling it taut before you pat it down. The fish must be wrapped as tightly as possible. Flip the fish so the flesh side is down. Cover the fish with another piece of plastic wrap. Put the salmon in the refrigerator and allow it to marinate overnight.

Finishing the salmon the next day. Remove the salmon from the refrigerator and clean the sugar and salt mixture from the fish by wiping it away with paper towels. If you must rinse it, do so quickly, under cold water.

Slice the salmon as thinly as possible. Serve on crackers with capers and grated lemon zest.

seared shrimp with garlic-almond sauce

VARIATIONS
You could serve
this sauce with
scallops, grilled
chicken skewers,
or lamb kebabs.

SUGGESTIONS
The shrimp would
be great grilled.

The first time I met Sharon, Shauna's best friend for twenty-five years, was at Shauna's fortieth birthday party. That was a trip. A bunch of friends flew in for the weekend. I was nervous. Who wouldn't be? Sharon is brilliant, hilarious (she truly is a comedian), and has known Shauna every moment of their lives since they were fifteen. Oh boy.

For the first evening of the weekend, Shauna's friends gathered at my restaurant. I stayed in the kitchen, cooking, putting all my love for Shauna into the food. This dish was one of the appetizers on the menu that month. When I came out to say hello, Sharon looked up at me, pointed to this sauce, and said, "Can you just make me a vat of this so I can swim in it and eat my way out?"

Sharon and I have been friends ever since.

Marcona almonds are the best of the almond family. Roasted in extra-virgin olive oil and slicked with sea salt, they're only recently available in the United States, so they seem like a rare commodity. While they are a bit more expensive than grocery store almonds, they are worth the price of admission. When you have a dish like this that has so few ingredients, then the quality of the ingredients truly shows.

1 cup roasted Marcona almonds
3 cloves garlic
1½ teaspoons each kosher salt and
   cracked black pepper
1 cup extra-virgin olive oil

Soda water, as needed
3 tablespoons argan or grapeseed oil
16 large shrimp (16/20 count),
   peeled and deveined, tails on

Pureeing the sauce. Put the almonds, garlic, and ½ teaspoon each of the salt and pepper into a food processor. Whirl them up until a paste is formed. With the food processor running, slowly drizzle in the olive oil until a thick sauce forms. If the sauce feels too thick, add soda water until the sauce has reached the consistency you desire.

Searing the shrimp. Set a large sauté pan over medium-high heat and add the argan or grapeseed oil. Season the shrimp with the remaining 1 teaspoon of salt and pepper. Add the shrimp to the pan and sear on one side for about 1 minute. Turn them over and sear the other side for 1 minute more. Remove the pan from the heat.

To serve, place some of the almond sauce in the middle of each plate and surround the sauce with the seared shrimp.

cold roasted pork tenderloin

VARIATIONS
This would also work well with beef tenderloin.

SUGGESTIONS
If you know the source of your pork, you can roast it with a blush of pink. If you must roast this to well-done, know that it will not be as juicy. This dish works well as an appetizer, along with a salad of arugula and pea vines. It's great over rice. The chutney would be fabulous with fish tacos.

Our friend Tara Weaver would probably strangle us if she did not find this recipe here. A lifelong vegetarian, Tara dabbled with eating meat in her early thirties. This was when we first became friends with her. Eventually, her pendulum swung back, and even farther: she began gravitating toward a raw-food vegan diet. However, when she first ate a thin slice of this pork, she talked about it for days. She wrote about it in her book, *The Butcher and the Vegetarian*. She craved it for months. And if we offer more to her now, she'll eat some again.

This is a simple dish to make, but the taste combination will leave you wanting more as well. There's something smoky, a bit of dark sweetness, a touch of juniper berry with the taste of gin. It's not too salty, but just salty enough. If you buy pork tenderloin cut from a pig that has been raised with care, this will be an especially flavorful piece of meat. • *Feeds 4*

TOMATILLO CHUTNEY
1 tablespoon cumin seeds
2 tablespoons extra-virgin olive oil
1 medium yellow onion, peeled and medium diced
1 clove garlic, peeled and minced
10 tomatillos, husked and quartered
¾ cup dry white wine
¼ cup chopped fresh cilantro
1 lime, zest grated and juiced

PORK TENDERLOIN
⅓ cup plus 2 tablespoons kosher salt
⅓ cup plus 2 tablespoons muscovado sugar, packed
1½ teaspoons finely chopped fresh rosemary
1½ teaspoons finely chopped fresh sage
Small pinch ground cloves
1 juniper berry, crushed (if you can find it)
2 pork tenderloins, about 12 ounces each
3 tablespoons extra-virgin olive oil

Toasting the cumin. The day before you plan to serve the pork, set a small sauté pan over medium heat. Drop in the cumin seeds and toss gently until they become fragrant, 1 to 2 minutes. Crush the cumin seeds in a spice grinder or using a mortar and pestle. (If you don't have either, you can smash them on a cutting board with the bottom of the pan.)

Sautéing the vegetables. Set a sauté pan over medium-high heat and pour in the oil. Add the onion and garlic and cook, stirring, until the onion is softened and translucent, 2 to 3 minutes. Toss in the toasted cumin and cook until it is fragrant. Throw in the tomatillos and stir everything around, mingling the vegetables until they are completely coated.

Making the chutney. Pour in the wine to deglaze the pan, scraping up the goodness from the bottom. Reduce the heat to low and simmer, stirring occasionally so the chutney does not stick to the bottom, until the tomatillos start to soften and wilt, about 10 minutes. Add the cilantro, lime zest, and lime juice. Take the chutney off the heat and let it cool to room temperature.

Marinating the pork. In a small bowl, combine the salt, sugar, rosemary, sage, cloves, and juniper berry. Spread the spice mixture over the pork tenderloins and wrap them tightly in plastic wrap. Put the pork in the refrigerator and allow it to marinate overnight.

Roasting the pork. The next day, wipe off the marinade from the tenderloins, rubbing everything off, but do not rinse. Preheat the oven to 375°F.

Set a large sauté pan over high heat and pour in the oil. Add the tenderloins and sear until the bottoms are golden brown, about 5 minutes. Watch the meat carefully because the sugars in the marinade could burn and sear the tenderloins on both sides.

Transfer the tenderloins to a roasting pan with a rack. Roast in the oven until the internal temperature reaches 155°F, 10 to 15 minutes.

Chilling the pork and serving. Remove the tenderloins from the oven. Let them cool to room temperature, then chill completely in the refrigerator. Slice the tenderloins thin. Spoon the tomatillo chutney over the pork tenderloins.

potato-mushroom tart

VARIATIONS
You could use any fresh mushrooms you want here, but dried mushrooms will be a disappointment. You could try a Gruyère cheese instead of the Parmesan, and Manchego or pecorino would be great too.

SUGGESTIONS
You could make this as an appetizer. Or serve it with a nice little salad for a summer lunch, with a little balsamic vinaigrette or reduction sauce.

Almost everybody loves mushrooms, but most people think mushrooms means button mushrooms or those god-awful mushrooms from a can. If you haven't experienced anything but those, then portobello, or shiitake, or cremini mushrooms can seem like "wild" mushrooms.

But true wild mushrooms live in the forests. And luckily for us, at the farmers' markets. Lobster mushrooms, cauliflower mushrooms, morels, hen of the woods, matsutakes, black trumpet mushrooms in the winter. There are so many to explore.

Making this tart gives you the chance to explore. We've specified portobello mushrooms for this recipe, only because we know that folks outside of the Pacific Northwest don't have the easy access to wild mushrooms that we do. Feel free to substitute any mushroom that is in season.

Mushroom tarts are standard in classical French cuisine. But I love mushrooms and potatoes together, from their connection of having been raised in the earth. • *Feeds 8 to 10*

---

3 to 4 large portobello mushrooms
4 tablespoons extra-virgin olive oil
Kosher salt and cracked black pepper
2 cups heavy cream
10 cloves garlic, peeled, 6 of them smashed and 4 thinly sliced
2 teaspoons finely chopped fresh rosemary and thyme combined, stems set aside
1 bay leaf
Small pinch freshly grated nutmeg

3 large eggs
2 cups thickly sliced button mushrooms
3 shallots, peeled and thinly sliced
½ white part of 1 leek, thinly sliced
Kosher salt and cracked black pepper
1 Tart Shell (see page 152, minus the sugar and cinnamon), unbaked, in a tart shell pan
3 medium russet potatoes, peeled and grated, squeezed to remove excess water
¼ cup freshly grated Parmesan cheese

Preparing the portobellos. Preheat the oven to 450°F. Stem the portobellos and remove the gills. Toss with 2 tablespoons of the oil and some salt and pepper. Place on a baking sheet and bake the mushrooms until they are sizzling and beginning to wilt, 5 to 6 minutes.

Heating the cream. Combine the cream, the smashed garlic cloves, ½ teaspoon each of salt and pepper, the stems of the rosemary and thyme, the bay leaf, and the nutmeg in a large saucepan over medium heat and cook, stirring, until the cream boils. Take the pan off the heat and allow the cream to steep for 2 to 3 minutes.

Tempering the eggs. In a bowl, whisk the eggs together. Pour ½ cup of the cream mixture into the eggs, whisking continuously. When that mixture is fully combined, slowly pour the remaining cream mixture into the eggs, whisking continuously. Pour the custard through a strainer and set it aside.

(continued on next page)

Sautéing the mushrooms. Set a large sauté pan over high heat and pour in the remaining 2 tablespoons of oil. Toss in the button mushrooms. Cook, stirring occasionally, until they have a good brown color, about 5 minutes. Add the shallots, leek, and sliced garlic and cook, stirring, until everything is softened and translucent, about 5 minutes. Toss in the chopped rosemary and thyme and cook until they release their fragrance, about 2 minutes. Stir everything up. Season with salt and pepper. Set aside to allow the mushrooms to cool.

Blind baking the tart shell at 375°F. See page 153 for instructions. Keep the oven on after the shell is baked.

Combining everything together. Combine the mushroom mixture and the custard. Toss in the potatoes and Parmesan cheese and mix to combine. Season with salt and pepper.

Baking the tart. Pour the mushroom and custard mixture into the prebaked tart shell. Carefully arrange the portobellos in a circle in the middle of the tart shell. Bake until the center of the tart is set, 35 to 40 minutes. Poke the custard in the center of the tart with a sharp knife, through the portobellos; the knife should come out clean. You should be able to jiggle the pan and not see any movement, and the tart should be tanned, but not entirely browned.

Cooling the tart. Take the tart out of the oven and let it cool in the pan on a wire rack until it has reached room temperature, about 1 hour. Remove the outer ring from the tart shell pan before serving.

gluten-free baking

Gluten-free baking is not like your mother's baking. Traditional baking is elastic and easy. You can stretch pizza dough, form air pockets in crusty bread, and make cookies in ten minutes without thinking too much.

But gluten-free baking, at first, seems far more difficult. You know why? There's no gluten in it.

However, if you give yourself some patient time to play, you'll figure it out. We have. Don't expect gluten-free baked goods to match the taste and texture of the original. Let them be themselves. Some of those treats might taste better to you than those with gluten flours, like banana bread with teff. Some baked goods might never match your conception of them, but does that mean you give up? What are you going to do, go without muffins the rest of your life?

You might need to add a bit more protein (an extra egg white, a splash of milk), as well as a binder like xanthan gum, to replace the gluten in a recipe. We usually use 1 teaspoon of xanthan gum plus ¼ teaspoon of guar gum for each cup of flour.

Sift each flour before you combine them all in a bowl, and then sift them again before you bake. This makes the final mixture one coherent flour.

Cookies, crisps, quick breads, and pie doughs are fairly easy to make gluten-free. Pie doughs are actually easier to make without gluten, because you can't overwork the crust, and you can just pat any spare pieces into the pan when you are done.

Refrigerate pie doughs, cinnamon roll dough, and cookies before you bake them. They need to rest for at least an hour, and ideally overnight. Let them sit out a bit before you work with them, to make the dough more pliable.

Be gentle with the doughs. The first time you roll out a gluten-free dough, it's not going to do what you want it to do.

When you make gluten-free cookies, don't overcream the butter and sugars. Mix them until they are just combined. This helps prevent spreading.

The hardest baked goods to make gluten-free are those that require a certain structure: some cakes, bread, puff pastry, croissants. Those are where gluten is especially necessary. We're still working on those. That doesn't mean you will never eat bread again. We make bread from the recipe in this book three times a week. But just expect a lot of interesting mishaps at first. You'll want to blame the recipe if it all goes woppy-jawed. Keep trying.

If you bake by weight instead of by volume[md]measuring out grams or ounces instead of scooping flours into a cup[md]your baking will be more successful and satisfying. Buy yourself a kitchen scale and start baking.

In short, you will have to do some tasks differently, creating new muscle memory, and playing with different ingredients than you did before. However, once you have learned, it will all feel familiar. Shauna bakes nearly every day for our web site, learning all the time. This just feels like baking to us both.

dinner service begins

Before I met Danny, I sometimes sat in a packed restaurant at 8 p.m. and wondered why it was taking so long to get my food.

You want to know what it's like right in the middle of dinner service?

"I'm at the sauté station. Frank is expediting, calling out orders: 'Okay, I'm going up on table sixty-five. We're going to need a rack of lamb and sauce for the rack of lamb. We also have a mixed seafood, so I need seafood for that, and the mixed seafood sauce, plus a halibut.' I put my head down and get to work.

"Past Frank, the grill guy is grilling lamb, salmon, swordfish, New York steaks, and veal chops. The pasta guy is making pastas, heating up lobster tail, and finishing asparagus risotto to order. It is loud in that kitchen, so the grill guy can't hear everything. The pasta guy has to look at the tickets and tell him.

"The people in the middle are working as a cohesive unit. One guy grabs the first bag of potatoes and puts dollops on the plates. The second guy puts down the deep-fried potato baskets. The guy with the pastry bag loops back around and fills the baskets with the mashed potatoes. The second guy follows behind and ladles butter sauce over the mashed potatoes. Boom boom boom. The first guy comes back around, grabs the sauté pan of the vegetable of the day, and fills the plates with the vegetables.

"I turn around and see all the burners full, the heat on my face, the spices on the shelf above me. There is nothing in my head except for the work that is before me.

"The grill guy passes down the sauté pan with the duck breast, sausage, and swordfish for the mixed grill.

"Frank picks up the pan of sweetbreads and a pan of sauce from me, tasting before he takes them to the plates. He puts the sweetbreads and sauce on the mixed grill plate, along with Cabernet lentils finished with chives. And then we finish the mixed seafood, the rack of lamb, and the halibut special the same way.

"And then everything comes together. Time to send out that table.

"I look up and watch the order tickets come out of the printer, loop up, and over, and hit the floor. Another 123 people to feed.

"This continues throughout the entire night."

• •

I have learned to never call him during dinner service.

crab cakes with shrimp mousse and avocado

VARIATIONS
Maryland lump crab would work well here too. But do not use imitation crabmeat here. Please.

SUGGESTIONS
These crab cakes go well with coleslaw or pickled cabbage.

Crab is one of my favorite foods of all time, along with avocado and artichokes. In fact, every year for my birthday, Shauna finds a way to combine those three foods for my birthday meal. You would think, therefore, that I would insist on nothing but crab in my crab cake.

I learned to make crab cakes with shrimp mousse at Papillon, the large French-Asian restaurant in Denver where I was the sous chef. We made crab cakes right and left at that place, at least sixty orders a night. Adding shrimp mousse is a way of stretching the crab, because shrimp isn't as expensive. However, it's more than a way to save money. The shrimps puff up in the cooking, which makes the crab cakes fluffy. Shrimp sweetens the crab a bit more too, giving this an unexpected flavor.

It's almost sacrilege to say in Seattle, but I prefer crab cakes with shrimp instead of standing alone. • *Feeds 4*

½ **pound shrimp, peeled and deveined, tails removed**
1½ **cups heavy cream**
½ **pound Dungeness crabmeat, shells carefully removed**
2 **cups gluten-free breadcrumbs**
2 **teaspoons mayonnaise (use homemade, if you can, or at least full-fat jarred mayonnaise)**

2 **teaspoons fresh lemon juice**
1 **tablespoon chopped fresh dill**
½ **teaspoon cayenne pepper**
Kosher salt and cracked black pepper
3 **tablespoons extra-virgin olive oil**
2 **ripe Hass avocados, tender yet firm to the touch**

Preheating the oven. Turn the oven to 450°F.

Making the shrimp mousse. Puree the shrimp in a food processor. With the food processor still running, slowly add the cream until the mixture is light and fluffy. Throw in half of the crabmeat and process again. Remove the mousse and place it in a large bowl. In a bowl, combine 1 tablespoon of the breadcrumbs with the mayonnaise. Fold this mixture into the shrimp mousse. Pour in the lemon juice. Sprinkle in the dill, cayenne pepper, salt, and pepper. Toss in the rest of the crabmeat and gently fold all the ingredients together; do not overmix.

Making a taster. Scoop a bit of the shrimp and crab mixture into your hands and form it into a cake. Coat the cake with enough breadcrumbs to cover. Set a large oven-safe sauté pan over medium-high heat and pour in 1 tablespoon of the oil. Put the crab cake in the hot oil and cook until the bottom is a crisp brown. Slide the pan into the oven and allow the crab cake to cook until it puffs up and looks good enough to eat, 4 to 5 minutes. Taste the crab cake. It should have just a tiny bit of heat and a smidge of dill and lemon juice. The crab should be the dominant taste. Adjust the seasonings according to your desires.

(continued on next page)

Making the rest of the cakes. Once you have the mousse seasoned to your taste, form the rest of the cakes; they should be about the size of the top of a pint glass, or 3 ounces each if you have a kitchen scale. Dip each crab cake into the breadcrumbs to coat.

Set the large sauté pan over medium-high heat again and add enough oil to coat the bottom of the pan. Place the cakes in the hot oil and cook until browned on the bottom. Flip them over and slide the pan into the oven. The cakes are done when they have a firm yet spongy texture with crisp brown outsides.

To serve, slice up the avocados and season them with salt. Place the slices over the top of each crab cake.

chicken braised in red wine

VARIATIONS
Instead of green beans, you could cook whatever green vegetable you are hankering for.

SUGGESTIONS
Serve this with roasted potatoes, mashed potatoes, or jasmine rice.

You might think of this dish as coq au vin, but technically coq au vin is made with an old rooster. The name doesn't matter so much—this chicken is still good. You're not going to see it served in the hippest restaurants of the moment. But it has been made for generations for a reason. Tender and juicy, with the robust flavor of red wine, this is comfort food at its best. It's deeply satisfying to eat.

And it's satisfying to make. You might be intimidated by all the ingredients and steps, but don't be. This is a good lazy-afternoon dish. Take your time. Don't rush, because that's where you'll burn the chicken or overcook the vegetables, and then you're screwed. If you cook to be done as quickly as possible, your food won't taste as good as this long-afternoon dish will. Make this a project, a chance to learn. • *Feeds 4*

2 whole chickens, broken down (if buying this in parts, use breasts and legs)
4 large carrots, peeled and chopped
2 stalks celery, chopped
2 large yellow onions, peeled and chopped
5 large cloves garlic, peeled
One 750-ml bottle Burgundy
Kosher salt and cracked black pepper
5 tablespoons extra-virgin olive oil
1 sprig fresh rosemary, roughly chopped

3 sprigs fresh sage, roughly chopped
1 tablespoon tomato paste
1 bay leaf
3 quarts chicken stock
4 slices smoked bacon, finely diced
1 cup peeled pearl onions
2 cups quartered button mushrooms
2 tablespoons finely chopped fresh thyme
1 cup green beans, topped and tailed
2 tablespoons cold unsalted butter

Marinating the chicken. The day before you plan to serve, if you are breaking down whole chickens, separate out the breasts and entire legs. Set aside the rest of the carcass to make a stock. If you have bought breasts and legs in separate packages, pull those out now. Put the chicken parts in a large bowl. Throw the carrots, celery, onions, and garlic into the chicken bowl. Pour in the wine. Cover with plastic wrap and refrigerate overnight.

Starting the next day. Preheat the oven to 425°F. Remove the chicken legs from the marinade. Place them on paper towels and pat them dry. Strain the wine into a large saucepan over medium heat and begin reducing it, skimming the scum from the surface as it arises.

Searing the chicken legs. Season the legs with salt and pepper on all sides. Set a Dutch oven over high heat. Pour in 2 tablespoons of the oil. Add all the chicken legs to the oil and sear on one side until they have formed a golden brown crust, 4 to 5 minutes. Turn them over and sear them on all sides. Remove them from the Dutch oven and set aside.

(continued on next page)

Sautéing the vegetables. Pour 1 tablespoon of the oil into the Dutch oven over medium heat. Add the carrots, celery, onions, and garlic to the hot oil and cook, stirring occasionally, until they are browned and softened, about 15 minutes. Throw in the rosemary and sage and cook until they become fragrant. Stir in the tomato paste until all the vegetables are coated. Add the bay leaf.

Making the braising liquid. Pour the reduced wine and the chicken stock into the Dutch oven. Bring to a boil. Add the chicken legs to the liquid. Place the lid on the Dutch oven and slide it into the oven. Cook until the internal temperature of the legs reaches 185°F, 35 to 45 minutes.

Rendering the bacon. While the chicken is cooking, put the bacon slices in another sauté pan over medium heat. When the slices are crisp, remove them from the pan and set them aside. Toss the pearl onions into the bacon fat in the pan and cook over medium heat until they are softened and almost caramelized, 15 to 20 minutes. Drop in the mushrooms and cook, stirring, until they are softened and wilted. Throw in the thyme and cook until it is fragrant. Season everything with salt and pepper—go easy because of the bacon. Take the pan off the heat.

Making the sauce. When the chicken legs have reached the right temperature, remove them from the braising liquid. (Keep the oven on at 375°F.) Strain the sauce and throw away the vegetables. Return the sauce to the Dutch oven and cook until it is reduced by half its volume, about 20 minutes.

Searing the chicken breasts. Meanwhile, set a large sauté pan over high heat and pour in the remaining 2 tablespoons of oil. Put the chicken breasts, skin side down, in the oil and cook them until the skin is crisp and golden, 3 to 4 minutes. Flip over the breasts and slide them into the oven. Roast until the internal temperature near the wing reaches 155°F, 10 to 15 minutes.

Cooking the green beans. Cut the green beans in half. Put the sauté pan with the onion and mushroom mixture back over medium heat. When the sauce is almost entirely reduced, throw the green beans into the sauté pan. Cook until the green beans are bright green in color but still crisp, 2 to 3 minutes. Take the pan off the heat.

Finishing the sauce. Drop the butter into the sauce and stir until it has become one with the sauce.

To serve, on each plate, ladle out enough sauce to cover the bottom of the plate. Make a mound of the vegetables. Arrange the chicken on top, with the meaty part of the breast facing up.

prosciutto-wrapped king salmon with wild mushroom risotto

VARIATIONS
This dish would work with other kinds of salmon, such as Coho or sockeye. You want a thick piece. If you don't want to eat pork, you could try wrapping this in grape leaves, which would work best on the grill. Of course, you can use any wild mushrooms in season for the risotto.

SUGGESTIONS
Keep the salmon rare to medium-rare for this fish.

There is no other mushroom like the morel. Earthy and smoky, with a lovely nutty flavor, morels sprout up wild from April to June. Their fleeting season makes them expensive, but they're worth it. You only need a handful of morels to flavor an entire dish. Their architectural texture relaxes in the heat of the risotto, releasing the rich smell of the woods.

Wild Alaskan salmon appears in the markets at the same time as morels around here. King salmon, sometimes called Chinook, is the most sought-after salmon: rich pink running to red, thick, and tender with a heft. We don't eat farmed salmon—you should know that "organic" salmon is always going to be farmed; you cannot categorize a wild fish—and so we wait, all year, for Alaskan salmon to appear.

We long for both fresh morels and Alaskan salmon all year long. When they appear, we celebrate by preparing this dish. • *Feeds 4*

WILD MUSHROOM RISOTTO
4 tablespoons extra-virgin olive oil
1 tablespoon unsalted butter
2 cups morels
1 medium yellow onion, peeled and finely diced
2 cloves garlic, peeled and chopped
1 tablespoon finely chopped fresh thyme
1 cup Arborio rice
½ cup white wine
1½ quarts mushroom stock (recipe follows), hot

Kosher salt and cracked black pepper
½ cup freshly grated Parmesan cheese

PROSCIUTTO-WRAPPED KING SALMON
4 fillets wild king salmon, about 6 ounces each, skin removed
12 slices prosciutto
3 tablespoons extra-virgin olive oil
1 teaspoon each kosher salt and cracked black pepper

Starting the risotto. Set a large saucepan over medium heat and pour in 1 tablespoon of the oil and the butter. Add the morels to the hot oil and butter and cook, stirring occasionally, until they soften and release their fragrance, 3 to 5 minutes. Add the onion and garlic and cook, stirring occasionally, until the onion is soft and translucent, about 10 minutes. Add the thyme and cook for 1 minute more.

Coating the rice. Toss in the Arborio rice and cook, stirring occasionally, until all the grains are entirely coated, about 2 minutes. Pour in the wine and cook, pushing the rice slowly in the pan, until the liquid is reduced by half its volume, about 5 minutes.

Adding the stock. At this point, pour the mushroom stock into the rice, 1 cup at a time, stirring gently. Stir and stir until the stock is absorbed into the rice. When the liquid is absorbed, but not dry, add more stock. Continue this process until all the stock is absorbed.

(continued on next page)

Making the risotto creamy. Taste the rice. It should have no crunch to it. Instead, it should be chewy and soft, without being mushy. Taste the risotto and season with salt and pepper, if necessary. Toss in the remaining 3 tablespoons of oil and the Parmesan cheese. Stir gently until everything is fully incorporated. Place the lid on the saucepan and allow the risotto to sit, covered, for 2 minutes, which will make the risotto beautifully creamy. Keep the risotto off to the side while you prepare the salmon.

Preheating the oven. Turn the oven to 450°F.

Preparing the salmon. Wrap each salmon fillet in 3 slices of the prosciutto.

Searing the salmon. Set a large oven-safe sauté pan over medium-high heat. Pour in the oil. Season the salmon with salt and pepper. Put the salmon, with the seam of the prosciutto down, into the hot oil. Sear the salmon until the prosciutto is browned, 3 to 4 minutes. Flip over the fish. Slide the pan into the oven. Cook the salmon until the internal temperature reaches 100°F to 120°F, depending on your preference, 5 to 7 minutes.

Bring the risotto back up to heat and serve with the salmon.

mushroom stock

• *Makes 1 ½ quarts*

2 tablespoons extra-virgin olive oil
2 pounds button mushrooms, roughly chopped
2 portobello mushrooms, roughly chopped
½ large carrot, peeled and roughly chopped
1 medium yellow onion, peeled and
  roughly chopped
2 stalks celery, peeled and chopped

5 cloves garlic, peeled
2 sprigs fresh rosemary
½ bunch fresh thyme
3 sprigs fresh sage
½ cup sherry
¼ cup dried mushrooms
  (whatever type you want)

Sautéing the vegetables. Set a medium stockpot over medium-high heat and pour in the oil. Add the button and portobello mushrooms, carrot, onion, celery, and garlic to the hot oil and cook, stirring, until they are softened and almost caramelized, but not burnt, 10 to 15 minutes. Toss in the rosemary, thyme, and sage and cook until they release their fragrance.

Deglazing the pan. Pour the sherry into the pot, scraping up all the goodness from the bottom. Cook until the sherry is reduced by half its volume. Add the dried mushrooms.

Making the stock. Pour in 2 quarts of water. Bring the stock to a boil, then turn the heat down to medium-low and simmer for 30 minutes. Turn off the heat and let the stock sit for 20 minutes. Strain the stock and keep hot for using in the risotto.

trout with almonds, grapes, quinoa, and kale with a lemon-marjoram vinaigrette

VARIATIONS
This dish also works well with salmon, halibut, flounder, or rockfish in place of the trout. You can use tarragon, basil, or cilantro in place of the marjoram. Instead of grapes, try orange slices or finely diced apples. And instead of the kale, try haricot verts or purslane in the summer.

SUGGESTIONS
This is a great grilled fish, if the trout is firm. You could also bake it or poach it.

My head chef in Breckenridge, Pierre, did pan-seared trout with lemon-marjoram butter and boiled potatoes. There were times when we had couscous on the menu, and I would make a small snack with couscous, adding a few grapes, lemon butter, and a sprig of marjoram. And I'd be hunky-dory. I couldn't make a piece of trout for myself. I would have been yelled at, for the expense. But the flavor combination stayed in my mind.

I had never eaten quinoa before I met Shauna. I had never even heard of it. When I first cooked it, I immediately thought, This is a nice substitute for couscous. I really love couscous, but I want to share my food with Shauna. So I started cooking quinoa.

Quinoa is not like couscous, which you can cover with water and walk away from while it cooks. You have to pay attention and be gentle with it. A few stirs help it to absorb the water. You can make it savory or sweet. We sometimes eat it for breakfast, steeped in spiced milk, with dried strawberries and fresh pears.

If you find you have leftover vinaigrette after making this recipe, drizzle some on grilled salmon, roast chicken, or on top of brown rice with sunflower seeds. • *Feeds 4*

LEMON-MARJORAM VINAIGRETTE
¼ cup fresh lemon juice
1 tablespoon chopped fresh marjoram
1 tablespoon finely chopped shallots
¾ cup grapeseed or canola oil
Kosher salt and cracked black pepper

QUINOA AND TROUT
¼ cup sliced almonds
2 cups red or ivory quinoa

Kosher salt and cracked black pepper
8 fillets rainbow or ruby red trout, about 4 ounces each, skin on
10 tablespoons extra-virgin olive oil
3 tablespoons finely chopped shallots
1 bunch kale leaves, picked from the stems and torn into pieces
½ lemon, juiced
1½ cups red or green seedless grapes

Preparing the vinaigrette. Combine the lemon juice, marjoram, and shallots in a medium bowl. Whisk them together, and then slowly drizzle in the grapeseed or canola oil, whisking the entire time. Taste the vinaigrette and season it with salt and pepper, if necessary.

Toasting the almonds. Preheat the oven to 350°F. Place the almonds in a small oven-safe sauté pan. Slide the pan into the oven and toast the almonds, tossing them a few times, until they are browned, 10 to 15 minutes; do not burn them. Set the almonds aside.

Cooking the quinoa. Fill a large saucepan with salted water and bring to a boil. Pour in the quinoa and cook, stirring occasionally, until it becomes softened and almost translucent, 10 to 15 minutes. The grain, when fully cooked, will burst with a tiny white ring around the middle. Strain the quinoa. Taste it and season with salt and pepper, if necessary. Set aside and keep warm.

Pan-roasting the trout. Season the trout with salt and pepper on both sides. Cut the fillets in half, cutting diagonally in the middle of the fish. Set 2 large sauté pans over high heat and pour 4 tablespoons of the olive oil in each pan. Put each trout fillet, skin side down, in the hot oil, moving the fish around a bit so it doesn't stick. As the trout cooks, its color will turn from dark to orange-ish, from the bottom of the fish up. When the orange color reaches the top, flip the fillets and turn off the heat in both pans.

Cooking the kale. Set another large sauté pan over medium heat. Pour in the remaining 2 tablespoons of olive oil. Add the shallots to the hot oil and cook, stirring, until they are soft and translucent, 2 to 3 minutes. Toss in the kale and cook, stirring, until it starts to wilt. Season with salt and pepper. Continue cooking until the kale has wilted, 2 to 3 minutes more. Add a bit of lemon juice and remove the kale from the heat.

To serve, place a mound of quinoa on each plate. Cover it with the kale. Place the fish on top, at an angle. Scatter the grapes around the dish and drizzle with the vinaigrette.

main dishes and dishwashers

After Danny and I fell in love, I started meeting everyone who is important to him. His friends, cousins, even his parents—none of them intimidated me as much as meeting Hortensia. When Danny calls me from the restaurant in a good mood, I know it is because (a) the food is going well and (b) he and Hortensia are joking around. If she comes to work in a foul mood, nothing can shake him from the worry that she is going to quit and go back to Mexico, or that she is angry with him.

"She knows me. She doesn't speak much English, but she always knows what is going on. She looks at the board and knows what needs to be fired. If I am out in the dining room talking to customers, and an order comes in, she starts firing. I wouldn't know what to do without her."

When I finally did meet Hortensia, we were both shy. It is quite clear we are the two most important women in his life. Luckily, I took one look at her—compact strength, her hair wet with sweat at the end of the evening, sharp bright eyes—and felt at ease. She looked at me with a shy smile. We giggled. Within a few moments, we were making fun of Danny, together. He beamed.

"I've had chefs I've respected deeply, fellow guys and women on the line who are my friends. But you know the people I respect the most in a restaurant? The dishwashers. Dishwashers are God's gift to the restaurant business."

I didn't realize this before I met Danny—dishwashers do far more than wash dishes.

"The night dishwashers at Papillon were responsible for peeling and cutting all the potatoes, in gallon buckets. Then they made the raviolis, with wonton skins, three hotel pans full. The dishwashers made the tomato concassé, washed all the greens, cut up the romaine, and made the crab cakes. They put away all the produce orders. They did most of the prep. And then they cleaned the front of the house and vac-uumed the carpets. During dinner service, they scrubbed stacks of hot sauté pans, polished all the glasses, and did dishes all night long, six days a week."

Danny's childhood friend, Hoa, came to the States from Vietnam with his mother when he was eleven. In order to make enough money to bring Hoa's older sisters to this country, his mother worked two to three jobs at all times. In the late afternoons and evenings, she washed dishes at several of the restaurants at the ski resort. Hoa helped her after his basketball games were over. It took a decade for her to bring her daughters to the States.

"Most dishwashers I worked with came across the border to get the job, living in a two-bedroom apartment with five to six other people. To them, being a dishwasher is not just about washing the dishes. It's their livelihood. They probably have another job on the side. The money they save buys a tractor back home. They are only here for their families.

"Some of them are probably here illegally, but no one ever asks. Most of the owners pay them cash, under the table. One of the dishwashers I worked with, for a couple of years, came by to say good-bye on his last day. I said, 'It was good to work with you, Raphael.'

"He shuffled his feet and said, 'Actually, my name is José.'

"He had lied about his name the entire time, because he was afraid that we would turn him in."

Never once, in all the years that I have eaten in restaurants, did I think about the dishwashers prepping my meal and washing my dishes. When I raved about a restaurant to friends, I only talked about the fabulous entrée and the genius chef who swirled the sauce on it.

Now that I know more about restaurants and eat his food every day, I still think Danny is amazing. But without Hortensia, he wouldn't be the chef he is.

poussin with red quinoa and rhubarb

VARIATIONS
You can do this with roasted chicken breast or quail instead of poussins. You can substitute chicken stock for the veal stock.

SUGGESTIONS
You can stuff the quail with already-cooked quinoa and rhubarb.

Rhubarb reminds me of my childhood. The rhubarb plant on the side of our yard didn't come to life until midsummer, but did we have some rhubarb down there. Every year, the plant grew bigger. My mom made rhubarb pies all summer, but I used to cut off a stalk, pour sugar on it, and eat it raw. Rhubarb is botanically a vegetable. That's why it works in savory dishes, where it offers crunch and a little zip.

I like the red quinoa with rhubarb. The nutty taste complements the rhubarb, and the white part of the rhubarb echoes the white stripe around the cooked quinoa. Poussin are little chickens, less than twenty-eight days old, sometimes called spring chickens. My French head chef in Breckenridge, who often got words wrong, used to yell at all of us young cooks, "You chicken spring!"

I always laugh when I make poussin, thinking of this. • *Feeds 4*

1 cup red quinoa
Kosher salt and cracked black pepper
4 poussins
10 tablespoons extra-virgin olive oil

One-half 750-ml bottle Madeira
2 cups veal stock (see page 148)
1 tablespoon unsalted butter
2 stalks rhubarb, large diced

Cooking the quinoa. Add 1½ cups of water and 1 teaspoon of salt to a medium pot and bring to a boil. Pour in the quinoa and cook, stirring occasionally, until it is softened and almost translucent; small white rings will appear in the middle of each grain when the quinoa is cooked. Drain the quinoa. Taste it and season with salt and pepper, if necessary. Set aside and keep warm.

Preheating the oven. Turn the oven to 500°F.

Roasting the poussins. Season the poussins with salt and pepper on all sides and smear them with 8 tablespoons of the oil. Place 2 poussins into a large oven-safe sauté pan, breast side up, and repeat with another sauté pan. Slide the pans into the hot oven and roast until the skin begins to brown, about 5 minutes. Turn the heat down to 400°F. Roast the poussins until the internal temperature of the legs reaches 180°F, 10 to 15 minutes. Take the poussins out of the oven and transfer them to a plate. Set aside.

Making the sauce. Pour the grease from the sauté pans and place them over medium heat. Pour half of the Madeira into each sauté pan and scrape the crispy bits from the bottom of each pan with a spatula. Cook until the Madeira in each pan is reduced by about half its volume, 6 to 8 minutes. Pour the Madeira from one sauté pan into the other. Pour in the veal stock. Cook until the liquid is reduced by half its volume, about 5 minutes. Swirl in the butter, cooking until it is fully incorporated into the sauce. Taste the sauce and season with salt and pepper, if necessary.

Sautéing the rhubarb. While the sauce is reducing, set a small sauté pan over medium-high heat. Pour in the remaining 2 tablespoons of oil. Add the rhubarb to the hot oil and cook until it begins to soften, about 5 minutes. Stir the sautéed rhubarb into the quinoa.

To serve, make a small mound of the quinoa and rhubarb on the plate, perch the poussin on top, and drizzle with the sauce.

black cod in black rice flour

VARIATIONS
Halibut in season would be great in place of black cod, and scallops in black rice flour always produce gasps. Generally, a thick white fish is good for the contrast. However, ahi tuna is pretty spectacular in black rice flour as well.

SUGGESTIONS
This dish goes well with a bok choy risotto.

Six weeks after Shauna and I met, she left for two weeks in Alaska. It nearly killed us both to be away from each other. But we got a fish special out of it.

One evening when she was in Alaska, Shauna told me about visiting the home of friends in Sitka, whose father is a commercial fisherman. Above the mantelpiece hung an enormous dead, stuffed fish, with its mouth gaping open. It wasn't pretty—there were weird gills and an angular beak to it—but it was magnificent, in its own ugly way. When Shauna asked the teenage girls about it, they said, "Oh, that's a black cod." Their father trolled for the enormous fish later in the summer.

The next day, I saw black cod at University Seafood. I'd just picked up a bag of Italian black rice as well. That night, I ground the rice into flour and dredged the thick fish in it. The pearly purple crust against the gleaming white flesh made a startling image.

As soon as Shauna returned home, I made this dish for her. Whenever we eat it, we remember Alaska. • *Feeds 4*

½ cup Italian venere black rice
4 fillets black cod, about 6 ounces each,
   at least 1 inch thick, skin removed

Kosher salt and cracked black pepper
2 tablespoons extra-virgin olive oil
2 tablespoons unsalted butter

Preheating the oven. Turn the oven to 450°F.

Grinding the rice into flour. Grind the black rice until it's a pearly gray-purple flour. A spice grinder will work just fine and a strong blender will work even better. Sift the black rice flour to remove any bigger bits of rice.

Dredging and searing the fish. Season both sides of the cod fillets with salt and pepper. Dredge each fillet in the black rice flour, coating only the side that did not have skin. Shake off the excess.

Set a large oven-safe sauté pan over medium-high heat, then add the oil and butter to the pan. When the butter is foaming, but not yet brown, add the fish to the pan, flour side down, and shake the pan around a bit so the fish doesn't stick. Cook until the rice flour forms a crust, 2 to 3 minutes. Flip over the fish and slide the pan into the oven. Cook the fish until the internal temperature reaches 120°F, 5 to 6 minutes.

braised balsamic rabbit

VARIATIONS
You could make this dish with chicken, if you wish.

SUGGESTIONS
This braised rabbit goes well with the Potato-Mushroom Tart (see page 199) or a watercress salad. It is best served hot.

Rabbit rocks. Everyone assumes it tastes like chicken, but I think it tastes a bit gamier. (That's good.) I first cooked rabbit at a luxury ski resort in Colorado, where we grilled the rabbit loin, braised the leg, and served the rabbit in its natural juices. Later, at Pierre's in Breckenridge, we braised rabbit in red wine and served it with lardons and boiled potatoes. And at Cassis in Seattle, I made rabbit with mustard hundreds of times.

It's not typical to braise rabbit in balsamic. Mostly, rabbit is braised in red wine, white wine, or mustard. But I played with the vinegar because balsamic has a syrupy sweetness that goes well with the faint sweetness of rabbit meat. Find an authentic young balsamic for this recipe. You're going to use a full cup here, and it would be a shame to waste the twenty-five-year-old bottle you bought in Italy on your honeymoon. • *Feeds 4*

2 rabbits, broken down into front and hind legs, and saddle/loin
Kosher salt and cracked black pepper
4 tablespoons canola oil
1 medium yellow onion, peeled and medium diced
1 leek, white part only, chopped

5 cloves garlic, smashed and peeled
4 to 5 sprigs fresh thyme, chopped
$\frac{1}{4}$ cup dry white wine
1 cup balsamic vinegar
2 quarts chicken stock
2 tablespoons unsalted butter

Preheating the oven. Turn the oven to 375°F.

Searing the rabbit. Season the rabbit pieces with salt and pepper. Set a large sauté pan over medium-high heat, then pour in 2 tablespoons of the oil. Place the rabbit legs in the hot oil, making sure not to crowd the pan. Sear until they are browned on all sides and transfer to a deep roasting pan. Sear the rest of the rabbit pieces in the same fashion and transfer them all to the roasting pan. Drain all the grease.

Sautéing the vegetables. Add the remaining 2 tablespoons of oil to the sauté pan and turn down the heat to medium. Add the onion and leek and cook, stirring occasionally, until they are browned and almost caramelized, 15 to 20 minutes; pay attention so they do not burn. Add the garlic and thyme and cook, stirring, until it is fragrant, about 2 minutes.

Making the braising liquid. Pour in the wine and vinegar and scrape up the goodness from the bottom of the pan. Cook until the liquid is reduced by half its volume, about 5 minutes. Pour in the chicken stock and bring to a boil.

Braising the rabbit. Pour the hot liquid over the rabbit. Cover the roasting pan with aluminum foil, leaving one of the edges loose so you can check the rabbit without burning yourself. Place the roasting pan on a burner turned to high. Bring the liquid back to a boil, checking through the loose edge of the aluminum foil. Slide the roasting pan into the oven. Cook until you can take tongs to the legs, squeeze, and the meat will fall off the bone, $1\frac{1}{2}$ to 2 hours.

Making the sauce. Lift the rabbit gently from the sauce with a slotted spoon. Remove any vegetables that cling to the rabbit pieces. Strain the sauce and throw away the vegetables. Pour the sauce into a medium saucepan and cook it over medium-high heat, skimming any fat that comes to the surface. Cook until it is reduced by half its volume, 15 to 20 minutes. Dip a spoon into the sauce. If you can run your finger down the back of the spoon and no sauce runs into that space, then your sauce is done. Whisk in the butter until it is incorporated into the sauce. Taste the sauce and season with salt and pepper.

To serve, place a piece of saddle and a front and hind leg, or half a rabbit, on each plate. Spoon the sauce over the rabbit.

pan-roasted rib-eye chop with potato-artichoke gratin

VARIATIONS
You can use artichoke hearts in a jar, if you need to save time. If you are allergic to eggs, you can make this without the egg whites. The gratin will not hold together as well, but it will still taste great.

SUGGESTIONS
If you don't have a barbecue, or want to make this in the middle of the winter, you can sear the steaks in a very hot pan and then slide them into a 450°F oven and cook until the internal temperature reaches 145°F to 150°F, about 10 minutes.

When most people think of rib eyes, they think of giant pieces of meat on the plates before them, with no accompaniment but the juices. Shauna once ate at a steakhouse in South Dakota where there were paper tablecloths, sawdust on the floor, and cows grazing just outside the window. They served her a rib eye so big that she ate the leftovers for breakfast, lunch, and dinner the next day. (And the only accompaniment was a giant orange piece of Texas toast.)

I just think of this scene in *The Great Outdoors*, where John Candy tried to eat a piece of beef the size of his head and couldn't do it. Meat shouldn't be eaten like that. Don't let a rib eye scare you. This cut of meat, from the rib between the short loin and the chuck, can be tremendously tender without being titanic.

Artichokes and potatoes are two of my favorite foods. Why not put them together? Artichokes, like the size of rib eyes, can be intimidating. But there's something satisfying about cutting them down yourself and eating the fresh heart. If it's early summer, and the smell of mesquite smoke and charred rare meat is coming off the grill, this is what I'm having. • *Feeds 4*

POTATO-ARTICHOKE GRATIN
2 cups heavy cream
1 small sprig fresh rosemary
2 cloves garlic, smashed and peeled
3 large russet potatoes, peeled and sliced
  ¼ inch thick
2 large artichokes, trimmed, heart removed
  and thinly sliced (see page 220)
Kosher salt and cracked black pepper

2 large egg whites, lightly beaten
1 cup freshly grated Parmesan cheese

RIB EYES
4 beef rib eyes, about 10 ounces each,
  bone in
2 tablespoons grapeseed oil
Kosher salt and cracked black pepper

Preheating the oven. Turn the oven to 425°F.

Heating the cream. In a small saucepan, combine the cream, rosemary, and garlic. Bring to a boil over medium-high heat. Remove the pan from the heat immediately and let the cream steep for 10 minutes. Strain the cream.

Assembling the gratin. Combine the potatoes and artichoke hearts in a bowl. Season with salt and pepper. Add the egg whites and toss to coat. Arrange a small layer of the potatoes and artichokes at the bottom of a medium baking dish. Add half of the Parmesan cheese and cover with the rest of the potatoes and artichokes. Pour the strained cream over the gratin and sprinkle with the remaining cheese. Cover with aluminum foil.

Baking the gratin. Bake the gratin for 15 minutes. Remove the aluminum foil. Bake the gratin until the top is golden brown and a sharp knife inserted into the potato comes out clean, about 10 minutes.

Preheating the grill to cook the rib eyes. Prepare the grill and get it smoking hot.

Seasoning the meat. Slather the steaks with the oil. Crunch salt and pepper onto both sides of each of the rib eyes and rub into the meat well.

Grilling the rib eyes. Find the hottest part of the grill, the sweet spot. Place the rib eyes on the grill and let them go. When you smell the steaks, check for marks on the bottom. Don't char the steaks, but look for dark streaks after about 3 minutes. (If there is too much oil on the steaks, the oil will drop down into the coals and splatter up again, which will give the steaks a burnt-oil taste.) Take your tongs, lift up the meat, and turn the steaks at a 45-degree angle; this will make crosshatch marks on the bottom of the steak. Grill for another 3 minutes. Flip the steaks and repeat the process, making the total cooking time about 12 minutes. Each steak will be different, so use your judgment as to when to turn the steaks. For medium-rare, the steak will feel like the muscled flesh between your finger and thumb when you are making a fist and your first two fingers are extended out.

Resting the rib eyes and serving. Put a small plate upside down on a larger plate. Drape the rib eyes over the small plate, which will allow the juices to run down. Do not stack the rib eyes, because that will create steam. Let the meat rest for 3 to 4 minutes. Cut the gratin into squares and serve it with the rib eyes.

how to cut up an artichoke

Whoever first looked at an artichoke and thought, "Food!," we salute you.

It's easier to cut up an artichoke than you think, and more satisfying than buying a jar of artichoke hearts. No matter how good the brand, those are weak substitutes for the real thing. Once you have eaten a fresh artichoke heart you have prepared yourself? Well, you'll see.

You need a sharp chef's knife and a paring knife. If you use a dull knife, you're going to cut the hell out of yourself.

You also need 2 quarts of cold water with lemon juice in it.

Cut off about 1 inch from the dome (top) of the artichoke. Slice off ⅛ inch of the stem.

Peel back all the leaves and toss them aside until you reach the pale chartreuse layer of leaves. (You can make a stock with the artichoke leaves, if you want.) Take your paring knife and trim the outer layers off the waist of the artichoke. Shave the rough outer edges of the stem of the artichoke with your paring knife.

Toss that artichoke in the water and repeat with any other artichokes.

Put a saucepan full of boiling salted water on high heat, with several lemons cut in half, juiced, and bobbing in the water. Throw the artichokes in the water. They will want to float. Push a strainer against them to keep them down. Cook the artichokes until you can slide a knife in and it falls out, about 30 minutes. Shock them in ice water.

Peel off the remaining rosette leaves on top. There will be thistly hair underneath all the leaves. Remove all of the hairs with your paring knife. What you have left is the artichoke heart, which is entirely edible. Slice it up and dip it in drawn butter or aioli (see page 266). Artichoke hearts are also great in pastas, with fish, and in potato gratins.

Enjoy.

there's a gluten-free table

Every night of our first few months together, I went into Danny's restaurant at the end of service. Walking in, even though the sign had been turned to closed, I'd wave hello to the women behind the bar and saunter back to the kitchen. After hugging Hortensia, the dishwasher, I'd kiss Danny. The state of his hair usually told the story. If every hair was neatly in place, he had been bored with the quiet night. If he looked like a combination of Albert Einstein and a snowboarder dude who just pulled his head out of a helmet, then I knew they had had a busy night. Tousling his hair, I'd ask him to tell the evening's stories.

Most of the time, he shooed me out of the kitchen, because he and Hortensia still had to clean. I'd wait at the bar with a glass of wine and talk to the girls while they dried wine glasses, biding my time. Some nights, however, Danny let me stay for a minute, because he was so excited to feed me something he had created that day.

One night, his smile grew wide at the sight of me. "Wait, you have to try this. It's from tonight's fish special."

He dipped his finger in a thick red sauce and plopped a big dollop in my mouth.

"Hmm." A hit of chiles, the heat of garlic, a slender thread of saffron, and extra-virgin olive oil. Heaven. I kissed him. "What is this?"

"Rouille," he said proudly, turning toward his reach-in for something else.

My face started to flush, and a faint vibration started ringing in my head. "Sweetie, what's in this?"

He named off all the ingredients I had spotted. And then . . . "Breadcrumbs."

"Bread?" I gulped.

He looked at me for a moment, and then went white. "Oh shit."

I ran to the bathroom, trying to rinse out my mouth, fighting back the tears. It was too late. The gluten had gone down. Nothing to do but wait out the three days of living in the bathroom and then crawling back into bed.

Danny felt worse than I did.

The next time I typed up the next month's menu for him, I stopped and said, "Wait, I can eat everything here."

"I know," he said.

"How did that happen?"

"Easy. I don't want to cook anything that I can't share with you. I don't need to use gluten."

I kissed him, of course. The French-trained chef had given up traditional roux and sauces, baguettes and crepes.

Over the past two years, gluten-free customers have trickled in, tentatively, and then swarmed in. Some of

them planned family vacations to Seattle so they could eat Danny's food. The menu is the same for everyone, every month. Most customers think they are eating pork belly, or sea scallops, or crab and avocado salad. But for some folks, it's much more. And much less.

Every night, Danny calls me from the restaurant and says, "There's a gluten-free table here." I love the proud joy in his voice. He calls to tell me about the man from down the street who comes in three times a week, sometimes ordering takeout, because he can't believe he can eat this well, and safely. Or the couple who sit down for a long dinner every Friday evening, at the same table, close to the kitchen so they can wave him over to thank him. He was especially teary the night that a couple came in for their thirty-fifth wedding anniversary celebration. The dinner Danny made for them was their first restaurant meal in fifteen years.

"I love seeing the excitement on their faces. Someone who has been recently diagnosed looks so scared. There's a progression throughout the evening, with people at first sitting hunched into themselves, like they're trapped in a cocoon. By the end, it's like they have burst through the shell and are free."

Those of you who are not gluten-free might not understand. What's the big deal?

If I eat at a restaurant where the waitress brings my salad with the croutons on it, I can't eat the salad. If the guy on the line makes my salad with the same pair of gloves with which he touched the croutons for another salad, I get sick. If he doesn't use a clean bowl for my salad, I'm down for the count. Think of all the ways that the equivalent of half a teaspoon of flour could get into my food, and you will understand the jubilation people feel when Danny cooks for them.

"Look, I'll be honest. I used to think that customers with food allergies were a real pain in the ass. I didn't entirely know what to do, because no one ever taught me about this in school. Was I doing the right thing? It frustrated me to stop the whirlwind on the line and take out a clean pan or make a new sauce. It threw me off my rhythm. I was younger then.

"But I find that feeding people who need to eat gluten-free (or dairy-free, peanut-free, garlic-free) has changed my perceptions of food. Most truly great food is gluten-free. You just have to approach it that way. I'd never cooked millet, teff, or quinoa before I met Shauna; I thought they were only allowed in vegetarian restaurants. Now I cook those grains every week, and I feel lucky. I love discovering new foods."

I know many folks who stay home, and miss the restaurant meal and the inspiration it can provide, because they are afraid of making a fuss. But in the hands of the right chef, creating a meal for someone with a food allergy is not only an interesting challenge, but also a privilege.

"I've always enjoyed looking at people's faces while they eat my food. But the faces of people who have been afraid to eat? They are more appreciative. If you are constantly worrying that you are going to be sick from every bite of food you eat, how much are you going to be enjoying your meal?"

It wasn't until I lived with Danny and listened to his restaurant lingo that I understood why it's called dinner service. Chefs, waitstaff, dishwashers—they work to serve the people who eat the food. Some of them may forget it, and some of the diners may not know it. I didn't understand this before I met him. But as I've seen Danny blossom from all the attention he has received for his restaurant, it's clear to me that he truly does live what he told me on our first date: "I cook because I can give people joy in the belly."

lamb chops with breadcrumbs, mustard, and lavender

VARIATIONS
I wouldn't change this combination. It's too good.

SUGGESTIONS
Serve the lamb chops with polenta and flageolet beans. Or with mashed potatoes and fennel salad. Asparagus in season would make this even more spectacular.

Pierre, my head chef in Breckenridge, invented this flavor combination. He used to make it with a rack of lamb. That was one of the most popular dishes I have ever seen in a restaurant. People ordered it as though they had never eaten meat before. We must have done twenty orders in one day, and that was in a forty-five-seat restaurant. That's how I got good at cleaning lamb.

When you learn what flavors go well together, you're going to create food that is at the very least decent. And sometimes you invent a crowd pleaser, like this one. The crunchy breadcrumbs, warm mustard, and savory herbs that have infused themselves into the meatiness of a good medium-rare piece of lamb taste of southern France in summer. • *Feeds 4*

2 slices gluten-free bread
2 teaspoons herbes de Provence
1 teaspoon dried lavender buds
8 lamb loin chops, about 5 ounces each

Kosher salt and cracked black pepper
¼ cup Dijon mustard
4 tablespoons extra-virgin olive oil

Making the breadcrumbs. If your bread is fresh, toast the slices in a 400°F oven, turning once during the baking, until the slices are browned, 15 to 20 minutes. (If your bread is not fresh, you will not need to toast it. Gluten-free bread is usually pretty dry by the third day after baking.) Break the toasted slices (or dry slices) apart with your hands and put the bread chunks into a food processor. Whirl them up until they are breadcrumbs.

Preparing to cook. Preheat the oven to 475°F. In a bowl, combine the breadcrumbs, herbes de Provence, and lavender buds.

Coating the lamb chops. Season the lamb chops with salt and pepper. Smear each of the chops with the mustard, on both sides. Dip the mustard-covered lamb chops in the breadcrumb mixture.

Searing the lamb chops. Set 2 large oven-safe sauté pans over medium-high heat and add 2 tablespoons of the oil to each pan. Place the lamb chops, 4 to each pan, in the hot oil and sear until the bottoms are browned, about 3 to 4 minutes. Flip the chops and slide the pans into the hot oven.

Roasting the lamb chops. Cook the chops until the internal temperature reaches 140°F, about 7 minutes. The chops should feel as firm as the muscle between your first finger and thumb when you are beginning to pinch your thumb and fingers together.

Pull the chops out of the oven and let them rest for 5 minutes. Serve.

gluten-free focaccia bread

VARIATIONS
If you are allergic to eggs, you can omit the egg here. The focaccia will be a little denser than the version with egg, but it will still taste good.

SUGGESTIONS
Try using the focaccia to make a sandwich with fig spread, salami, prosciutto, and fresh mozzarella.

One mention of a food that interests us, and we're off.

Our friend Luisa, who writes a food blog called The Wednesday Chef, spent a good part of her summer in Italy, with her family there. Clearly feeling nostalgic for her time there, Luisa spent weeks trying to replicate her grandmother's focaccia bread. The photographs of her last, successful attempt left us both a little dazed. We wanted some.

Of course, we had to change it quite a bit, since hers contained gluten.

I was shocked to find that most authentic Italian focaccia breads contain a potato. But it makes sense. Boil the potato and then put it through the ricer and you have a light-as-air starch. Focaccia breads are lighter than other breads. The egg white, beaten to stiff peaks, adds lightness here too, like a soufflé. Try this bread with rosemary or oregano. It's a little taste of Italy, right in your kitchen. • *Feeds 8*

1 large Yukon gold potato, peeled and quartered
1 envelope (2¼ teaspoons) active dry yeast
1 tablespoon sugar
1 cup warm water (about 110°F)
1 cup (120g/4.2oz) tapioca flour
¾ cup (95g/3.4oz) sorghum flour
⅔ cup (129g/4.5oz) potato starch
½ (102g/2.2oz) cup sweet rice flour

1 teaspoon xanthan gum or an equal amount of psyllium husks
½ teaspoon guar gum or an equal amount of psyllium husks
2 teaspoons fine sea salt, plus extra for sprinkling
1 large egg, separated
3 tablespoons olive oil, plus extra for greasing pan and sprinkling
2 teaspoons finely chopped fresh rosemary

Ricing the potato. Put the potato quarters into a large saucepan with cold water and enough salt to make the water taste like the ocean. Bring to a boil, then cook over medium-high heat until a knife inserted into the potato slips out easily, about 20 minutes. Drain the potato and set aside. When the potato has cooled enough for you to work with it, press it through a fine-mesh sieve, using the back of a ramekin or a large wooden spoon. (If you own a ricer, use it here.)

Proofing the yeast. Combine the yeast and sugar in a large wide-mouthed bowl. Add the warm water. (Run the water over the inside of your wrist. When it feels like the temperature of your skin, the water is ready.) Stir together gently. Give the yeast 10 to 15 minutes to proof.

Combining the flours. Sift the tapioca flour, sorghum flour, potato starch, and sweet rice flour through a fine-mesh sieve into the bowl of a stand mixer. Stir in the xanthan gum, guar gum, and salt.

Making the dough. Add the egg yolk, oil, yeasty water, rosemary, and the riced potatoes to the dry ingredients. Run the stand mixer with a paddle attachment on medium speed until the dough comes together, about 5 minutes. When you first stop the mixer, the dough will look like a firm ball, and then it will start to slump off the paddle attachment. The dough will have the consistency of thick cake batter.

Finishing the dough. Beat the egg white until it is stiff. Gently fold it into the dough. Set the bowl in a warm place and allow the dough to rise until it has doubled in size, about 1 hour.

Preparing to bake. Preheat the oven to 450°F. Grease both sides of a piece of parchment paper with oil and lay it down in a 9-inch pie pan.

Baking the focaccia. Push the dough into the prepared pan and smooth the top with a rubber spatula. Sprinkle on olive oil and sea salt, if you wish. Slide the focaccia into the oven and put a large oven-safe sauté pan filled with ice cubes on the rack beneath it. Bake until the top is browned and the internal temperature of the bread reaches at least 180°F, about 25 minutes.

Cooling the focaccia. Allow the focaccia to cool in the pan for at least 10 minutes. Tip it onto a wire rack and cool for another 30 minutes. Enjoy.

black rice with chickpeas, bok choy, and tamari sauce

VARIATIONS
You can make this with vegetable stock or water. It won't thicken up as well, but it will taste good.

SUGGESTIONS
This dish goes well with fish and seafood, particularly with scallops and fat prawns. True decadence? Butter-poached lobster.

When Shauna and I were in Italy for our honeymoon, we had the joy of spending the day with Judy Witts-Francini. Judy, an expat American married to a man from Tuscany, ran a cooking school in Florence. (She has since closed it, sadly.) For our wedding present, she offered us two spots in the class. With a clutch of other people who loved to cook, we made our way through the central market with the exuberant Judy. Stands selling aged balsamic vinegars, butcher stalls with caulfat and entire roosters, baskets full of forest mushrooms—such profusion left us both a little stunned.

Afterwards, we returned to Judy's apartment to cook. Of everything we ate that day, our lasting favorite was a black rice and chickpea dish. Family farmers in Tuscany attempted to achieve a rice like the "forbidden" black rice in China. Their venere black rice, grown in salt marshes, is even more flavorful.

When we came home, I made a dish at the restaurant like this, but with the tastes of the Pacific Northwest. Shauna says she could eat this at least once a week, just to feel like she is in Florence again. • *Feeds 4*

2 tablespoons canola oil

2 large yellow onions, peeled and finely diced

2 tablespoons thinly sliced garlic

1 cup dried chickpeas, soaked overnight

¼ cup extra-virgin olive oil

2 tablespoons finely chopped fresh cilantro

1 tablespoon grated lemon zest

Kosher salt and cracked black pepper

4 tablespoons sesame oil

1 medium nub ginger (about the size of a thumb), peeled

1 stalk lemongrass (same size as the ginger), smashed

1 kaffir lime leaf (if you can find it)

2 cups Italian venere black rice, rinsed under cold water for 15 minutes

4 medium baby bok choy, cut in half lengthwise

1 cup wheat-free tamari

1 cup chicken stock

2 tablespoons butter

Cooking the chickpeas. Set a large saucepan over medium-high heat and add the canola oil. Add 1 of the onions and 1 tablespoon of the garlic and cook, stirring, until softened and translucent, about 10 minutes. Add the soaked chickpeas and pour in enough water to cover by 1 inch. Bring to a boil, then turn the heat down to low and simmer until the chickpeas are especially tender, about 1 hour. (If your dried chickpeas are old, they may soak up all the water before turning tender. If so, cover them with water again and keep cooking.) Drain the chickpeas. Combine the chickpeas with the olive oil, cilantro, and lemon zest and stir to coat. Season with salt and pepper, about 2 teaspoons each. Set aside to cool.

Cooking the rice. Set another large saucepan over medium heat and add 1 tablespoon of the sesame oil. Add the remaining onion and cook, stirring, until it is softened and translucent, about 10 minutes. Add the remaining 1 tablespoon of garlic and cook, stirring, until it is fragrant, about 1 minute. Drop in the ginger, lemongrass, and lime leaf and stir. Pour in the black rice and enough water to cover by 1 inch. Cook the rice, covered, until it is fork-tender but still has a bit of bite, 35 to 40 minutes. Cool the rice to room temperature. Remove the ginger, lemongrass, and lime leaf. Combine the chickpeas and rice in a large sauté pan and set aside.

Sautéing the bok choy. Preheat the oven to 450°F. Toss the baby bok choy with salt and pepper and the remaining 3 tablespoons of sesame oil. Set a large sauté pan over medium-high heat. Add the bok choy, flat side down, and cook until the flat sides are browned a bit, 3 to 4 minutes. Pour in ½ cup of water and cover the pan. Turn off the heat and allow the bok choy to steam for 5 minutes.

Making the sauce. Remove the bok choy from the pan. Return the pan to high heat. Add the tamari and bring it to a boil. Turn the heat down to low and cook until the tamari is reduced by half its volume, about 5 minutes. Pour in the chicken stock and bring it to a boil. Reduce the heat to low and cook until the liquid is reduced by half its volume, about 5 minutes. Add the butter and stir it into the sauce as it melts.

Finishing the dish. Add a touch of water to the sauté pan with the combined rice and chickpeas. Heat over medium-high heat until warm, about 3 minutes.

To serve, spoon some rice and chickpeas on each plate, then some bok choy on top, and drizzle the sauce around the plate.

sage polenta fries with parsley pesto

VARIATIONS
For a slightly different flavor, try olive oil or grapeseed oil instead of the canola. You can certainly try other herbs besides sage. If you cannot eat dairy, soy or rice milk will work well here.

SUGGESTIONS
Before serving, top the polenta fries with a bit of lemon zest, for a quick taste of sunshine.

This recipe is easy to make, and the rewards are rich. But it does require patience. Instead of using quick-cooking polenta, please find authentic cornmeal. Stir and stir, savoring every physical sensation for 30 to 40 minutes. That means low, slow heat. You can't make this as quickly as you want to eat it.

And then you wait. Wait for the polenta to chill. Really, you should probably refrigerate it overnight. And this means being patient enough to plan ahead the night before. It's worth it.

When these are finished, they are wonderfully crunchy on the outside, with the creamy give of hot polenta inside, following close behind. Smell a hint of the garlic and the waft of the sage. Listen to the crackling of the polenta, the crisp of the Parmesan. Take a bite.

All that patience paid off. • *Feeds 4*

PARSLEY PESTO
3 tablespoons pine nuts
2 bunches fresh Italian parsley, leaves picked
¼ cup freshly grated Parmesan cheese
1 clove garlic, peeled and chopped
1 cup extra-virgin olive oil
½ lemon, juiced
Kosher salt and cracked black pepper

POLENTA FRIES
2 tablespoons extra-virgin olive oil
2 large shallots, peeled and thinly sliced
1 teaspoon thinly sliced garlic
1 teaspoon finely chopped fresh sage

2½ cups whole milk
1½ cups water
1 cup gluten-free fine yellow cornmeal
  (not all are gluten-free because of
  manufacturing practices)
1 tablespoon butter
¼ cup freshly grated Parmesan cheese
2 ounces soft goat cheese (chèvre)
Kosher salt and cracked black pepper
½ cup cornstarch for dredging
  (this measurement is an estimate)
4 large eggs, beaten
1 cup gluten-free breadcrumbs
¼ cup canola oil

Toasting the pine nuts. Set a small sauté pan over medium heat. Add the pine nuts and toast them, tossing occasionally, until browned, about 10 minutes; do not burn the pine nuts.

Making the pesto. Place the parsley, Parmesan cheese, garlic, and toasted pine nuts in the food processor. Whirl up the ingredients until they are pureed. With the machine still running, slowly drizzle in the olive oil. Add the lemon juice. When the puree has the consistency of a runny paste or loose sauce, turn off the food processor. Taste the pesto. You should taste every ingredient, in balance. If not, add more of what is missing. Season with salt and pepper.

Sautéing the vegetables for the polenta fries. Set a large sauté pan over medium-high heat and pour in the olive oil. Add the shallots and garlic to the hot oil and cook, stirring, until the shallots are softened and translucent, 3 to 4 minutes. Toss in the sage and cook until it is fragrant, about 2 minutes.

Making the polenta. Add the milk and water to the sauté pan. As soon as the liquids come to a boil, pour in the cornmeal and reduce the heat to low. Stir the mixture with a steady hand until the polenta becomes one mass and pulls away from the sides of the pan, 30 to 40 minutes. (The time will vary, depending on the kind of polenta you are using.)

Finishing the polenta. When the polenta is ready, add the butter, Parmesan cheese, and goat cheese and stir and stir until they are incorporated. Taste the polenta and season with salt and pepper, if necessary.

Chilling the polenta. Immediately pour the polenta into a baking dish or roasting pan. Using a rubber spatula, evenly spread out the polenta about 1 inch thick. Transfer to the refrigerator to chill for at least 2 hours, but preferably overnight.

Preparing the polenta fries. Cut the chilled polenta into French-fry-size shapes. (You don't want shoestring potatoes, but you probably don't want giant wedges either. Aim for the middle.) Season the polenta with salt and pepper, if necessary.

Setting up an assembly line. Dredge the polenta fries in the cornstarch, coating well. Dip the fries in the frothy eggs. Finally, roll each of the fries in the breadcrumbs. Make a plate of prepared fries.

Heating the oil. Bring a large sauté pan to high heat. Pour the canola oil in. Heat the oil to 350°F to 375°F.

Frying the polenta fries. Carefully put the polenta fries into the hot oil. Allow the fries to bubble away happily until they are browned, 3 to 4 minutes. Remove with a slotted spoon and place on a plate covered with a paper towel.

To serve, drizzle some of the parsley pesto on a plate and top with the polenta fries.

cooking for the chef

I am in the kitchen, a glass of red wine on the countertop, music playing, onions sizzling in the sauté pan. I have missed this intimate satisfaction of cooking alone.

Close companions in the hours we are together, Danny and I lead different lives when we are apart. Most of my life is spent sitting in front of the computer, and I have to schedule exercise with friends. He does not sit down once in ten hours. I write sentences in my head, wonder about stories, and work hard to create these little black words on the white page. He can go hours without talking. I can't eat gluten. He can, and does, at the restaurant.

That's what keeps it interesting between us.

Time to sear the pork shoulder.

For a while, I was willing to wash the dishes and peer over Danny's shoulder, trying to figure out what he was doing. Then, I became his prep cook, peeling the carrots and practicing dicing. My garlic is minced much more evenly now. Let's be honest—I used peeled garlic from a jar and a garlic press before I met Danny. When I began cooking a few simple dishes at his side, I expected him to be the alpha to my beta. I expected him to tell me how to make polenta the *right* way.

After I made polenta for him the first time, it took him two days—and much cajoling from me—before he told me how he makes polenta at the restaurant. And that was only because I wanted to put up a recipe on the website. He has never let me feel bad that I don't cook as well as he does.

Whether or not we like to acknowledge it, there is a constantly shifting dynamic of power in a relationship. At a moment's notice, I could teach him about Rasputin or the bombing of Hiroshima. The ending of James Joyce's Ulysses inspired me to get the word yes tattooed on my wrist. Danny asks me to proofread every important e-mail he writes.

But I didn't know how to chop an onion when I met him. Even though I know now, I will never chop onions as well as he does.

After all those years as a teacher, it's good to be a student again.

I'm still standing at the stove, humming. Even if my dishes will never look as good as his do, I make them.

He is cooking for other people, and I am cooking for us.

Caraway seeds, bay leaves, and garlic cloves slide into the stock.

Most people are too intimidated to cook for a chef. However, like most of the chefs we know, Danny loves simple foods full of flavor, soft mounds of food he can mix together with his fork into one bite.

Before he met me, Danny stopped for slices of pizza or a hot dog from a stand on the way back to his apartment, and a six-pack of beer. He appreciates any food I make him.

For dinner, I make hearty soups. Soft polenta with sautéed kale and a poached egg on top. Braised chicken thighs. Slow-cooked stews. Roasted lemon chicken and potatoes. A warm apple crisp for late in the evening after work. Comfort food.

Dice the carrots, onions, and celery. Throw in a leek as well.

What I make for the two of us to share at the end of the night has to be able to simmer and bubble for hours, or be ready before I leave to pick him up, to be warmed up when we return. Danny doesn't drive. About seven years before I met him, he suffered a seizure, and the doctors suspected epilepsy. They advised him not to drive. He gladly complied. So he has not been behind the wheel of a car since.

So in the fall and winter, I braise meats for us. I'm fascinated by the fact that braising takes a muscled cut of meat and changes its composition with low, slow heat. Early in our relationship, I made some braised chicken thighs with a crème fraîche and lemon zest pan sauce. To my disappointment, the thighs were tough, the meat almost brittle. "Sorry, I cooked them too long," I told him.

"No, sweetie, you didn't cook them long enough."

And so I braise locally raised pork in whole-grain mustard and chicken stock, or the cheap cuts of meat I have never made before. Danny's happy when he comes home and there's meat. However, he is also happy if I make Thai red rice in the rice cooker, sauté up some vegetables, toss on some champagne vinaigrette, and top it off with sunflower seeds. Really, if there are sunflower seeds, he's happy.

He's just happy I cooked something for him.

Slide it into the oven.

At the end of the evening, I climb in the car to pick him up, a pork shoulder braising in low heat. Even though some people might hate this routine, I love the meditation of driving in the dark, thinking through the day. And our time to and from the restaurant, talking, is almost our favorite time together, debriefing the hours apart and singing along to songs on the radio. When we walk through the front door, he takes a deep whiff, closes his eyes, and looks at me gratefully.

I love feeding him.

braised pork stew with cabbage and caraway

VARIATIONS
Beef would work well, if you use a top round roast. Sirloin would be decadent.

SUGGESTIONS
Roasted or boiled potatoes would be good with this, as would creamy polenta.

If you're in the kitchen on a cold day, and you smell this wafting from the oven, you feel warm.

Pork shoulder is one of those cuts of meat that turns tender with long, slow cooking. Don't use loin—that would be a waste. Pile on cabbage and caraway, which blend in a friendly fashion, and you have a solid winter dish. It's sturdy and simple, a meal you can make in the afternoon and let it braise away while you lounge on the couch, throw snowballs outside, and visit with family. And then you'll make little satisfied sounds together at the table. • *Feeds 4*

¾ cup plus 2 tablespoons Dijon mustard

2 tablespoons finely chopped fresh rosemary

2½ pounds pork shoulder butt roast, cut into 3-inch cubes

4 tablespoons canola oil

2 medium carrots, peeled and medium diced

4 stalks celery, medium diced

1½ medium yellow onions, peeled and medium diced

4 tablespoons caraway seeds

2 bay leaves

3 cloves garlic, smashed and peeled

1 quart chicken stock

10 new potatoes, cut in half

2 tablespoons kosher salt

2 cups quartered button mushrooms

½ white part of 1 leek, medium diced

1 tablespoon finely chopped fresh sage

2 tablespoons butter

1 tablespoon yellow mustard seeds

2 cups roughly chopped cabbage

Marinating the pork roast. The day before you plan to serve, in a small bowl, combine 2 tablespoons of the mustard and 1 tablespoon of the rosemary. Coat the pork butt with the mixture. Refrigerate the pork overnight to marinate.

Searing the pork. The next day, set a Dutch oven (or large saucepan) over high heat and add 1 tablespoon of the oil. When the oil is hot enough that the pork will sizzle when it hits the pot, add the pork pieces. Allow them to sear until the bottoms are browned. Turn the pork pieces and continue searing until all sides are browned. Take the pork out of the Dutch oven to rest.

Preparing to simmer the pork. Add 1 tablespoon of the oil to the Dutch oven over medium-high heat. Add 1 of the carrots, 2 stalks of the celery, and 1 of the onions to the hot oil and cook, stirring occasionally to make sure the vegetables do not burn, until they are caramelized, 5 to 7 minutes. While the vegetables are caramelizing, toast the caraway seeds in a separate pan over medium heat, stirring occasionally, until they are fragrant, about 5 minutes. Add 2 tablespoons of the toasted caraway seeds to the caramelized vegetables (mirepoix). Throw in the bay leaves, 2 garlic cloves, and pork. Cover with the chicken stock. Bring it all to a boil and turn it down to a gentle bubbling. Simmer until the meat surrenders to the tongs at your touch, 1½ to 2 hours.

Boiling the potatoes. Place the potatoes in a pot with cold water to cover and the salt. Bring to a boil, then reduce the heat to a simmer. Simmer the potatoes until they are fork-tender, 15 to 20 minutes. Drain the potatoes and set them aside.

Making the sauce. When the meat is tender, remove it from the stock. Strain the stock, discarding the vegetables. Add the remaining 2 tablespoons of oil to the Dutch oven over medium-high heat. Add the remaining carrot, celery, and onion, along with the mushrooms, leek, and remaining garlic clove. Cook, stirring, until the vegetables are soft and the onions are translucent, about 10 minutes. Stir in the remaining 1 tablespoon of rosemary, the remaining 2 tablespoons of caraway seeds, and the sage. When the herbs are fragrant, pour in the stock you set aside and bring it to a boil. Spoon in the remaining ¾ cup of mustard, the butter, and the mustard seeds. Reduce the heat to medium-low and allow the sauce to reduce until it has thickened, about 15 minutes.

Finishing the stew. When the liquid has thickened, toss in the cabbage, pork pieces, and cooked potatoes. When they are heated, serve the stew.

tuna-noodle casserole

VARIATIONS
Clam juice will work in place of the fish stock if you don't have the time to make the stock from scratch.

SUGGESTIONS
When we want to kick up this recipe a notch, we sear 2-inch-thick pieces of ahi tuna and perch them on top of each serving of the casserole.

This isn't the tuna-noodle casserole my mother made. That was cream of mushroom soup, cheap tuna from a can, bow-tie pasta, and Ruffles crunched on top. (Shauna's mother used Pringles.)

There's something to be said for comfort food. Great food doesn't have to come in swirls of sauces or dots of foam. Sometimes, the simple food is the best. But true comfort comes from truly good food. This is a recipe where the quality of the ingredients matters.

A few unexpected touches enhance the basic goodness of this dish, the fishiness of it, the richness of it. • *Feeds 4*

2 tablespoons extra-virgin olive oil
2 cups quartered cremini mushrooms
½ large yellow onion, peeled and small diced
4 cloves garlic, peeled and thinly sliced
1 leek, white part only, thinly sliced
5 sprigs fresh thyme, leaves finely chopped
2 tablespoons sweet rice flour
2 cups whole milk
1 cup fish stock (recipe follows)
½ cup heavy cream
¼ teaspoon cayenne pepper

1 teaspoon each kosher salt and cracked black pepper
Two 5-ounce cans good-quality albacore tuna
1 cup freshly grated Parmesan cheese
½ cup freshly grated semifirm goat cheese (we like Drunken goat cheese here)
8 ounces gluten-free pasta of your choice (see page 60 for homemade gluten-free pasta recipe), slightly undercooked
Potato chips, optional

Preheating the oven. Turn the oven to 450°F.

Starting the sauce. Set a large sauté pan over medium-high heat and pour in the oil. Add the mushrooms to the hot oil and cook, stirring occasionally, until they start to steam and hiss, about 5 minutes. Add the onion, garlic, and leek and cook, stirring, until the onion and leek are softened and translucent, about 5 minutes. Stir in the thyme and cook until the herb is fragrant.

Dusting the vegetables with flour. Sprinkle the sweet rice flour into the pan and scrape up the browned parts on the bottom of the pan. Dusting the sautéed vegetables with the flour will help thicken the liquids when you add them.

Finishing the sauce. Add the milk, fish stock, cream, and cayenne pepper, stirring constantly so the liquids do not burn. Allow the liquid to come to a gentle boil. When the first bubbles appear on the surface, turn the heat down to low. Keep scraping the sides of the pan, because the roux will stick as it boils up, and you want to catch that flavor. Allow the mixture to simmer until it starts to thicken, about 10 minutes. Taste the sauce and season it with salt and pepper, if necessary. The sauce will be seasoned properly when you can taste everything in the dish. Add the tuna to the mix. Sprinkle in the Parmesan cheese and goat cheese, which will thicken the sauce even more.

Baking the casserole. Place the cooked pasta in a large casserole dish. Pour the sauce over the pasta and stir well. You could crush some potato chips on top, if you are looking for true authenticity. Bake until the top is browned and bubbling, about 10 minutes. Spoon a healthy portion of the tuna-noodle casserole onto each plate and serve.

fish stock

• Makes 1 gallon

3 pounds halibut bones
2 medium yellow onions, peeled
  and large diced
1 white part of leek, large diced
3 ribs celery, large diced

½ bunch thyme, chopped
2 bay leaves
½ pound button mushrooms, sliced
2 tablespoons peppercorns
2 tablespoons salt

Place the halibut bones in a large saucepan. Cover them with cold water and bring the water to a gentle simmer. Skim the scum that will rise to the surface of the water; there will be a fair amount. Pay close attention.

Toss in all the remaining ingredients except the salt. Bring the water to a simmer.

If you are cooking other dishes during this time, you can add any garlic and onion skins you happen to have.

Simmer the stock for 1½ hours.

Toss in the salt. Cook the stock for an additional 5 minutes.

Strain the stock through cheesecloth into a large bowl. This will make it a clean, clear stock.

bean bake casserole

VARIATIONS
Try chorizo instead of ground beef. Or, make this vegetarian by leaving out the meat and finding refried beans not fried in lard. If you cannot eat dairy, there are dairy-free cheeses and vegan sour cream out there.

SUGGESTIONS
Try making your own refried beans sometime. You probably won't go back to the can.

When Danny and I first visited his hometown of Breckenridge, Colorado, his sister-in-law, Patty, brought out a dish of this casserole. His eyes grew wide. His mother made this when he was a child. "So did mine!" I told him, and we traded stories. My mother made the most delicious chicken enchiladas, with a white sauce she crafted seemingly out of thin air. Except for the nights when it was breakfast for dinner, that meal was my favorite. But I also loved this casserole with corn tortillas, ground beef, avocados, and plenty of cheese.

When Danny and I returned home from the restaurant one night, and I came out of the kitchen bearing a Pyrex casserole dish full of this cheesy baked goodness, his face stretched open in happiness.

The joy of this recipe is that you can make it a dozen different ways. If you want to take the time to make your own homemade corn tortillas, or braise some heirloom beans in leaf lard, or find some authentic chorizo to spice up the meat mix, you're going to have an extraordinary meal in your hands. Or if you're pressed for time, you can also make it fast. Good refried beans out of a can (the kind that squelch when you stick in the spoon). Cheddar cheese and Monterey Jack released from plastic wrappers. Even those black olives already sliced, in a can. Fresher is better, of course. But the easy way still tastes pretty damned good. • *Feeds 8*

SPANISH RICE
1 fresh poblano chile
2 tablespoons canola oil
½ medium onion, peeled and chopped
1 teaspoon chopped garlic
1 teaspoon tomato paste
1 tablespoon chili powder
2 teaspoons ground cumin
½ cup chopped tomatoes (please use canned tomatoes if it's not tomato season)
1 cup white rice (we like basmati or jasmine rice)
1 teaspoon each kosher salt and cracked black pepper
3 cups chicken stock

BEAN BAKE CASSEROLE
1 pound ground beef
20 corn tortillas
One 16-ounce can refried beans
1½ cups shredded Cheddar cheese
1½ cups shredded Monterey Jack cheese
½ cup pitted black olives
1 cup salsa
4 avocados, peeled, pitted, and cut into chunks
1 cup sour cream

Roasting the poblano for the rice. Preheat the oven to 500°F. When it has come to heat, throw in the poblano chile. Turn the chile every once in a while, until the skin starts to blacken and blister. Remove the chile from the oven and put it into a bowl. Cover the bowl with plastic wrap and let the chile sit until it cools. Peel the chile, remove the seeds, and cut it into large pieces.

Turn down the oven to 450°F.

Making the Spanish rice. Set a large sauté pan over medium-high heat and pour in the oil. Add the onion and garlic and cook, stirring, until the onion is softened and translucent, about 10 minutes. Add the tomato paste, chili powder, and cumin and cook until they release their fragrance, about 3 minutes. Add the tomatoes, the roasted chile, and the rice, stirring to coat. Season with salt and pepper. Add the chicken stock. Bring to a boil, then reduce the heat to a simmer. Cook until the rice is soft and fluffy, about 20 minutes.

Browning the beef. Set a large sauté pan over medium-high heat and add the ground beef. Cook, stirring occasionally, until the beef is thoroughly browned, about 10 minutes.

Assembling the casserole. Line the bottom of a casserole dish with some of the corn tortillas. Scoop in a third of the ground beef, a third of the Spanish rice, $\frac{1}{3}$ of the refried beans, $\frac{1}{3}$ cup of each of the cheeses, a third of the olives, and a third of the salsa. Top that with another layer of corn tortillas, and then another third of the beef, third of the rice, $\frac{1}{3}$ cup of each of the cheeses, third of the olives, and third of the salsa. Repeat the layering one more time. Top everything with another layer of corn tortillas and sprinkle with the remaining $\frac{1}{2}$ cup of each of the cheeses.

Baking the casserole. Slide the casserole dish into the oven and bake until the top is golden and bubbly, about 40 minutes. Scatter the avocado and sour cream over the top of the warm cheese and serve.

warm rice salad

VARIATIONS
You could use black rice in place of the Thai red rice. An herb vinaigrette—rosemary, thyme, parsley, and marjoram—would work well here too.

SUGGESTIONS
The salad would be even heartier with roasted chicken, turkey breast, or pork tenderloin.

After our first few months together, falling in love and eating duck confit, port reduction sauce, and plenty of bacon, Shauna insisted we had to start eating more healthfully. She didn't tell me about it. She just started making dinners like this one. I'd come home from the restaurant, not having eaten for hours, and I needed food. She knows how much I love sunflower seeds, so if what we ate was topped with those and some champagne vinaigrette, I loved it. It took me months to realize we were eating "healthy" meals.

Artichokes are God's gift to the world. They are so sensual. I first started eating them when I was a kid, dipping them in melted butter and lemon juice. I loved coming home and seeing artichokes on the kitchen counter, which meant my mom had bought some for dinner that night. Oh, it was such a treat.

Shauna knows this about me. She threw fresh artichokes into this salad, some avocados, and Thai red rice. It's nutty, with a heft to it. Minute rice is just wrong. Real rice has a taste. It turns out that healthy can be memorably delicious too. • *Feeds 4*

3 fresh artichoke hearts (see page 220)
1 lemon
2 medium tomatoes
¼ cup champagne vinegar
1 teaspoon Dijon mustard
1 teaspoon minced shallot
Kosher salt and cracked black pepper
¾ cup plus 2 tablespoons extra-virgin olive oil
1 cup Thai red rice
½ medium yellow onion, peeled and sliced

2 tablespoons unsalted butter
½ pound wild mushrooms (chanterelles, lobster, or porcini, whichever is in season)
1 medium yellow onion, peeled and large diced
1 tablespoon minced garlic
1 teaspoon finely chopped fresh rosemary
1 large ripe Hass avocado, tender yet firm to the touch, peeled and finely diced
¼ cup sunflower seeds

Cooking the artichoke hearts. Set a pot of salted water over high heat. When the water has come to a boil, add the artichoke hearts. Cut open the lemon, squeeze the juice into the water, and throw the lemon halves into the water. Turn down the heat to medium-low and cover the pot. Simmer until the artichoke hearts are tender to the knife, about 30 minutes. Drain and set aside to cool.

Blanching and chopping the tomatoes. Bring a large saucepan of salted water to a boil, using enough salt to make the water taste like the ocean. Mark a small X on the bottom of the tomato with a paring knife. Carefully add the tomatoes to the boiling water and cook until the skin starts to slip off, just 5 to 10 seconds. (Don't let the tomatoes stay in the water for much longer, or you will start to cook them.) Transfer the tomatoes to a bowl of ice water to cool quickly. Remove the tomato skins, which should slip off fairly easily. Cut the tomatoes in half and remove the seeds. To chop the tomatoes, slice each tomato one way, and then slice them the other way.

(continued on next page)

Making the vinaigrette. Place the vinegar, mustard, shallot, salt, and pepper into a blender and whirl them up. Slowly drizzle in ¾ cup of the oil until everything has started to blend and the sound in the blender drops in tone, about 2 minutes. Set aside. (You will have vinaigrette left over for other salads.)

Cooking the rice. Set a large saucepan over high heat. Add the red rice, sliced onion, butter, some salt and pepper, and 1½ cups of water and bring to a boil. Reduce the heat to low, cover the pan, and simmer until the rice has absorbed all the water, about 20 minutes. Stir the rice and taste—you want light and fluffy, with a tiny crunch.

Sautéing the vegetables. Set a large sauté pan over high heat and pour in the remaining 2 tablespoons of oil. Add the mushrooms to the hot oil and cook, stirring, until they release their juices and start to soften, 5 to 6 minutes. Add the large-diced onion and the garlic and cook, stirring occasionally, until the onion is softened and translucent, about 10 minutes. Toss in the rosemary and cook until the herb is fragrant.

Composing the salad. Place the rice in a large bowl. Throw in the sautéed vegetables, the artichoke hearts, and the tomatoes, then toss to combine. Slowly drizzle in enough of the champagne vinaigrette to dress the salad to your liking. Taste the salad and season with salt and pepper, if necessary. Garnish the salad with the avocado and sunflower seeds.

It's a cold, snowy day. Hours before, you seared off venison shanks, a beautiful piece of meat with a color like caramel. The shanks have been simmering in liquid in the oven, slowly, and the smells entice you to enter the kitchen. Take a fork to the meat and watch it fall apart, tender to the bone. Your first bite is melt-in-the-mouth meat, then you taste the rich buttery sauce, and the sensual texture of comfort floods in.

Braising is a great way to use less expensive pieces of meat that might be tough and transform them into something tender. You can be a vegetarian and braise—fennel, escarole, collard greens, and cabbage with caraway. But really, this is a meat technique. Osso buco. Rabbit. Beef or veal cheeks. Ribs. Pork belly.

Braising forces you to slow down.

Once you understand the technique, you can move away from recipes. Here's a basic structure for how to braise:

- Marinate the meat overnight (wine with garlic and herbs or a dry-rub marinade)
- The next day, heat up the stock.
- Pat the meat dry and season it with salt and pepper.
- Sear the meat, to create flavor and add contrast between the crisp sear and tender inner part.
- Strain any liquids from the marinade into another pot. Reduce.
- Roast the mirepoix in a hot pan.
- Add the reduced liquid to the mirepoix.
- Pour in the stock.
- Throw in aromatics—herbs, peppercorns, or tomato paste.
- Place the meat back in the pot.
- Cover the pot and braise it, at 325°F to 375°F. You can also braise on the stovetop. Take out the meat when it is entirely tender.
- Strain the liquid. Reduce it. Make a sauce.
- Eat.
- Don't rush it.

Every braise you do will only be a slight variation from this process. Once you have the memory of these steps in your head, you can braise whatever you want. And use a slow cooker, if that makes it easier for you. A slow cooker is essentially a

plates coming back

"How's it going?" I ask. Danny's standing outside of the restaurant, on one of his few breaks during dinner service.

"Okay."

"What's wrong?" If he doesn't talk immediately, something's wrong.

"Oh, some woman's plate came back with three bites left."

He won't be able to let this go all evening.

When I made myself dinner, I never once thought about how the food looked on the plate. When friends came over, I put food in big bowls and balanced serving spoons on the

edge. Perching chicken on top of a mound of rice seemed unnecessary to me. But that's because I was only thinking about the taste and eating as fast as I could.

"I've had dreams about plate presentations. Plating is an artistic expression. If you just slop the food on a plate, the food might taste like a million bucks, but people don't know it until they put the first bite in their mouths. You don't want your food to look like it came off an assembly line."

Danny has shown me that taste is only one part of a meal. "I look at what's going on in the plate, what the colors are in each part of the dish. I might squeeze sauce from a bottle instead of spooning it, because I want the straight lines. Or I build height, which allows diners to see all the textures of a dish. It also brings the smell closer to their nose. Playing a little makes the food more exciting."

Even when he cooks for us at home, on a Monday night, Danny bends over the plates, spreading out the slices of roasted chicken breast over the black rice. Because it's not a solid breast plunked down, I can see the mushrooms poking out between the chicken slices, the crispy skin falling toward the broccoli rabe, the tiny black rice grains clinging to all the vegetables. He takes a ladleful of sauce and pours it through a tiny strainer, no bigger than the bottom of a wine glass, and waits for the sauce to drip, slowly, on the plate. Arranging the plate in a pleasing fashion takes no more than one extra minute than if he had just slung it on there. Watching him makes me even hungrier.

That's a big part of being a chef—how the food looks.

"At some places, like Papillon, there was a definite system. Dollop. Basket. Mashers. Sauce. Vegetables on top. Meat on the side. I thought it was boring to plate it the same way every time. After all that repetition, I was bored.

"Sometimes at the restaurant, the way I am plating a dish is different by the end of the evening than it was at the beginning. As long as the plates going to the same table are consistent, I don't mind. It's good to mix it up. That's how

I learn what makes a dish most appealing in the first few days of the new menu."

So what do I do if I want to make a plate interesting? Swirl things? Make little dots?

"I'm not a big fan of the dots. They seem pretty prissy to me. You can do what you want—and experiment a lot—but the main point is that the design of the plate should come out of the way the food tastes. Stacks are good. I love a deconstructed dish, three component parts side by side. Everything should enhance the flavor of the food. Garnish with something that is in the dish."

When I was a kid, the only decoration I saw on restaurant plates was a wilted piece of parsley. It took me years to realize that parsley was actually edible.

"Even if you garnish with something that is not in the dish, make sure it complements the flavors already there. Roasted spring onions would go well with fish and chips and a malt vinegar reduction, for example."

Lately, it seems that plenty of chefs are smearing thickened sauces on plates. Danny helped me see why they do it.

"If the smear increases the taste of the food, it's not just a decoration. Just slow down and figure it out."

You've probably seen those articles in women's magazines that teach us how to portion our food for proper health. A piece of chicken should be the size of a deck of cards! Somehow, the idea of eating playing cards never inspired me to take out my measuring tape and ensure I was eating just enough. My portions were pretty haphazard. If you want to learn how to eat just enough food to sate you but not too much, eat at a good restaurant.

"Food should be enjoyed, not inhaled. It's wasteful to give people too much food. If you give people enough food to stuff them, you are losing money. You want them to slow down and really savor it. You want to keep them a little bit hungry, too, because that way they'll want dessert."

With all that preparation and thought, and the way he wipes every plate before it goes out to make sure there is not one errant drip, it's no wonder that Danny feels hurt when a plate comes back not entirely finished. "If something comes back, even one bite, I always ask the server what happened. Sure, it happens once in a while that I undercook a piece of meat in all the rush. And maybe they don't like chives, and they weren't listed on the menu. I can't write every ingredient in the description of the dish."

When I have eaten at his restaurant, I watch him come out of the kitchen, stand on the little ledge, up on his toes, and crane his neck to see if everyone is enjoying the food. If it's not such a busy night, he comes out to talk to all the customers, the chef as wandering minstrel. Often, he looks at the empty plates of the people smiling up at him and says, "Oh man, it looks like you didn't enjoy that food at all." He's friendly and jovial, forming connections with guests who will come back again and again. But really, underneath all the banter, he is checking out the plates to see if everyone enjoyed the food.

"I like it when it looks as though people have licked their plates. I wish everyone did."

So when he calls me in the evening, upset because one plate came back with a few bites left, I remind him to remember the other sixty plates that came back clean. And then I ask, "Did you get a look at whose plate it was?"

Sometimes it's a customer who doesn't know that most fish is best served medium-rare and thinks it was undercooked. But nine times out of ten, it was a young woman, on a date, who didn't order dessert either.

"I just don't get that. I think it's dumb. Why try to convince some guy that you don't even know that you don't eat much? You're only cheating yourself."

As a woman who has always had more curves than hollows, this always makes me grin. And then I remind him of how well the rest of the night went. He always focuses on the one person who thought the food was just okay.

"Chefs just want everyone to enjoy all the food. Plates coming back keeps us humble."

fennel salad with rainier cherries, radishes, and raspberry vinaigrette

VARIATIONS
French feta would work here instead of the Parmesan. You could use Bing cherries instead of Rainiers if you want a darker color.

SUGGESTIONS
Buy a mandoline for this salad, if you don't already own one. The fennel needs to be paper thin, as do the radishes.

Cherries in season are one of the most beautiful things in the world. By the time cherries arrive in the markets in July, I'm craving that bite of intense sweetness that leaves the jaw aching.

Bing cherries cling to the pit, a treasured stubbornness I tackle every June. Rainier cherries are more yielding, a soft yellow and red blush bite. By the time the Rainiers arrive, I'm ready to do something with cherries besides eat them out of hand.

This salad has a hint of licorice flavor from the fennel, the pepper bite of the radishes, and the twinge of vinegar to soften the sweetness of the cherries. Shauna could eat this salad all summer long.

Cherries in January just depress me, however. Please, make this only in the summer. • *Feeds 4*

RASPBERRY VINAIGRETTE
¼ cup raspberry vinegar
¾ cup extra-virgin olive oil
Kosher salt and cracked black pepper
Pinch sugar

FENNEL SALAD
2 heads fennel, thinly sliced
2 bunches radishes (as fresh as you can find), trimmed and thinly sliced
1 pound fresh Rainier cherries, pitted, stemmed, and cut in half
4 ounces Parmesan cheese

Making the vinaigrette. Add the vinegar to a blender. With the machine running, drizzle in the oil. Taste the vinaigrette and season with salt, pepper, and a touch of sugar, if necessary.

Making the salad. Place the fennel and radishes in a bowl of ice water for 30 minutes. Shake them dry. Compose the salad with the fennel, radishes, and cherries. Toss with a smidge of the vinaigrette. Thinly slice the Parmesan cheese with a peeler and place the slices on top of the salad.

curried red lentil puree

VARIATIONS
If you are allergic to tomatoes, you can make the dip without them and still have something tasty.

SUGGESTIONS
Serve this with crackers, corn chips, or warm, crusty bread.

Years ago, my head chef at Pierre's in Breckenridge grilled veal loin with lentils that smoked and simmered. I remembered that dish one morning in Seattle and made a smoky red lentil–tomato soup as the special that night. People ordered it in droves.

The next day, the soup sat before me on the line. Later, during dinner service, I'd thin it out with stock or soda water. But in that moment, hungry, I dipped crackers into the thick soup because I had forgotten to eat.

That's where this red lentil puree was born. I curried the lentils instead of smoking them and somehow liked them even more. I don't know why, and this is going to sound crazy, but this puree reminds Shauna and me of bean dip. It's much more nutritious, of course, but this is a good way to introduce your kids to lentils. At nearly every dinner party or potluck party, friends ask if we are making this dip. Now, you can too. • *Feeds 4*

3 tablespoons extra-virgin olive oil
½ medium red onion, peeled and small diced
2 cloves garlic, peeled and thinly sliced
1 tablespoon curry powder (preferably freshly ground Madras)
¼ cup medium-diced tomatoes

1 cup red lentils
2 cups vegetable stock
2 tablespoons roughly chopped fresh cilantro
1 teaspoon fresh lemon juice
Kosher salt and cracked black pepper

Sautéing the vegetables. Set a large saucepan over medium-high heat and pour in 2 tablespoons of the oil. Add the onion and garlic to the hot oil and cook, stirring, until the onion is softened and translucent, about 5 minutes. Sprinkle in the curry powder and cook until it is fragrant. Drop in the tomatoes and cook until they absorb the flavor of the curry powder and start to release some of their juices, 2 to 3 minutes.

Simmering the lentils. Scoop the lentils into the saucepan. Pour in enough stock to cover the lentils by 1 inch. Bring the liquid to a boil, then reduce the heat to low and simmer until the lentils are tender, 10 to 15 minutes. Spoon a few into your mouth and feel if you want to eat them. Strain the lentils but keep the stock.

Making the puree. Place the lentils in a blender. Pour in a quarter of the stock. Blend until the lentils are thoroughly pureed. Pour in more stock, depending on the consistency. You want the blender to run easily, but you also want the puree to be thick enough for a dip.

Transfer the puree to a large bowl and stir in the remaining 1 tablespoon of oil, the cilantro, and the lemon juice. Taste the dip and season it with salt and pepper, if necessary.

making vinaigrettes

Once you start making vinaigrettes from scratch, you'll never go back to bottled dressings again. Bottled dressings are full of stabilizers and corn syrup, ingredients meant to let them sit on grocery store shelves for months. If you make your own vinaigrette, all you need is vinegar, mustard, salt, pepper, and oil. The difference in the taste is night and day. And the basic ingredients are much cheaper than the bottled dressings.

Honestly, I don't understand why people believe that making vinaigrettes is beyond their reach. It's the easiest kitchen task.

All you need is 1 part vinegar to 3 parts oil. You don't even need to measure. Just pour each of them into a plastic squeeze bottle and eyeball it. Plop in a smidge of Dijon mustard and a pinch of kosher salt and pepper. Shake it up. Vinaigrette. Maybe you like more vinegar or less. Find your own taste. You can squeeze the vinaigrette directly onto the salad from the bottle.

If you want to emulsify the vinaigrette, so that it stays stirred in the bottle for a week, combine the ingredients in the blender. Add some fine-diced shallots (or garlic or onion, if you want).

Once you have this method down, experiment with different flavors. Buy different vinegars, such as sherry vinegar or raspberry vinegar. (Omit the mustard for fruit vinaigrettes.)

You can make the simplest vinaigrettes easily. If you want to be more complex, you can make your own flavored oils, or roast tomatoes and whirl those in. There's plenty of room to play.

Please, make your own vinaigrette.

rabbit with mustard

VARIATIONS
If you do not make the rabbit stock, you can use chicken stock to replace it. You could make this as chicken with mustard, if the rabbit intimidates you. Roast the breast and braise the leg instead.

SUGGESTIONS
Serve the rabbit with roasted potatoes and diced bacon. You could also sear the rabbit liver, if you are game.

Each night of the week at Cassis, a French country bistro in Seattle where I was the sous chef, we served a classical French dish. Every Tuesday afternoon, I broke down rabbits and made stock. Every Wednesday, I braised the rabbits in the stock and served plates of rabbit with mustard that evening.

Wednesdays were, by far, the most popular choice with the diners. I made this dish every week for two years, and I still love to make it.

I love the entire process of making this dish. But the final moment, digging in with the fork, is equally rewarding. You taste the rich stock, the warmth of the mustard, the smokiness of the bacon that goes in as a garnish. And there is the juiciness of the rabbit, so much more so than chicken, the sauces around it creamy and rich, but without any cream. I could eat plates of this every week and still be happy.

If you have never cooked rabbit, and you are looking at this recipe, intimidated, just know you can do it. Instead of thinking, I've never cooked this before, so I bet I'm no good at it, try to take this on as a challenge. You don't want to spend the rest of your life eating the same food, over and over. You don't want to miss this dish. • *Feeds 4*

3 whole rabbits, broken down into forelegs, hind legs, saddles (also known as bone-in loin), and the remaining bones (your butcher can do this for you)
2½ cups Dijon mustard
2 large carrots, peeled, quartered lengthwise, and large diced
4 large stalks celery, large diced

2 large yellow onions, peeled and large diced
10 cloves garlic, smashed and peeled
1 tablespoon tomato paste
Kosher salt and cracked black pepper
6 tablespoons extra-virgin olive oil
5 sprigs fresh thyme
2 cups dry white wine
1 tablespoon unsalted butter

Preparing the rabbit. The day before you plan to serve the rabbit, preheat the oven to 500°F. Pull out the saddles and hind legs of the rabbits and smear them with ½ cup of the mustard. Put them in a bowl, cover with plastic wrap, and marinate overnight.

Making the rabbit stock. Place the remaining rabbit bones in a roasting pan. Slide the pan into the oven and cook until the bones have color, about 30 minutes. Put the bones in a stockpot. Add ½ cup of water to the pan in which you roasted the bones and put it on the stovetop. Bring the water to a boil and scrape the goodness from the bottom of the pan, then add this water to the stockpot. Throw in half of the carrots, half of the celery, half of the onion, and half of the garlic. Add the tomato paste and enough water to cover by 2 inches. Simmer for 4 to 5 hours, skimming the scum as you go. Strain the stock and allow it to cool to room temperature. Refrigerate overnight.

Sautéing the rabbit. The next day, pull the mustard-covered rabbit pieces from the refrigerator and season with salt and pepper. Set a large sauté pan over medium-high heat and add 2 tablespoons of the oil. When the oil slides around the pan easily, add the rabbit pieces; do not crowd the pan. You will have to do this in batches, adding more oil to the pan each time. Sear the rabbit until the bottom turns a lovely brown color, about 3 minutes. Turn the rabbit pieces over and sear the other side. Put the browned rabbit pieces into a Dutch oven.

Preheat the oven to 375°F.

Cooking the mirepoix. Drain the fat from the bottom of the sauté pan and set it over medium heat. Pour in 2 tablespoons of the oil. When it has come to heat, add the remaining carrot, celery, onion, and garlic and cook, stirring occasionally, until the mirepoix has caramelized, about 15 minutes. Add the thyme and cook until it is fragrant.

Deglazing the pan. Pour in the wine to deglaze the pan and scrape up the goodness from the bottom. Cook until the wine has almost evaporated. Pour the vegetables into the Dutch oven with the rabbit. Cover with the rabbit stock. Set the Dutch oven over high heat and bring the liquid to a boil.

Braising the rabbit. Cover the Dutch oven and slide it into the oven. Cook until the thigh meat is tender to the tongs, 2 to 2½ hours.

Making the sauce. Remove the rabbit from the Dutch oven. Strain the sauce and return it to the pot. Bring it to a boil over medium-high heat. Whisk the remaining 2 cups of mustard into the sauce until the mustard is incorporated. Once the sauce begins to reduce and thicken, after about 10 minutes, add the butter. Whisk the sauce until it is emulsified.

To serve, place a rabbit leg and half of the saddle on each plate. Spoon the sauce over the rabbit.

cassoulet

VARIATIONS
Cassoulet is more of a suggestion than a set recipe. Every region in France has a different way of doing it. Some people make cassoulet with duck stock or sausage, and some with preserved duck or goose. Find your way.

SUGGESTIONS
Serve this with a salad. You'll want something light.

One night a week at Cassis, we served cassoulet. All week, we prepped for it. We made duck confit, lamb sausages, and rendered duck fat for that casserole. Days in advance, people called in for reservations for cassoulet day. On rainy Seattle Sundays, cassoulet was the right food for hunkering down into the evening.

There's nothing sophisticated about cassoulet. It's richly flavored peasant stew. That's what's funny about the name. People hear cassoulet and think it's too difficult to make. French women who live in the country make this every week. As long as you don't mind being patient, and using more than one kind of meat at a time, you can make cassoulet. The anticipation alone makes it worth it. So does the look on your friends' faces when they sink their spoons past the breadcrumbs into the braised pork and sausages, and look up at you knowing you are about to make them happy. • *Feeds 8*

1½ pounds pork shoulder, cut into
   2-inch cubes
4 teaspoons each kosher salt and cracked
   black pepper
4 tablespoons olive oil
1 carrot, peeled and cut in half
2 stalks celery, cut in half
1 large yellow onion, peeled and
   chopped in half
10 cloves garlic, peeled
1 cup dry white wine
1 quart veal stock (see page 148) or
   chicken stock
1 bay leaf

3 cups dried white beans, soaked in water
   to cover overnight
½ medium white onion, peeled and finely
   diced
One 28-ounce can San Marzano tomatoes,
   chopped
1 large sprig fresh rosemary
1 pound smoked pork belly (you can use
   unsliced bacon, if you wish)
4 duck confit legs (see page 186)
8 lamb sausage links, about 3 ounces each
   (feel free to substitute pork sausage)
4 cups gluten-free breadcrumbs
1 cup duck fat (see Resources, page 283)

Preheating the oven. Turn the oven to 350°F.

Searing the pork shoulder. Season the pork with 2 teaspoons each of salt and pepper. Set a large sauté pan over medium-high heat and pour in 1 tablespoon of the oil. Sear the pork until it has a beautiful brown crust on the bottom, about 5 minutes. Turn the meat and sear on the other side. Remove from the heat and transfer the pork to a Dutch oven.

Roasting the vegetables. Pour 1 tablespoon of the oil into the sauté pan in which the pork was seared. Add the carrot, celery, and yellow onion and cook over medium heat, stirring occasionally, until they begin to caramelize, about 10 minutes.

Making the braising liquid. Add 5 of the garlic cloves and cook until they are fragrant. Deglaze the pan with the wine, scraping the bottom for all the goodness. Cook until the liquid is reduced by half its volume, about 5 minutes. Pour in the stock and bring to a boil on high heat.

Braising the pork. Pour the contents of the sauté pan into the Dutch oven. Toss in the bay leaf and slide the Dutch oven into the oven. Cook until the meat is delightfully tender, 2 to 2½ hours.

Cooking the white beans. Set the large sauté pan that held the braising liquid over medium heat and pour in the remaining 2 tablespoons of oil. Add the white onion and cook, stirring, until it is softened and translucent, about 10 minutes. Stir in the tomatoes, the remaining 5 cloves of garlic, the rosemary, and the remaining 2 teaspoons each of salt and pepper. Add enough cold water to cover by 2 inches. Cook until the beans are tender, 45 minutes to 1 hour. Strain the beans. Discard the rosemary and garlic, but keep the tomatoes. When the pork is done, take the Dutch oven out of the oven. Remove the pork from the Dutch oven and strain the stock, setting it aside.

Assembling the cassoulet. Increase the oven temperature to 425°F. Cut the smoked pork belly (or bacon) into 8 pieces. Arrange the pieces in the bottom of a 4-quart casserole dish. Spoon the white beans on top of the belly. Separate the duck legs at the joint and arrange in the dish, with a sausage nestled next to each one. Spread the braised pork shoulder around the dish evenly. Pour in the reserved stock so that it's almost three-quarters of the way up the baking dish. Top the entire dish with the breadcrumbs. In a small pan, gently heat the duck fat until it is melted, then drizzle it over the top of the breadcrumbs.

Baking the cassoulet. Slide the casserole dish into the oven. Bake the cassoulet until the breadcrumbs have browned and the internal temperature of the sausages reaches 185°F, about 1 hour. The rest of the meat should be juicy and tender.

sweetness at the end of the evening

"I love desserts. Desserts are such a great way to end the meal. Plus, they make great breakfasts when you have to work in the morning. Desserts don't have to be complicated to be memorable. My mom made a great apple crisp. Warm out of the oven, that was my favorite food in the world. S'mores on camping trips out in the mountains. Just a touch of sweetness."

My mom made perfect apple pies, the crust dome-high with a little slit in the middle where I could peer down and see the cinnamon-bathed apples softening in the heat. We ate a lot of packaged baked goods too, which I couldn't eat now, even if I could eat gluten. But I loved that we always

had sweets in our house.

Before I met Danny, I had a raging sweet tooth that sometimes roared out of control. After he started feeding me his food, my sweet tooth started to tame itself. My preferences changed. Because I had been better at baking than making savory foods, my desserts were always the most interesting part of the meal. That was no longer true when Danny made smoked duck breast and wild rice with a sauce made of duck stock, blood oranges, crème de cassis, and kiwis.

I still love a great dessert, however. We had a corn crème brûlée with candied bacon at Tilth in Seattle that I'm still thinking about two years later.

Pastry chefs come from a special breed. They not only have to learn how to make all the traditional desserts—brûlées, flans, tarte Tatins; ice creams, cream puffs, and truffles—but they have to constantly reinvent themselves in sugar and cream. If pastry chefs are working at a restaurant that moves its menus through the seasons and delights in different ingredients, a standard crème brûlée at the end of a meal might make the experience fall flat. Instead, how about a rosemary crème brûlée with chocolate sea-salt shortbread? Our friend, Dana Cree, makes incredible desserts that leave us breathless, like dark chocolate terrine with ginger, cumin cashews, and sesame; or Pyrat rum and walnut praline ice cream with drunken prune topping. She works vigorously, meticulously, her head bent down toward the foods before her, fully focused. Dana uses sweetness as her base taste, and swirls in savory hits. Danny starts with the savory, but folds in fruit juices or liqueurs.

They are both chefs.

"In culinary school, we had two classes in baking. Cheesecakes and raspberry tarts. Basic stuff. Even though the first year's class started at four in the morning—and on Saturdays we started at one in the morning—I still loved it. We were responsible for stocking the bakeries upstairs, and the two restaurants the school ran, and we cleaned everything. But I learned how to make croissants and I was especially proud of a sun-dried tomato and rosemary bread. My second-year instructor said I had a good eye for it. But the savory stuff excited me even more."

Now, Danny is the pastry chef too. The kitchen and restaurant are so small that he doesn't have the space for a separate pastry chef. Danny does it all. For that reason, the desserts are simpler than Dana's. He has all the prepping and planning and cooking to do, the restaurant on his shoulders. "Either I do them myself or I buy the desserts, and I just won't do that." After I came along, and he turned the restaurant gluten-free, I sometimes worked as his unofficial pastry chef. I didn't know how to make sassafras ice cream—I'd sure like to learn, though—but I could make gluten-free chocolate–peanut butter brownies. Danny made the vanilla bean ice cream from scratch, and a rich chocolate sauce, and the diners were happy.

"At first, making desserts without gluten was hard. I wanted to do cakes, but I couldn't figure out how to do a genoise without gluten. The carrot cake turned out great, though. The chocolate pancakes made with teff and caramelized bananas, based on a recipe by Marcus Samuelsson—those were a big hit. And the blue cheese cheesecake with a fig crust sold out every night."

As with the savory foods, not being able to use gluten inspired Danny to new, sweeter heights.

"I just don't understand it when people don't order dessert."

Danny calls me from the restaurant sometimes, to complain that the desserts aren't selling. Over the course of the month, they do fine. If there's one evening where the dessert orders are light, he starts to worry. Should he have done something differently? Are they not good enough?

"Sweetie, you forget. Not everyone can afford dessert."

Many times I've been out to dinner with girlfriends, and we all ordered entrées and lived on the bread in place of appetizers. (I don't do that anymore.) We wanted dessert, but we couldn't afford it. Sometimes, we'd split a piece of chocolate cake with six forks.

But to Danny, dessert is the final note of what should be a food symphony. Not having dessert is like the Beatles' song that finishes *Abbey Road*, "Her Majesty," which deliberately leaves off the last chord, leaving the listener hanging.

Danny, however, always orders dessert when we go out to eat. It's his way of honoring the pastry chef and exploring every part of the place.

We visited San Francisco as part of the publicity tour for my first book. While we were there, we ate at the new restaurant where our friend, Shuna Fish Lydon, was the pastry chef. She personally marked up the menu for us, noting everything I could eat and what I had to avoid. She also instructed everyone on the line exactly how to feed me. We ate beautifully with our friends, and at the end of the evening, we were nearly full. However, we could not go without one of Shuna's desserts. To our surprise, and awe, Shuna sent out one of everything for us, any dessert she could make gluten-free. The table was filled with spiced hot chocolate with handmade honey marshmallows. Almond milk gelée with woodleaf peach and blackberry granita. Honey-cumin pot de crème with an heirloom apple–walnut–white fig salad. Citrus soufflé, fennel shortbread, lemon sherbet, and pine nut–date–anise–arbequina oil relish. I had to go without the shortbread, but at that point I was thrilled. We were stuffed. After thanking Shuna, profusely, we all groaned and moved slowly toward the BART.

We will always remember those desserts.

"I love that sweet, satisfying taste at the end of the meal. Almost as good as kissing you."

blue cheese cheesecake with fig crust

SUGGESTIONS
This would be a great dessert to take to a dinner party. Watch everyone be impressed.

VARIATIONS
We are big fans of Point Reyes blue cheese for this cheesecake because of its clean taste. You can substitute other blue cheeses, but be aware that an especially big blue taste might overpower the cheesecake.

We came up with the idea for this dessert while we sat in a restaurant called Salt, in Vancouver, B.C. After eating local cheeses and charcuteries, and sharing a wine flight, we admired the dessert: blue cheese cheesecake. Our mouths wanted to try it, but Shauna couldn't eat the gluten-filled crust. So we went home and made it instead.

I'm not a fan of blue cheese, at all. But this cheesecake made me rethink that position. It has just a hint of pungent blue cheese, the creaminess of both blue cheese and cream cheese, and the sweetness of sugar. I served it at the restaurant for a month. People were surprised. They thought it would be too weird for their sensibilities. Instead, it was the most popular dessert by far.

We make the crust for this cheesecake from the fig cookies in Shauna's first book. While we think that's ideal, you can also use packaged gluten-free shortbread cookies mixed with fig jam, if you wish. Find a way to make this cheesecake. You don't want to miss it. In fact, our friend Tara says this entire book is worth the price for this recipe. • *Feeds 16*

10 gluten-free fig cookies (we use the recipe from Shauna's first book, *Gluten-Free Girl***) or 10 store-bought gluten-free shortbread cookies plus 2 tablespoons fig jam**
Butter for greasing pan
16 ounces cream cheese (two 8-ounce boxes)

16 ounces good-quality blue cheese
1½ cups sugar
½ teaspoon salt
2 teaspoons vanilla extract
4 large eggs, at room temperature
1½ cups sour cream

Preheating the oven. Turn the oven to 350°F.

Making the crust. Whirl up the fig cookies (or the shortbread cookies and jam) in a food processor until they are the consistency of breadcrumbs. Butter a 9-inch springform cheesecake pan. Press the cookie crumbs into the bottom of the pan about a quarter of the way up the sides. Wrap the bottom of the cheesecake pan in a double layer of aluminum foil. Slide the pan into the oven and bake for 10 minutes. Set the crust on a wire rack to cool slightly.

Preparing to bake. Turn down the oven to 325°F. Bring a kettle of water to a boil.

Making the filling. In a food processor, beat the cream cheese and blue cheese together until they are a creamy consistency, about 4 minutes. Keeping the food processor running, add the sugar and salt. Let the food processor run until the mixture starts to be frothy, about 4 minutes more. Add the vanilla, and then the eggs, one by one, allowing the food processor to run a full minute between each egg. This will make the cheesecake light. Mix in the sour cream at low speed. Pour the batter into the crust.

Baking the cheesecake. Put the springform pan into a roasting pan large enough to leave some room on all sides. Pour in the boiling water, enough to come halfway up the sides of the cheesecake pan. Bake until the top is firm (no jiggle), nicely browned, and perhaps a little cracked, about 1½ hours. Turn off the oven and prop the door open a bit, perhaps with a wooden spoon. Let the cheesecake cool about 1 hour, as the water cools.

Cooling the cheesecake. Pull the roasting pan out of the oven. Pull out the springform pan and take off the aluminum foil.

Place the cheesecake pan on a wire rack and set aside until it has come to room temperature. Cover loosely with aluminum foil. Refrigerate for at least 4 hours, preferably overnight. When you are ready to serve, remove the sides of the springform pan and slice the cake.

chocolate mousse with jam and crème fraîche

VARIATIONS
If you want a darker taste, substitute the semisweet chocolate with bittersweet. Try orange marmalade or raspberry jam with the mousse.

SUGGESTIONS
You can make your own crème fraîche, if you like. It's simple to make.

The other day, good friends of ours admitted they had never made chocolate mousse before. Okay, you might think, neither have I. But one of them was the food editor for one of the leading Seattle newspapers.

There's something that seems impossible about chocolate mousse. The taste is so rich, the texture so decadent that we assume it must be difficult. However, once you have made it successfully, you will never be intimidated by it again. Mousse just takes a bit of time and patience.

For this dessert, you need extraordinary jam to stand up to the mousse. June Taylor, in Berkeley, makes her jam in small batches, using heirloom fruits in season, cooking slowly, with no pectin. This dessert occurred to me after we bought a jar of cherry-almond jam from her stand at the San Francisco ferry terminal farmers' market. You can find it online as well. • *Feeds 4*

8 ounces semisweet chocolate
  (make sure it's gluten-free)
4 tablespoons (½ stick) unsalted butter
⅛ teaspoon salt
1 teaspoon vanilla extract
4 large eggs, separated
¾ cup heavy cream

½ teaspoon cream of tartar
2 tablespoons sugar
4 tablespoons thick, high-quality
  cherry jam
1 teaspoon sea salt
½ cup crème fraîche

Melting the chocolate. Set a large pot of water at a gentle boil. Place a metal bowl on top of it. Lower the chocolate and butter into the metal bowl. Stir with a rubber spatula, evenly, until they are both melting. Pinch in the salt and continue stirring until the mixture has entirely melted. If the pot is boiling too much, the edges of the chocolate will burn; if you scrape that into the mousse, then your mousse will taste terrible. Pay attention. Add the vanilla, remove from the heat, and stir.

Whisking in the egg yolks. Whisk in the egg yolks, one at a time, incorporating each completely before starting the next. Once they are all whisked in, let that mixture cool to room temperature.

Whipping the cream. Whip the heavy cream to stiff peaks in your stand mixer, if you have one. (If not, use your biceps.) Spoon into a separate bowl and set aside.

Beating the egg whites. Thoroughly clean and dry the mixer bowl. Then, using the whisk attachment on high speed, beat the egg whites with the cream of tartar until they form stiff peaks. Pour in the sugar and beat the mixture until it is stiff.

Folding in the egg whites. Fold a quarter of the egg whites into the chocolate mixture with a rubber spatula. Stir gently until they are completely incorporated. Fold in the rest of the egg whites until there is no visual trace of the egg whites.

Finishing the mousse. Slowly, gently, fold the whipped cream into the chocolate mixture. When the cream has joined forces with the chocolate completely, the mousse is done.

Chilling the mousse and serving. Chill the mousse for at least 2 hours before serving it. Spoon the jam into the bottom of a martini glass. Scoop in the chocolate mousse. Pinch some sea salt on top of the mousse. Top with the crème fraîche.

make your own crème fraîche

Find some good fresh cream, one that is not ultra-pasteurized. Let it sit out for a bit to come to room temperature. Combine the cream and a few tablespoons of buttermilk in a small saucepan. Heat it until it is about 85°F. (That will take no time at all.) Put the mixture in a jar. Place the lid on it. Allow the jar to sit in a warm place in the house for a day or two, stirring every morning. One morning, you'll lift off the lid, put in a spoon, and let out a gasp. Crème fraîche!

carrot cake with ginger frosting

VARIATIONS
You can use golden raisins or walnuts, or both. If you cannot eat dairy, you can use nondairy "buttery" sticks in place of the butter.

SUGGESTIONS
You can also add a small amount of ginger juice with the carrot juice, when you are making the cake, if you have your own juicer.

Before the first bite of every gluten-free baked good, I pause and wonder—will this bite be worth it? So many gluten-free cakes, while well-meaning, taste as though the baker used sawdust instead of butter. I think we can promise you that a bite of this cake will be worth your trouble.

The secret here is to reduce fresh carrot juice to a puddle. The rich flavor of carrots weaves itself into the cake and helps to keep everything moist, as well. In this new world of baking, I've learned to adapt what I know from savory cooking. I once watched my head chef make a carrot vinaigrette, with cilantro, by reducing a pint of pale carrot juice to a dark orange quarter-cup. Oh, the flavor was so amazing that I have always remembered it. We tried it one day in our carrot cake and danced around the kitchen when we tasted it.

Some of us like a lot of stuff in our carrot cake. You can add the raisins and the walnuts if you like. We like ours plain, and moist, and topped with this spicy ginger frosting. • *Feeds 8 to 12*

2 cups fresh carrot juice
Canola oil for oiling parchment paper
⅔ cup (75g/2.6oz) almond flour
½ cup (60g/2oz) tapioca flour
¼ cup (30g/1oz) sweet rice flour
¼ cup (30g/1oz) superfine brown rice flour
1 teaspoon xanthan gum or an equal amount of psyllium husks
¾ teaspoon guar gum or an equal amount of psyllium husks
1 teaspoon baking powder
1 teaspoon salt
1 teaspoon ground cinnamon
½ teaspoon ground nutmeg
½ teaspoon ground ginger
¼ teaspoon ground cloves
16 tablespoons (2 sticks) unsalted butter at room temperature

½ cup packed dark brown sugar
½ cup white sugar
4 large eggs, plus 2 large eggs, separated
1 orange, zest grated
1 teaspoon vanilla extract
1 cup peeled and grated carrots
⅓ cup chopped walnuts (optional)
⅓ cup golden raisins (optional)
Pinch cream of tartar

GINGER CREAM CHEESE FROSTING
8 ounces cream cheese
16 tablespoons (2 sticks) unsalted butter at room temperature
1 tablespoon ground ginger
⅛ teaspoon ground cardamom
3 to 4 cups powdered sugar

Reducing the carrot juice. In a small saucepan over medium heat, add the carrot juice. Allow the juice to come to a small boil, then turn down the heat to low. Ignore the juice for a while and let it slowly reduce, coming back to stir it occasionally. After about 20 minutes or so, the juice should be dark in color and reduced to about ¼ cup. Take it off the heat and let it cool.

Preparing to bake. Preheat the oven to 350°F. Cut a circle of parchment paper to fit a 9-inch cake pan. Grease both sides of the paper with oil and place it in the pan. *(continued on page 260)*

Combining the dry ingredients. Sift the almond flour, tapioca flour, sweet rice flour, and brown rice flour into a bowl and stir to combine. Sift the combined flours into another bowl. Add the xanthan gum, guar gum, baking powder, salt, cinnamon, nutmeg, ginger, and cloves. Stir and set aside.

Working with the wet ingredients. Beat the butter and sugars together until they are creamy and fluffy. Add the 4 eggs and the 2 egg yolks, one at a time, beating for 1 minute before adding the next egg. Add the orange zest and vanilla. Pour in the reduced carrot juice and stir.

Marrying the two together. Sift the dry ingredients into the liquids and beat until they are combined. By hand, add the carrots, walnuts (if using), and raisins (if using). The cake batter should be quite thick, but you should still be able to work a rubber spatula through it easily.

Incorporating the egg whites. In a clean, dry mixing bowl, beat the 2 egg whites with the cream of tartar until they form stiff peaks. Gently, fold the stiff egg whites into the cake batter until they are entirely incorporated.

Baking the cake. Pour the batter into the prepared cake pan. Slide the pan into the oven and bake until a knife inserted into the center of the cake comes out clean and the top is golden brown, about 45 minutes. Transfer the pan to a wire rack and let the cake sit for 15 minutes before removing it from the pan. Turn the cake out onto the rack, turn it right side up, and let it cool completely before frosting it.

Making the frosting. In a mixing bowl, combine the cream cheese, butter, ginger, cardamom, and powdered sugar until they are smooth. Start with 3 cups of powdered sugar, then add more if you want the frosting thicker and sweeter. Spread the frosting on the top and sides of the cake.

chocolate–peanut butter brownies

VARIATIONS
If you cannot eat dairy, you can use nondairy "buttery" sticks in place of the butter.

SUGGESTIONS
Remember that the quality of the chocolate determines the quality of these brownies, so choose accordingly. Serve these with a dollop of ice cream or whipped cream on top. If you want, you can cut each brownie in half and put a layer of jam between the two halves for a peanut butter and jelly brownie.

Sometimes, my favorite cooking is trying to recreate the flavors of my childhood. I find that I keep circling back to what I ate in a small town in Colorado in the 1970s. While I really can't eat most of the boxed and processed foods anymore, because they don't taste good to me, I still want the giddy discovering of when I was a kid.

I loved Reese's peanut butter cups growing up. And I do love brownies. Why not combine them? That's what these brownies are—gluten-free candy bars, in baked form. But they're better than those candy bars. If you take the time to bake, you have the satisfaction of knowing you made it yourself.

Shauna made these for a month as one of the desserts of the restaurant, and we served them with a scoop of ice cream and hot chocolate sauce. Are you surprised that we ran out of them every night? • *Feeds as few or as many as you wish*

Canola oil for greasing pan
Sweet rice flour for dusting pan
8 tablespoons (1 stick) unsalted butter, cut into large chunks
4 ounces unsweetened chocolate, (make sure it's gluten-free)
⅓ cup (40g/1.4oz) oat flour (make sure it is ground from certified gluten-free oats)
⅓ cup sweet rice flour

1 teaspoon xanthan gum, or an equal amount of psyllium husks
1 teaspoon baking powder
½ teaspoon salt
1 cup sugar
2 large eggs
1 teaspoon vanilla extract
4 tablespoons peanut butter, at room

Preparing to bake. Preheat the oven to 350°F. Grease an 8-inch square baking pan with oil. Dust it with sweet rice flour.

Melting the chocolate and butter. Set a large pot of water at a gentle boil. Place a metal bowl on top of it. Lower the butter and chocolate into the metal bowl. Stir with a rubber spatula, evenly, until they are both melting, taking care not to burn the mixture. When it has all melted and become one, take the pot off the heat. Cool to room temperature.

Combining the flours. In a bowl, combine the oat flour, sweet rice flour, and xanthan gum. Sift the mixture through a fine-mesh sieve into a large bowl. Stir in the baking powder and salt.

Making the batter. Whisk the sugar into the chocolate mixture. Next, whisk in the eggs and vanilla. Stir in the dry ingredients until the mixture is just combined.

Baking the brownies. Pour the batter into the prepared pan. Dollop the peanut butter onto the top of the batter. Gently, swirl the peanut butter into the batter with a spoon. Smooth the top of the batter. Set the pan on the middle rack of the oven. Bake until a knife inserted into the middle of the pan comes out clean, about 25 minutes. If some batter remains on the knife, continue baking in 3- to 5-minute increments until the brownies are done. Cool completely before slicing into pieces as large or small as you like. Or, grab a fork.

burnt garlic

Sometimes, when Danny and I walk down the sidewalk, he stops as we pass a restaurant. "Do you smell that?" I do. Something acrid and pungent, a familiar smell gone wrong.

"Burnt garlic. God, I hate that smell."

Danny can spot the smell of burnt garlic from five hundred yards away. He has me noticing it too. There are few smells more bothersome to the nose.

"Burnt garlic smells like laziness. It's not hard to catch the garlic before it burns. It's about paying attention. And the thing about it is, if you do burn it, and think you can hide it, you're deluded. Try wine sauce, more cheese, a ton

of salt and pepper, whatever you want. It's not going to work. Every bite of food will taste like burnt garlic."

When I pick up Danny at the end of the night, most of the time we are ecstatic to see each other after ten hours apart. But some nights, we are exhausted. He might have spent the evening in the weeds, buried up to his knees, annoyed by servers who can't seem to pronounce a dish correctly, and embittered by the perceived slight of one of his coworkers. That restaurant is tiny, with only a few employees, and they get on each other's nerves quickly. "Sometimes I like small places, but sometimes they are too much." Normally kind and accommodating, Danny can occasionally make a night of words held back and a quick angry glance into agony for the people working with him. Danny doesn't shout. He's not one of those television chefs who puff up their chests and bellow. He boils, and then he simmers.

And when he climbs into the car on those nights, tired and pent-up, he gives it all to me.

"When you sauté mushrooms, you are supposed to cook the garlic first. But if you go too fast, you're going to burn the garlic. So put the mushrooms in first, and then the garlic. It doesn't go strictly according to the rules, but it works. You still have to pay attention, because you can still burn the garlic, but it's not so easy."

Maybe I've had a long day at the computer, alone, feeling inadequate. Staring at a blank screen and trying to create something from nothing kicks me in the teeth. Much as I love to write—and am thrilled I no longer have to attend faculty meetings—this life leaves me alone much of the day. Most the time, I love the fact that I keep the house in line, pay the bills, run the website, keep the car gassed up, and do the laundry. But there are days when I despair that friends get starred reviews in *Publishers Weekly* and I can't write a damn sentence I like to save my life. Then I feel stupid for being so petulant, and there's no one else in the room to distract me from myself. I can't call Danny, because he's in the middle of dinner service, and I have a deadline

I have to meet. So I look forward to those reunions at the end of the evening. When he climbs in the car to complain about the same situation again, I sigh into the darkness as I drive us away.

"If you're making a big batch of tomato sauce and you burn the garlic, you're fucked. If you continue on like nothing happened, and it's a ten- or fifteen-gallon of tomato sauce, that's a lot of money you've wasted. Not just the product, but the prep time. If you have a dishwasher doing the prep work, that's a lot of time from that other person. It's not a wham-bam thank you ma'am. That's time."

Danny starts complaining after a quick kiss. Someone sent a plate of fish back. His assistant stood with her back to the refrigerator, watching him instead of working. Hortensia was in a bad mood. The manager, who has threatened to quit a dozen times, bitched at him all evening until she stepped into the bathroom and came back trembling with sudden nervous energy and no attention span. It's pretty obvious what she had been doing.

I've heard it all before, this evening just a variation on an old theme. Shy since he was a child, Danny never learned to stand up for himself or say anything confrontational straight out. Most nights, I feel for him, and listen. However, sometimes I just want to shout, "You always focus on the one person who doesn't like your food. You never told your assistant that you don't want her to just stand around so you can't expect her to read your mind. Hortensia was grumpy because you were fuming and ruined her mood in the kitchen. And you suspect that [the manager] does coke, but you've never talked to the owner. Why don't you just say something?"

I know that yelling won't change anything. I grew up in a family where people yelled, and I'm determined not to copy that. I remember what Danny told me they taught him in school: "(1) Chef is always right. (2) If Chef is wrong, refer back to rule #1. Say 'Yes, Chef,' and move on. Talk to him or her about it later."

Danny says, "Some people in restaurants aren't really the best equipped to deal with tough emotional situations. A lot of us are hotheaded, depending on the chef and the kind of mood he or she is in. I've been screamed at. Some of the people who work in restaurants have a fairly high divorce rate.

"One of my chefs 86ed the rack of lamb at 7 p.m. one night, even though nothing else was getting sold. He was pissed that no customers were buying the specials he had put together that day, and he figured that if he wouldn't let them buy the lamb, they would have to buy his creations. His wife, who worked the front of the house, was so furious at him that he slept at the restaurant that night. He grabbed himself a bottle of Scotch, drank most of it, and passed out on one of the banquettes.

"I don't want that, my love."

Neither do I.

"When you burn the garlic, you have to stop what you are doing and start all over. You can burn the garlic in a relationship too."

We are almost home, and we aren't really talking. I can feel the snit building up, and I start to follow it, even though I don't feel good in my stomach. We've had a few fights over the time we have known each other, and neither of us enjoyed them. The rest of those days tasted like heirloom tomato sauce with burnt garlic.

Early on, I shared this quote by Karl Jaspers with Danny, something that has informed me every day since: "Grief appears when communication fails." We've been teaching each other how we want to be treated.

"You have to throw out the burnt garlic and start over. If you try and mask the burnt garlic, and work on that dish like nothing happened, then it's going to be a shitty dish."

Danny looks over at me, takes a breath, and says, "I smell burnt garlic."

I let go of my breath and turn toward him.

roasted garlic and white bean spread

VARIATIONS
You can use onions instead of shallots, sage or thyme instead of the rosemary. Basil would work well too. Use this recipe as your template and play.

SUGGESTIONS
You will have roasted garlic left over. Keep it wrapped up in the refrigerator for later use, when you can fold it into pastas, soups, and scrambled eggs. Or you can use it to make Garlic Flan (see following page).

People love garlic or they hate it. Some of my customers are allergic to it. Our friend Cindy won't eat it. She's a great cook, but we still feel bad for her, missing out on this. Garlic opens every ingredient it touches, infusing the food with its warmth and building a depth of flavor.

If you roast garlic and fold it into this spread, people who are wary of garlic might be more open to it afterwards. It's a great dip for cocktail parties or a late-afternoon snack. You could also use it as a base for making a sauce for fish, if you want. As well as being delicious, this spread is healthy for you. Remember, you don't have to eat boring, tasteless food to be healthy. • *Feeds 4*

1 large head garlic
4 tablespoons extra-virgin olive oil
Kosher salt and cracked black pepper
1 cup dried cannellini or great northern
   beans, soaked overnight

1 sprig fresh rosemary
1 large shallot, peeled and sliced
1 lemon, zest grated and juiced
1 tablespoon finely chopped fresh Italian
   parsley

Roasting the garlic. Preheat the oven to 350°F. Cut the head of garlic in half, horizontally. Drizzle both halves with 1 tablespoon of the oil and season with salt and pepper. Put the garlic in a small sauté pan and cover it with aluminum foil. Roast in the oven until the garlic is soft enough that you can squeeze the cloves out of their skins, 45 minutes to 1 hour.

Cooking the beans. Set a large saucepan over high heat and add the beans. Cover the beans with cold water by 2 inches. Toss in the rosemary. Bring the water to a boil. Turn the heat down to medium and allow the beans to simmer until they are very tender to the fork, about 45 minutes. You don't want a bit of crunch in them. Drain the beans.

Sautéing the shallots. Set a sauté pan over medium heat and pour in 1 tablespoon of the oil. Put the shallot in the hot oil. Sauté the shallot until it is soft and translucent, 2 to 3 minutes. Do not allow it to brown.

Making the spread. Pour three-quarters of the beans, 1 teaspoon of the roasted garlic, and the sautéed shallot into a food processor. As the beans are pureeing, drizzle in the remaining 2 tablespoons of oil. Taste the puree. If you like more garlic in your puree, add it here. Season with salt and pepper.

Transfer the bean puree back to the bowl of whole beans. Toss in the lemon zest and parsley. Pour in 2 teaspoons of lemon juice. Taste the puree—you want a hit of lemon, roasted garlic, beans, salt, and pepper. Season with salt and pepper and whatever else you might need.

Refrigerate the spread until it is cool.

garlic flan

VARIATIONS
You could make these flans with basil, marjoram, or sage. You could make a curried version of this by adding a teaspoon of curry powder when you boil the cream. Try tarragon with fennel fronds.

SUGGESTIONS
These flans are the perfect garnishes for lamb chops. The roasted garlic and roasted chicken would dance well. Anything that goes well with garlic would work with these. Serve them as an antipasti with sliced prosciutto or Spanish ham. Or make lemon garlic flans with lemon zest. For real decadence, drizzle some aged balsamic vinegar on top of each flan.

Roasting garlic sweetens the bitterness and calms the sharpness we all identify with raw garlic. Roasted garlic has this miraculous ability to enhance the flavors of other foods, rather than asserting itself with a blare, the way that raw garlic can.

This flan is a savory version of dessert flan, a little appetizer that goes especially well with lamb. What scares people about flan is the idea of tempering the yolks. If you dump all of the hot cream all at once into the yolks, you will make scrambled eggs. If you do curdle the eggs, you might be tempted to strain the liquid and still try to use it, but those eggs will screw up your flan. Start again. Take your time. This requires patience. • *Feeds 4*

1 large head garlic
1 tablespoon extra-virgin olive oil
2 teaspoons each kosher salt and cracked black pepper
Butter for greasing ramekins

1½ cups whole milk
½ cup heavy cream
1 bay leaf
1 sprig fresh rosemary
4 large egg yolks

Roasting the garlic. Preheat the oven to 350°F. Cut the head of garlic in half, horizontally. Drizzle both halves with the oil and season with 1 teaspoon each of salt and pepper. Put the garlic in a small sauté pan and cover it with aluminum foil. Roast in the oven until the garlic is soft enough that you can squeeze the cloves out of their skins, 45 minutes to 1 hour. [If you have leftover roasted garlic from making the Roasted Garlic and White Bean Spread (see page 264), use it here.] Keep the oven on.

Preparing to make the flans. Set a kettle of water over high heat. Butter eight ¼-cup ramekins.

Pureeing the roasted garlic. Puree 1 tablespoon of the roasted garlic in a food processor. (Reserve the rest of the roasted garlic for another dish.)

Heating the cream. Set a large saucepan over medium-high heat and add the milk and cream. Drop in the roasted garlic puree, bay leaf, and rosemary. Bring the liquid to a boil, then take it off the heat.

Tempering the eggs. In a mixing bowl, whisk the egg yolks. Pour a quarter of the hot cream mixture into the egg yolks, stirring continuously. Keep adding the cream, in a continuous stream, into the egg yolks until it is all incorporated. Pinch in the remaining 1 teaspoon each of salt and pepper and stir. Strain the liquid through a fine-mesh sieve.

Baking the flans. Pour the mixture into the buttered ramekins. Put the ramekins in a large roasting pan or baking dish. Slide the roasting pan into the oven and leave the door open. Remove the ramekin from the left-front position. Pour the boiling water into the empty space in the roasting pan, halfway up the ramekins. Place the ramekin back in the roasting pan. Arrange aluminum foil over the ramekins and poke a few holes in it with a paring knife. Bake until the flans are set, 25 to 30 minutes.

Finishing the ramekins. Remove the ramekins from the oven and from the roasting pan. Allow them to cool to room temperature, then refrigerate. The flans taste best cold.

aioli

VARIATIONS
There are endless variations on aioli. Try tarragon, basil, or cilantro aioli, with about 1 table-spoon of the herb. Kalamata olive aioli is particularly fantastic. How about curry aioli?

SUGGESTIONS
We love homemade aioli in deviled eggs, steamed ar-tichokes, poached fish, and any vari-ety of sandwiches.

Go to the grocery store and let your eyes follow the rows and rows of jars of mayonnaise. Their eggy-white surfaces are a bland expanse. By their sheer volume alone, one would think that it is darned near impossible to make mayonnaise. Surely, this one is beyond us.

Of course, that's not true.

Many people who have been gluten-free for years avoid commercial mayonnaise. That's because the gospel of gluten-free said that distilled vinegars, which are in almost all commercial mayonnaises, contain gluten. The good news? They do not. Even if those vinegars are distilled with gluten-containing substances, the final product is gluten-free. However, that doesn't mean that we should run out and buy jars of mayonnaise. Not when the homemade version tastes so much better. With a bit of attention, and a good food processor, making mayonnaise will take less time than a run to the grocery store. And a bit of raw garlic makes it aioli. • *Makes 2 cups*

1 large egg
1 egg yolk
2 cloves garlic, peeled and finely chopped
1 teaspoon Dijon mustard

2 teaspoons fresh lemon juice
1 cup canola oil
Kosher salt and cracked black pepper

Making the aioli. Add the egg, egg yolk, garlic, mustard, and lemon juice to a food processor. (You can make aioli by hand, but it is much easier and more fail-safe in the food processor, trust me.) While the machine is running, slowly drizzle in the oil, until it is thick and creamy. Season with salt and pepper.

Fixing your mistakes. If you add the oil too fast, the aioli will separate, so go slowly, slowly, slowly. If it does separate, take the mixture out of the food processor, and start over. Add another egg and egg yolk to the food processor and blend them. Slowly, slowly add the separated aioli. That should do the trick.

roasted garlic soup

VARIATIONS
If you are lactose intolerant, you can skip the heavy cream and add lactose-free milk instead.

SUGGESTIONS
If you have a really sharp mandoline, buy some elephant garlic, peel it, slice it fine, and put it on a baking sheet and bake it at 250°F for 30 minutes, with a bit of extra-virgin olive oil on top. Garnish the soup with the crispy garlic bits.

If you are making this soup for a date, someone you want to kiss, you might skip this soup. If you've already decided to get married, it may not matter. • *Feeds 4*

1 large head garlic, separated into cloves and peeled
⅓ cup extra-virgin olive oil
1 large yellow onion, peeled and roughly chopped
1 teaspoon finely chopped fresh rosemary

1 russet potato, peeled and cut into 1-inch cubes
4 cups vegetable stock
½ cup heavy cream
Kosher salt and cracked black pepper
¼ cup finely chopped fresh chives

Roasting the garlic. Preheat the oven to 350°F. Put the garlic cloves in a large saucepan and add the oil. Cover with aluminum foil. Roast in the oven until the garlic is soft enough that you can squeeze the cloves out of their skins, 45 minutes to 1 hour. Strain the cloves and reserve the roasted garlic oil.

Cooking the soup. Set a Dutch oven over medium-high heat and add 2 tablespoons of the roasted garlic oil. Add the onion and cook, stirring, until it is softened and translucent, about 10 minutes. Add the rosemary and cook until it releases its fragrance. Stir in the roasted garlic and potato cubes, then pour in enough vegetable stock to cover the vegetables by 1 inch. Cook until a knife inserted into a potato piece cuts through easily, about 15 minutes.

Pureeing the soup. Puree the soup in a powerful blender or food processor until it is entirely smooth. Continuing to puree, drizzle ¼ cup of the roasted garlic oil into the soup. When that is done, slowly pour in the cream.

Finishing the soup. Taste the soup and season with salt and pepper, if necessary.
To serve, ladle the soup into bowls and garnish with the chives.

meals at midnight

"At the end of a shift, depending on what time it was, I caught a bus, if I got out early enough. If I missed the 10:30, I'd have to wait until the 11:30. I'd sit at the bar and have a glass of wine, waiting. Maybe one of the girls would give me a lift, and ask if I'd want to go out for a drink. Love to, I'd say."

Music playing, I'm standing at the stove, cooking bacon. Sizzle and spit, fat rendering out. The sky outside the window is dark, the room inside is warm. It's almost 10:30, time to leave soon.

Danny says, "When I worked at Cassis, I'd go have a beer

at the Roanoke Tavern with Laurie. She was just a friend. We got along really well, but I never thought of dating her. I learned early on not to date anyone at work. I went years without dating anyone."

I bash the lemongrass with the back of the chef's knife, the way he taught me, and the herb releases its scent from beneath my fingers. For a moment, I stop prepping and lean in.

"When I lived in New York, there was a bar next door to Gramercy Tavern. Every once in a while, I'd grab a beer there with one of the guys I worked with. But not often. It was hard to make friends there. Mostly, I was alone in that city."

I strip the rosemary from its woody stem, chiffonade the basil into slices that unfurl when I lay them down. The egg yolks under the palms of my hands meet the ground beef, and begin the juicy wriggle that will meld them together, into one.

"After I reached my apartment, I'd still be up for another hour or two. I'd watch TV, drink a six-pack of beer. I'd replay the day in my mind while I sat there, what went wrong at dinner service, leave myself notes about what to do the next day."

Onions are chopped and pushed into a tidy pile. The carrots sit in tiny dices, huddled next to the green slivers of celery stalks. Humming along to a song I have only recently learned, I pull the veal stock from the refrigerator. Time to start cooking.

Danny was so lonely before we met. Almost forty, he didn't know if he would find someone to share a meal with at the end of the night.

I had more people in my life than he did. For the first year of my website, I made a different meal every night. I'd have friends over, give out leftovers for lunch at school, and find my way back to the kitchen. But at the end of the evening, I was the only one doing the dishes. I thought I would always be alone.

Now, I want to have a home-cooked meal waiting for him at the end of his long night. I know. How June Cleaver of me. But there it is. I want to cook for my husband. He has made all those people happy in the belly, all evening. I want to make him happy now.

When I was growing up, and sat under the spell of every sappy love song on the radio, I wondered. (You know those songs.) I wanted it. Oh boy, did I long for that imagining.

(Embarrassing admission: I remember a moment of deep keening, listening to Olivia Newton-John's "Xanadu," while developing photographs in a darkroom with a boy I loved, at twelve.)

But could that imagined love be real?

None of those fantasies comes close to capturing it. Every love song I play for him is just a finger pointing, guiding him toward my feelings. I will never convey it with these words.

As I start the meat braising, I think of the night of Valentine's Day, when he brought home pickled cabbage—magenta pink—in a Ziploc bag from the restaurant, late at night. He knows how much I love everything pickled. When I asked him how he made it, he could tell that I was already going into work mode (I could put it on the blog!) before I had even tasted it. He put his finger to his lips, and then to mine, and said, "Not now. Just eat it." I took a bite, and sighed. Sweetly puckering at the lips and whispering of spices. Pepper? Bay leaves? Cloves. A touch of sugar. Vinegar? He nods. Champagne vinegar, it turns out, along with salt. After a few bites, I didn't ask him for the recipe. I simply settled into bed and lay my head upon his chest, felt his arm around my shoulder, and fed him pickled cabbage.

Sighing at the memory, I turn back to that night's meal. Every meal with him feels like a gift.

"Dinner with you is my favorite part of the day. I get to spend time with the one I love. I missed you. A dozen phone calls doesn't do it."

And so we sit, in the kitchen, talking about the night as we dig into meatloaf, or three-cheese lasagna. Ours is the only light still on in that quiet residential neighborhood. We lift spoons filled with veal paprika, or twirl forks in the arugula-fig salad and talk about how good the food tastes, together. It's the two of us, huddled over the table, eating and talking, late into the night.

And the next day, it all happens again.

three-cheese lasagna

VARIATIONS
If you would like to make this vegetarian, simply remove the sausage. If you cannot eat dairy, you can make this a cheese-less lasagna and add extra sausage and other vegetables to fill it out.

SUGGESTIONS
Use this recipe as a template. You can try ground pork, ground beef, or lamb in place of the sausage, oregano in place of the basil, and store-bought gluten-free lasagna noodles if you want to save time.

Lasagna makes me feel warm in the tummy. It's comfort food, and it's even better the day after you make it. Making a few choices, like using fresh herbs and cheese you grate yourself, can make this old favorite into something fresh. • *Feeds 8 to 10*

1 recipe fresh gluten-free pasta (see page 60), rolled out in sheets (see directions below)
8 tablespoons olive oil
2 medium yellow onions, peeled and large diced
5 cloves garlic, peeled and thinly sliced
3 tablespoons chiffonade fresh basil
One 32-ounce can diced tomatoes
1 cup water

4 teaspoons each kosher salt and cracked black pepper
2 pounds sweet Italian sausage, sliced
1 pound button mushrooms, quartered
1 large red bell pepper, chopped
2 tablespoons fresh oregano, chopped
1 cup fresh ricotta cheese, at room temperature
2 cups shredded fresh mozzarella cheese, drained of water
1 cup freshly grated Parmesan cheese

Making the pasta. Roll out the pasta as thin as you can into 8 large sheets. Set aside.

Making the sauce. Set a large saucepan over medium-high heat and pour in 2 tablespoons of the oil. Add half of the onions and three of the cloves of garlic to the hot oil and cook, stirring occasionally, until the onion is softened and translucent, about 5 minutes. Add the basil and cook until it releases its fragrance, about 2 minutes. Add the tomatoes and water and stir everything together. Turn down the heat to medium-low and simmer for 10 minutes. Taste the sauce and season with some salt and pepper. Puree the sauce in a blender until smooth, then pour in 2 tablespoons of the oil and blend. Taste the sauce again to see if you need more seasoning. Set aside the sauce.

Sautéing the sausage mixture. Set a large sauté pan over medium-high heat and pour in the remaining 4 tablespoons of oil. Add the sausage and cook, stirring occasionally, until it is browned. Remove the sausage from the pan. Add the remaining onion, the mushrooms, and the red pepper and cook, stirring occasionally, until the mushrooms are browned and the pepper is softened, about 5 minutes. Add the remaining garlic, the oregano, and the browned sausage and cook, stirring, until the oregano and garlic are fragrant, about 3 minutes.

Preheating the oven. Turn the oven to 450°F. Pull out an 8½ x 11-inch casserole dish.

Making the lasagna. Put two sheets of the pasta side by side to cover the bottom of the casserole dish. Scoop in 1 cup of the sausage mixture, followed by ⅓ cup of the ricotta cheese, ½ cup of the mozzarella cheese, ¼ cup of the Parmesan cheese, and ½ cup of the tomato sauce. Repeat the layering until the casserole pan is filled. Finish with a layer of pasta, the last of the pasta sauce, and the remaining mozzarella and Parmesan.

Baking the lasagna. Cover the pan with aluminum foil and slide it into the oven. Bake for 20 minutes. Remove the foil and bake until the cheese is browned and bubbly, about 10 minutes.

veal paprika

VARIATIONS
If you don't want to cook veal, you could make this with pork shoulder butt. You could use sweet paprika instead of smoked. If you cannot eat dairy, use for a vegan sour cream.

SUGGESTIONS
Veal paprika goes well with mashed potatoes or jasmine rice. This is best made the day before. Let it sit in the stew liquid overnight, and eat it the next day. If you do this, before cooking the stew, you should strain the stock, throw out the mirepoix, bring the liquid to a boil, and proceed from there.

We made this at Papillon every Friday, as the lunch special of the day. The slow braising, the veal and the paprika, the mushrooms and onions, the good veal stock that had been simmering for two days—man, this was good. For Friday lunches, the dining room was stuffed full of diners.

Use good paprika with this, not the stuff that has been on your shelf since your mom gave it to you when you moved into your first apartment. Good sticky rice is wonderful with this. My life grew even more full when I taught Shauna how to make this, and she started making it for dinner for the two of us at midnight. • *Feeds 4*

1½ pounds veal stew meat (preferably shoulder or top round), cut into 2-inch chunks
1 teaspoon each kosher salt and cracked black pepper
½ cup extra-virgin olive oil
1 large yellow onion, peeled and large diced
1 large carrot, peeled and large diced
2 large stalks celery, large diced
8 large cloves garlic, peeled and chopped
2 tablespoons smoked paprika (Pimentón de la Vera)

1 teaspoon Piment d'Espelette (optional)
½ cup dry white wine
1 quart veal stock (see page 148) or chicken stock
3 cups quartered button or cremini mushrooms
2 medium carrots, peeled and medium diced
1 medium yellow onion, peeled and sliced
½ cup sour cream
2 tablespoons finely chopped fresh chives (optional)

Searing the meat. Season the veal with salt and pepper. Set a Dutch oven over medium-high heat. Pour in 4 tablespoons of the oil and put the meat in the hot oil. Sear the cubes until the bottoms are browned, about 1 minute. Turn the meat and sear on all sides until it is entirely browned, about 5 minutes. Remove from the pan and set it aside.

Sautéing the vegetables. Pour 2 more tablespoons of oil into the Dutch oven. Put the onion, carrot, celery, and about three-quarters of the garlic in the hot oil. Sauté until the vegetables are soft and the onion is translucent, about 5 minutes. Spoon in the smoked paprika and Piment d'Espelette (if using). Cook until the smell perfumes the room, about 3 minutes.

Deglazing the pan. Pour in the wine and scrape up all the goodness from the bottom. Cook until the wine is reduced by half its volume, about 5 minutes.

Making the stew. Splash in the stock and bring the liquid to a boil. Reduce the heat to low and lace the meat in the stew. Simmer the stew on the back of the stove until the meat is meltingly tender, 2 to 3 hours.

Finishing the dish. When the meat is tender, strain the liquid and discard all the vegetables. Set the meat and liquid aside. Put the Dutch oven back onto a medium-high burner and pour in the remaining 2 tablespoons of the oil. Place the mushrooms, carrots, and onion in the hot

oil and cook until they are soft, about 10 minutes. Toss in the remaining garlic and cook until it releases its fragrance, about 3 minutes

Pour the cooking liquid back into the pot and bring it to a boil. Turn down the heat to low. Simmer the sauce until it is reduced by a quarter of its volume, about 15 minutes.

Whisk in the sour cream. Reduce the liquid until it begins to thicken, about 5 minutes. Toss in the meat and cook long enough to heat it.

Serve with chopped chives on top, if you wish.

danny's favorite meatloaf

VARIATIONS
Some people prefer rolled oats to breadcrumbs in their meatloaf. If you are gluten-free, make sure to use certified gluten-free oats.

SUGGESTIONS
This meatloaf goes best with baked potatoes and sour cream. (We never eat anything else with it.) Mashed potatoes are great too. The glaze would also work well on roasted chicken or a pot roast.

Whenever I called home from the restaurant and asked Shauna what was for dinner, and she said meatloaf, I did a little dance in the kitchen. As much as I like inventing new foods and reinventing myself as a chef, at home I want comfort foods.

Of all the comfort foods, this is probably my favorite. It's a filling dinner. This, with baked potatoes and sour cream, and a little vegetable? It always reminds me of home. My mom used to make meatloaf and hers was kick-ass. I loved making sandwiches with it the next day. And there was a place in Denver I went to, at least once a week, the Cherry Cricket. They had a grilled meatloaf sandwich. That was a big-ass piece of meatloaf. So good.

Meatloaf is masculine comfort food.

To have my wife making it for me, with gluten-free breadcrumbs, so we can share it together? This makes me happy. • *Feeds 4*

½ teaspoon canola oil for greasing pan
2½ pounds ground beef (about 15% fat, not extra lean)
½ large yellow onion, peeled and finely diced
3 large eggs
½ cup gluten-free breadcrumbs
2 tablespoons minced garlic
2 tablespoons finely chopped fresh oregano
1 tablespoon finely chopped fresh Italian parsley

1 tablespoon chiffonade fresh basil
3 to 4 dashes Worcestershire sauce
1 teaspoon Dijon mustard
Kosher salt and cracked black pepper
2 cups chicken stock
2 cups ketchup
5 cloves garlic, smashed and peeled
1 sprig fresh rosemary

Preheating the oven. Turn the oven to 425°F. Grease a 9 x 11-inch loaf pan with the oil.

Making the meatloaf. In a mixing bowl, combine the ground beef, onion, eggs, breadcrumbs, garlic, oregano, parsley, basil, Worcestershire sauce, and mustard. Season with salt and pepper. Stir everything together well. Make a small patty of the meat mixture and cook it like a tiny hamburger in a skillet over medium-high heat. Take a taste to determine if the meatloaf is seasoned the way you like. Adjust the seasonings, if needed.

Baking the meatloaf. Put the meat mixture in the greased loaf pan. Cover with aluminum foil and bake for 45 minutes.

Preparing the glaze. As the meatloaf is baking, combine the chicken stock, ketchup, garlic, and rosemary in a large saucepan. Bring to a boil, then reduce the heat to a simmer. Allow the sauce to reduce until it is the consistency of molasses, about 15 minutes. Strain the glaze.

Glazing the meatloaf. Remove the foil from the meatloaf at 45 minutes. Using a pastry brush, evenly spread the glaze over the top of the meatloaf. Put the meatloaf back in the oven and bake, brushing the top of the meatloaf every 15 minutes or so, until the internal temperature reaches 185°F, about another 45 minutes.

Allow the meatloaf to rest 10 minutes in the pan before cutting and serving.

arugula-fig salad with blue cheese and warm bacon vinaigrette

VARIATIONS
In the winter, you can try this with frisée or mâche. Oranges would work well too. Avocados would be a great substitute for the fleshiness of the figs.

SUGGESTIONS
Use warm plates for this salad. The bacon fat will solidify on a cold plate. Dried figs do not work well in this salad.

Bacon. Blue cheese. Figs. Oh, do they go together. Fresh figs in season are sensuous, meant to be eaten slowly off the lips. Blue cheese and bacon have this richness too. And this salad really should be made in the early autumn, when the weight of the summer shifts into something lighter.

The warm bacon vinaigrette lends a kick to this. The acidity of the vinegar cuts the sweetness of the figs, the sharpness of the blue cheese, and the peppery punch of the arugula.

After eating one of my salads with warm bacon vinaigrette, Shauna asked me to move in with her. Watch out—you don't know what will happen if you make this salad for someone else.

• *Feeds 4*

2 slices high-quality smoked bacon
1 tablespoon canola oil
1 shallot, peeled and thinly sliced
4 teaspoons red wine vinegar
½ teaspoon Dijon mustard

Kosher salt and cracked black pepper
1 large bunch fresh arugula (about ½ pound)
1 pint fresh figs (black Missions are good here), quartered
4 ounces tangy blue cheese

Rendering the bacon. Cut the bacon slices into ½-inch pieces. Set a large sauté pan over medium heat and pour in the oil. Add the bacon to the hot oil and cook until it is crispy. Remove the bacon from the pan and pour off the bacon fat (reserving it for later) except for a small skim at the bottom of the pan.

Making the bacon vinaigrette. Add the shallot to the sauté pan over medium heat and cook until it is translucent, about 5 minutes. Turn off the heat. Add the vinegar to the shallot and whisk the mixture. Stir in the mustard. Pour into a small bowl and set aside.

Pour 4 tablespoons of the reserved bacon fat into the sauté pan in which you cooked the vinaigrette. (If you do not have 4 tablespoons, because the bacon you chose was lean, then make up the difference with canola oil.) Heat the fat over medium heat. When the fat is hot, vigorously whisk in the shallot mixture until it becomes a coherent mixture. Taste, then season with salt and pepper. Remove from the heat.

Composing and serving the salad. Drizzle the arugula with the bacon vinaigrette and toss. Arrange onto plates. Garnish with the figs and blue cheese. Top with the reserved bacon pieces.

sweet and savory, mixed together

We walk into the kitchen to make dinner together. As he does every night, Danny kneels on the floor before me, lifts up my shirt, and talks to my belly. "Hi there!" he says in his cartoon voice. He talks about his day. He kisses my belly. And then he looks up at me. I hold his head in my hands, and we smile at each other.

At forty years old, I was pregnant for the first time.

What did I want to eat? Meat. That bacon party happened for a reason, after all. My body craved protein as though I were a Russian weight lifter at the Olympics. Pork, mostly, but all meats, beans, nuts, safe seafood, eggs, and cheese. (I hated the fact that I was not supposed to eat unpasteurized or raw cheese, or meat cooked less than well-done. No raw eggs—this takes away homemade mayonnaise and cookie dough. And also, missing sushi nearly killed me.) Milk. Good lord, I drank three glasses of milk a day, avidly. I don't even like milk. Or I didn't.

One morning, Danny made us roasted potatoes and eggs, the way he does most mornings. He makes the best roasted potatoes I have ever eaten, and on some days he threads roasted onions through the pile of them too. That morning, I took one look at the plate, and then used my fork to shove every sliver of onion to the side.

"What are you doing?" he asked me, incredulous.

"I don't know why, but I just can't have onions right now."

"Okay," he said, shrugging his shoulders. He had already learned not to question this.

So had I. I learned to trust my body, fully.

Suddenly, every vegetable seemed repugnant to me. The texture of salads grossed me out entirely. What? This isn't me.

"All my times of cooking before, I was feeding the public. This time, along with feeding you, I was feeding somebody I helped create. Somebody I hadn't met yet but I already loved dearly. Every time I made something, and I

would put it under your nose, there'd be a pow, a push, a nudge, a hello. Hey, you in there. Do you like that?"

I felt the first movements in my belly, like champagne bubbles bouncing against my abdomen. When I felt it, I stopped and gasped, and rubbed back hello. And then I reached for Danny's hand.

There were ineffably beautiful moments, on Mondays when he was away from the restaurant, or in the mornings before he had to prep for the day. The first time we saw the little tadpole swimming in waters deep in my body, that little heart thrumming, a sweep of hummingbird wings beating against a small circle. The first time we heard the heartbeat, tiny horse hooves pounding out their rhythm, or the longer ultrasound, when we saw the spine, ten toes wriggling, small hands furling, and even a quick wave at us before a turn. Those experiences put us in a place beyond words.

Even after all this time together, Danny still remains a mystery to me, at times. He knows me better than any other human being, and yet every day I say something that surprises him so much he throws back his head and laughs without making any noise. Sometimes, when I wake up in the morning, I throw my arm over him and open my eyes. There are times that I startle and think, Who is that? As Danny becomes more comfortable to me, like braised meat on a Sunday in winter, he feels increasingly separate from me as well. Home for him meant dark green trees against snow-covered mountains just outside his bedroom window. Home for me meant concrete and smoggy skies. He has spent his life standing in front of a stove, unsure about his spelling or how to express himself. I have spent my life talking and writing, and hacking up onions with a blunt knife. We are both still learning who we are, and learning each other. He is uncannily good at loving me, and he still doesn't know me entirely.

"I never want to think of myself as a great chef. I still have so much more left to learn."

What would our lives be like when we added a third member to our home, someone we created and yet entirely her own? We only knew her movements in my belly, the shape of her head on ultrasound, the fierce kicks she gave to my ribs that seemed to suggest a spirit alive in there. We only knew that our daughter would feel deeply familiar, and also a stranger, the minute she was born.

Everyone knows that having a baby changes you. We thought we were prepared for that, and tried to ready the house. How could we have known that we knew nothing at all? That the night of her birth she would stop breathing and have to spend two weeks in the ICU, the two of us holding hands over her isolette, willing her to live? That when she came home, healthy and alive, Danny would decide to stop drinking, sobered by the idea of missing any part of her life for alcohol? That only a couple of months later, he would quit the Seattle restaurant, not working as a chef for the first time in his adult life, because we needed to write his stories for this book? That we would both feel split open by the love we feel for her when she smiles and makes a farting noise with her mouth in glee, and I laugh and say, "Just like her papa."

We knew none of that when we stood in the kitchen, Danny kneeling before me, talking to our daughter through my belly. All we knew is that we loved each other, and loved her, in the warm light of that room.

We could not wait to introduce her to food.

smoked-salt caramel ice cream
adapted from david lebovitz

VARIATIONS
The taste of this ice cream is especially addictive because the caramel is nearly burnt. But you don't want burnt caramel. Burnt caramel is awful. If you do burn the caramel, fill up the saucepan with hot water and boil it. This will help clean the pan. If you are new to making caramel, and intimidated by it, you can go a little lighter on the caramel and not take it to the almost-burnt stage.

SUGGESTIONS
You will have smoked salt left over from this recipe. Pinch it on top of grilled steaks or pork chops. You can use it for curing meats. Top sautéed kale with it, or grilled vegetables. Play with your food.

The sweetness hits first, and then the dark caramel with a hint on the edge of burnt. The smoke lingers and kicks in at the end, on the roof of your mouth, after the last of the ice cream is gone. We owe the original salted caramel ice cream to our friend David Lebovitz, one of our favorite people and pastry chef extraordinaire. This is his recipe for salted caramel ice cream. Except, we had the idea of smoking the salt ourselves. Since we didn't own a smoker at the time, we created an easy home smoker with half hotel pans (stainless steel rectangular pans used in restaurants, available at restaurant supply stores) that went on the stove. Bingo.

And why does this recipe go with the story of Shauna being pregnant with our daughter? How do you think I got her pregnant? I made her some of this ice cream. • *Makes 2 pints*

2 cups applewood chips, soaked in water for at least 1 hour
1 cup coarse sea salt (buy the best kind you can)
5 large egg yolks
1½ cups baking sugar (a super-fine sugar used for baking, available in grocery stores; it makes better ice cream)

4 tablespoons (½ stick) unsalted butter
2 cups whole milk
1 cup heavy cream
¾ teaspoon vanilla extract

Smoking the sea salt. Take a 4-inch half hotel pan (see headnote) and line it with aluminum foil. Put the soaked applewood chips on the aluminum foil (soaking them well prevents burning). Place a 2-inch perforated half hotel pan on top of that. Pour the salt into a little cup made out of aluminum foil. Place that in the middle of the perforated pan. Cover the pan with aluminum foil.

Place the hotel pans directly onto a burner on medium heat. Turn on your hood fan or open a window, because you will have smoke. As soon as smoke emerges from the hotel pans, turn off the burner. Leave the salt in there for 15 to 20 minutes, depending on how smoky you want the salt. Take off the aluminum foil and retrieve the salt. (If you have a smoker at home, use that here. And if this sounds too complicated, you can buy smoked sea salt.)

Preparing to make the custard. Find a large metal bowl in your kitchen. Pour in enough ice cubes to fill the bowl a third full and enough water to make the ice cubes float. Find another metal bowl small enough to nest inside the larger one. Put out all your ingredients near the place where you are going to make caramel. Put a medium-sized bowl on a wet towel on the counter. Put the egg yolks in this bowl.

Making the caramel. Find a solid, sturdy spoon, something to stand up to the caramel. If you burn yourself, you're going to cry like a little girl. Put a large heavy-duty saucepan over medium-high heat and pour in the sugar. Stir constantly, methodically. After a while, the sugar will begin

(continued on next page)

to dissolve and turn clear. Watch for it to melt, like a big pile of snow in warm water. The sugar will begin to clump together, like hard-packed crunchy snow. Then it will break down and you will see little pockets of the sugar beginning to caramelize. Be gentle with your stirring but keep stirring. (If the phone rings, let the voice mail pick it up.) As the sugar begins to turn a caramel color, you have to watch it carefully. Add the butter and stir. The sugar will grow darker and darker, just short of burning. When the sugar is the color of maple syrup, take it off the heat. Stir in 1 teaspoon of the smoked sea salt. Save the remaining smoked sea salt for other meals in your kitchen.

Making the custard. Begin to pour the milk and cream into the caramel, slowly. Put the saucepan back on the burner. The caramel will seize up and become hard as cement, so you might think you have ruined it. You have not. Continue pouring the milk and cream and stir until you have run out of milk and cream. This will take time. When the milk and cream heat up, and the caramel reheats, it will all come together.

When the milky caramel comes to a boil, whisk the egg yolks together in the bowl that you placed on a wet towel. Slowly pour ⅓ to ½ cup of the milky caramel into the egg yolks, whisking continuously. Make sure the bowl remains on the wet towel or the bowl will fly across the room and you will have hot caramel all over your hands. Continue whisking in the milky caramel until the saucepan is empty.

When the caramel is fully incorporated into the egg yolks, pour that mixture back into the

saucepan. Stir the custard over medium heat, scraping the bottom as you go, until the custard reaches a temperature between 160°F and 170°F on a candy thermometer.

Chilling the custard. Pour the custard through a fine-mesh sieve into the small metal bowl. Place that bowl on the large bowl filled with ice water, add the vanilla, and stir the custard. Leave the custard on the ice bath, coming back to stir it occasionally, until it is completely chilled. Move the custard to the refrigerator and allow it to sit overnight.

Making the ice cream. The next day, freeze the custard in your ice cream maker according to the manufacturer's directions. The final ice cream will be softer than commercial ice creams because the salt keeps it from freezing hard.

recipe list

resources

Alter Eco
2325 Third Street, Suite 226
San Francisco, CA 94107
(415) 701-1212
www.altereco-usa.com
This fair-trade company buys directly from farmers in third-world countries and sells to consumers all over the world. Their quinoa is particularly high quality (try the black quinoa!), but they also sell rice, coffee, chocolate, teas, olive oil, and unbleached sugars.

Anson Mills
1922-C Gervais Street
Columbia, SC 29201
(803) 467-4122
www.ansonmills.com
The folks at Anson Mills have made it their mission to bring back heirloom grains that were near extinction in modern America. Their antebellum coarse white grits are the best we have ever eaten, and we try to always have some in the house. Not everything milled by Anson Mills is gluten-free, but they maintain good practices to keep the grits, cornmeal, polenta, rice, rice flour, and buckwheat separate from the gluten ingredients in the warehouse.

Bob's Red Mill
5000 SE International Way
Milwaukie, OR 97222
(800) 349-2173
www.bobsredmill.com
Without Bob's Red Mill, we wouldn't be able to bake. Our pantry is always filled with their little bags of gluten-free grains and flours. They maintain a separate milling facility for gluten-free products, so look for the red symbol of a line through a grain of wheat on the bags. All the flours we use in this book are available through Bob's Red Mill. Their website is a fount of good information on the gluten-free life as well.

Chef Shop
1415 Elliott Avenue West
Seattle, WA 98119
(800) 596-0885
www.chefshop.com
Oils, nuts, beans, June Taylor marmalades, sea salts of all kind—these are the staples of Chef Shop. Run by people who truly love food, Chef Shop sells the best of all categories of comestibles. They also have agreements with Native American tribes in Alaska to sell Copper River salmon and sablefish directly from fishermen to customers.

D'Artagnan
280 Wilson Avenue
Newark, NJ 07105
(800) 327-8246
www.dartagnan.com
Every chef in America must know D'Artagnan by now. Their meats and poultry, both fresh and cured, are used in some of the best restaurants in this country. We promise you that duck confit is easy to make. However, if you want to buy it instead, this is your place. In addition, the veal D'Artagnan sells has been raised humanely, on a small cooperative farm where the calves roam freely. This might make you feel better about that veal stock.

Gustiamo
1715 West Farms Road
Bronx, NY 10460
(877) 907-2525
www.gustiamo.com
Umbrian lentils, Sicilian olive oil, Roman coffee from Caffe Sant'Eustachio—Gustiamo has all the best ingredients that Italy has to offer, directly from the Bronx.

La Buona Tavola
1524 Pike Place
Seattle, WA 98101-1527
(206) 292-5555
www.trufflecafe.com
If you're in Seattle, you can stop by this tiny stall in Pike Place Market where we bought the wild truffle honey on our second date, the one that later topped our potato-leek soup. If you're nowhere near Seattle, you can order the honey—along with oils, vinegars, and whole truffles—online.

Lotus Foods
601 22nd Street
San Francisco, CA 94107
(866) 972-6879
www.lotusfoods.com
This wonderful company uses sustainable practices worldwide to bring "exotic" rice to the U.S. while benefiting the farmers. Their Bhutanese red rice is the basis for one of our favorite salads in the book, and their Madagascar pink rice is an almost spicy heirloom you most likely have not tried. If you think you know rice, you probably haven't eaten some of these varieties yet.

Monterey Bay Aquarium
www.montereybayaquarium.org/cr/seafoodwatch.aspx
No, we are really not suggesting you go to the aquarium to pick out your fish for dinner. The Monterey Bay Aquarium runs Seafood Watch, one of the best

centers for understanding sustainability in fish. Their pocket guides to sustainable seafood—available online—are enormously helpful in deciding what fish are best to eat, both for you and the environment. (They even have an iPhone app!)

Rancho Gordo
www.ranchogordo.com

Steve Sando, who founded and runs Rancho Gordo, is kind of a god to us. Frustrated by the lack of good ingredients indigenous to the Americas (beans, grains, and corn), he made connections with growers and enticed them to grow heirloom varieties of these foods. If you have never tasted a Vallarta bean, you have never really eaten good beans. Rancho Gordo sells dozens of different beans, as well as amaranth and quinoa, chili powders, good Mexican cinnamon, and dried corn.

Ritrovo
309 South Cloverdale, Suite D-11
Seattle, WA 98108
(866) RITROVO
www.ritrovo.com

Ilyse and Ron at Ritrovo import foods from small farms and producers in Italy, particularly from Tuscany. Their venere black rice inspired the black rice dish in this book. Fresh popcorn with Ritrovo truffles and salt is one of Shauna's guilty pleasures. And their Il Macchiolo pasta is the best gluten-free pasta you can buy.

Sonoma County Poultry
P.O. Box 140
Penngrove, CA 94951
(800) 953-8257
www.libertyducks.com

Revered by chefs across the country for their meatiness, the ducks from Sonoma County Poultry are raised humanely on farms in northern California. They sell all parts of the duck, including breasts (which you can use for the duck breast ravioli in this book) and fat. If you eat duck at The French Laundry in Napa, Coi in San Francisco, or Tilth in Seattle, you will be eating

Sonoma County Poultry.

The Spanish Table
1426 Western Avenue
Seattle, WA 98101
(206) 682-2827
thespanishtable.com

We're lucky enough to be able to walk into The Spanish Table on Western Avenue, just down from the Pike Place Market. Most weeks, when Danny worked at his last restaurant in Seattle, we stopped for smoked paprika, sherry vinegar, and sometimes for Jamón Ibérico. With stores in Berkeley, Santa Fe, and Mill Valley, as well as an online shopping option, The Spanish Table is open for you too.

The Teff Company
(888) 822-2221
www.teffco.com

The founder of the Teff Company, Wayne Carlson, lived in Ethiopia in the 1970s, as an aid worker during the civil wars. This is where he first encountered teff, the tiny gluten-free grain with a nutritional wallop. He brought teff seeds back to Idaho, where the growing conditions suited the plant, then started this company, which sells whole-grain teff and teff flour across the country. If you have ever eaten teff, you've probably eaten from this company.

World Spice
1509 Western Avenue
Seattle, WA 98101
(206) 682-7274
www.worldspice.com

Sometimes we walk into World Spice just to take a deep whiff. The mingled scents of cinnamon, curry powder, and vanilla beans, plus dozens more, all gathered in one store are enough to make us grateful for our noses. The folks who run World Spice collect the best spices from around the world and make them available to us. And you.

Zingerman's
620 Phoenix Drive
Ann Arbor, MI 48108
(888) 636-8162
www.zingermans.com

A delicatessen, a bakery, a creamery, a sit-down restaurant, and one of the world's best online sources for fine food all around the world—that's Zingerman's. We love the fact that this purveyor of great olive oils, vinegars, cheeses, and chocolates is located in Ann Arbor, Michigan, rather than Manhattan or Los Angeles. Besides, they have a Bacon of the Month Club. What more do you want?

index